ENTREPRENEURIAL
FINANCE

ENTREPRENEURIAL
FINANCE

Finance and Business Strategies for the Serious Entrepreneur

Second Edition

STEVEN ROGERS

**Gordon and Llura Gund Family Professor of Entrepreneurship
Director, Larry and Carol Levy Institute for Entrepreneurial Practice
J.L. Kellogg School of Management, Northwestern University**

WITH ROZA MAKONNEN

New York   Chicago   San Francisco   Lisbon
London   Madrid   Mexico City   Milan   New Delhi
San Juan   Seoul   Singapore   Sydney   Toronto

5 6 7 8 9 0   QFR/QFR   1 5 4 3 2 1

ISBN 978–0–07–159126–3
MHID   0–07–159126–5

McGraw-Hill books are available at special quantity discounts to use as premiums and sales promotions, or for use in corporate training programs. To contact a representative, please visit the Contact Us pages at www.mhprofessional.com.

This publication is designed to provide accurate and authoritative information in regard to the subject matter covered. It is sold with the understanding that neither the author nor the publisher is engaged in rendering legal, accounting, or other professional service. If legal advice or other expert assistance is required, the services of a competent professional person should be sought.

——From a Declaration of Principles jointly adopted by a Committee of the American Bar Association and a Committee of Publishers.

CONTENTS

Chapter 4

Financial Statements   81

Chapter 5

Financial Statement Analysis   103

Chapter 6

Cash Flow Management   149

Chapter 7

Valuation   179

Chapter 8

Raising Capital   229

Chapter 9

Debt Financing   237

Chapter 10

Equity Financing   275

Chapter 11

Financing for Minorities and Women   315

Chapter 12

Taking a Job with an Entrepreneurial Firm   327

Chapter 13

Intrapraneurship: Corporate Entrepreneurship   345

It is morning at Opryland in Nashville, Tennessee, a place where young crooners from Charlie Pride and Johnny Cash to Garth Brooks and the Dixie Chicks have realized their dreams. Not far away is the Grand Ole Opry—country music's equivalent of the Broadway stage—and a full day of work is about to begin. But this morning, the visitors have business, not music, on their minds. This is a conference for future entrepreneurs from around the country. Their schedules are packed with seminars on financing, marketing, and operations. Here is a sample: "Business Start-Up Essentials," "How to Find Money-Making Ideas," and "Designing Products."

Of course, none of this would be particularly noteworthy except when you consider that these conventioneers are aged seven to ten—and they are not the youngest group here. There is another set of entrepreneur seminars for kids aged four to six. It's called the "Kidpreneurs Konference," sponsored by *Black Enterprise* magazine and Wendy's, and this sixth annual event is a sellout. Nearby, the kids' parents, all entrepreneurs or future entrepreneurs themselves, are packed into their own seminars. If there ever was a doubt that this is the glory age of the entrepreneur, a few days with these "titans of tomorrow" should put that notion to bed.

I write this book, this story of opportunities, because I have been blessed with so many of my own. It's said that a good entre-preneur always sees sun in the clouds and a glass half full. My wife,

Michele, and my daughters, Akilah and Ariel, laugh at me when I tell them that I have gone through life always believing that when I walk through a door, the light will shine on me, no matter who else is in the room. Like every good entrepreneur, I believe in myself, but I also have enough humility to know that one does not go from the welfare rolls on Chicago's South Side to owning three successful companies, sitting on the boards of several Fortune 500 companies [S. C. Johnson & Son (formerly S. C. Johnson Wax), SuperValu, AMCORE Financial, and Harris Associates, a $60 billion mutual fund], and teaching at the finest business school in America without a healthy supply of luck—and a handful of caring people.

The first entrepreneur I ever met was a woman named Ollie Mae Rogers—the oldest daughter in a family of 10 kids, and the only one among them who never graduated from high school, let alone college. Fiercely independent, she left home at the age of 17 and got married. The marriage, I believe, was simply an excuse to leave home. Leaving home meant that she got her independence, and if she was nothing else, Ollie Mae, my mother, was a fireball of independence. When my older brother, my two sisters, and I buried her a few years ago, the eulogy fell to me. I described my mother as a Renaissance woman filled with paradoxes. She was a tough and gutsy woman whose extensive vocabulary flowed eloquently although she barely finished the tenth grade.

I like to think of my mother as an eccentric "mom-and-pop" entrepreneur. Growing up, we were like the old *Sanford and Son* television series—selling used furniture at the weekend flea markets on Maxwell Street on Chicago's South Side. Nearly every Saturday and Sunday morning, my older brother, John, and I were up at 4 a.m. loading my mother's beat-up jalopy of a station wagon until we could fit no more "merchandise" on the seats, in the trunk, and on the roof. When I talk to prospective entrepreneurs, I tell them to go sell something at a flea market. You need to really live, breathe, and feel the rejection of hustling for "sells."

When I think back on it now, I realize that my mother just loved the art of the deal, and this, among other things, became part of my being. It was common for my mother to leave our space at the market and go shopping, leaving the operations to my brother and me—the savvy and sophisticated five-year-old business maverick. That is how I learned to sell, negotiate, and schmooze a customer. I started my first little business venture in that very same market: a shoeshine stand. People would stroll by, and I'd lure them in with the oh-so-memorable pitch line: "Shine your shoes, comb your hair, and make you feel like a millionaire."

As far back as I can remember, I always held a job. When we weren't working the flea markets, my brother and I found other jobs; from helping the local milkman make his deliveries to working as a stock boy at the neighborhood grocery store, we did what we needed to do. By the time I reached high school, I was plucked out of the Chicago public schools by a nonprofit organization called A Better Chance, a private national program that identifies academically gifted minority kids from low-income communities and sends them to schools where their potential can be realized. (I now serve on the organization's board of directors). I was sent to Radnor High School in Wayne, Pennsylvania. I played on the football team, and when the season was over, I worked as a janitor's assistant to help send some money home to my mother.

My mother started running a small used-furniture storefront, and when I came home for the summer breaks, she stopped working and turned the operation over to me. So by the age of 15, I had to manage a few employees, open and close the business, negotiate with our customers, and run the daily operations. My mother, unbeknownst to her, was nurturing a budding entrepreneur. She truly is the reason that my brother, my sisters, and I have all gravitated to leadership positions in our professional lives. My brother is a supervisor of probation officers, my older sister, Deniece, owns her own delivery business, and my youngest sister, Laura, is manager of a McDonald's restaurant.

I went on to attend Williams College (I am a former trustee), where, for the first time, the money I made was all mine. It's where I met my future wife, Michele, and between the two of us, we must have had every job on the darn campus. Williams is a liberal arts school, and at the time there were no finance courses or any other business classes to be found on campus. I majored in history. During my senior year at Williams, I took an accounting class at nearby North Adams State College. After graduating from Williams, I worked for Cummins Engine Company. At Cummins, I worked as a purchasing agent with a start-up venture in Rocky Mount, North Carolina, called Consolidated Diesel Company

(CDC). At CDC, I was responsible for developing a new supplier organization, and it was there that I got my first taste of finance. It was a position that put me smack-dab in the middle of the expense line item "cost of goods sold" because I was ultimately responsible for buying several engine components. The greatest benefit of this experience was the negotiating skills that I continued to develop.

After four years, I left and was accepted at Harvard Business School (I am a former trustee), where I received my first formal education in finance. That was the main reason that I attended business school: I knew that I wanted to be an entrepreneur, and I knew that if I was going to be successful, I needed to understand finance. My introductory finance class was taught by Professor Bill Sahlman. When I told him about my meager background in the subject, he told me to relax, that any novice can understand the subject with a little common sense. Though he never told me this, I quickly realized that the subject was made easier by having an outstanding professor, like Sahlman, who could teach a user-friendly finance course that combined academic theory and real practices into a powerful lesson.

While I was at Harvard, I recognized what many entrepreneurs find out the hard way: being a successful entrepreneur is not easy. I knew about the failure rate, and I was never really interested in starting a company from scratch. I wanted to buy an existing business. It's funny when I think back about all the jobs that I had as a kid. My older brother always had the same job first, so even back then, I was taking over an existing enterprise. I decided that going the franchise route was the smartest thing for me to do, and I applied for the franchisee program at McDonald's. My plan was to eventually buy a large number of the stores and become a fast-food mogul. Out of 30,000 applicants for the franchisee program that year, McDonald's accepted 50, and I was one of them.

The program required future franchisees to work 15 to 20 hours a week (for free, of course) over a two-year period. I actually did my fast-food tour of duty with the McDonald's right around the corner from Harvard. So during my second year at Harvard Business School, my classmates would come in and see this hulking second-year MBA student, decked out in the official McDonald's pants and shirt, dropping their fries into the grease and cleaning the stalls of the bathroom. Of course they were thinking, "What the hell are you doing?" But I learned a valuable lesson over the years: you're making an investment in yourself, and why should you care what someone else thinks? I believe this is an important lesson for everyone. There's a certain level of humility that all entrepreneurs must have. You want to talk about risks? Taking risks is not just about taking risks with your money; it is about risking your reputation by being willing to be the janitor. If you don't have that mindset and you can't handle that, then entrepreneurship is not for you.

After graduating from HBS, I still had a year to go with the McDonald's ownership program. In order to earn money, I accepted a consulting job with Bain & Company. During the week, I would fly all over the United States on my consulting assignments, and on the weekends, I would return to the Soldiers Field Avenue McDonald's in Boston and put in the hours required. Once I had completed the program and it was time for me to buy my own McDonald's, I could not come to terms with the corporation on a price for the store it wanted to sell. We went around and around, and finally I decided that maybe franchising was not for me after all. Like my mother, I am not very good at taking orders, living my life in a template designed by someone else, and doing what someone else believes I should do. My experience with McDonald's was phenomenal, and I have nothing but respect for the company, but it was time for me to purchase my own business.

Eventually, after working with a business broker, I settled on purchasing a manufacturing business. Before I sold the company and left for my dream job of teaching at Kellogg, I had purchased an additional manufacturing firm and a retail business. Being your own boss and running your own business is both an exhilarating and a frightening prospect for most people. This is a club for hard workers. If you want an 8-to-5 job, do not join. This is a club whose members flourish on chaos, uncertainty, and ambiguity. These are people who thrive on solving problems.

By picking up this book, you have singled yourself out as someone who wants to learn. This book is designed for existing and future entrepreneurs who are not financial managers but want a simple and practical approach to understanding entrepreneurial finance. This is not a traditional, boring, "comprehensive" how-to book, because that is not what most prospective or existing entrepreneurs need, nor is it the way I teach. Most academicians have never worked in business, and the "real-world practices" component is conspicuously missing from their teaching arsenal. My approach is to combine legitimate and important academic theory with real-world lessons. In my class, I call this "putting meat on the carcass."

But this is not just a book of war stories. Just as I do in my classes, I have made every effort to ensure that the reader gets tangible tools that can be used to improve the potential for entrepreneurial success. The entrepreneur needs to know financial formulas and how to use them to spot problems or seize opportunities.

Like Professor Sahlman, I subscribe to the "this is not brain surgery" approach to finance, and I stress the fact that everyone can, and, more importantly, must, learn finance. I believe that the baseball always finds a weak outfielder, and the same principle holds true for entrepreneurs: if finance is a weakness, the entrepreneur will be haunted by it. This book is intended for individuals who have little background in financial management, people who have taken entrepreneurship courses, and those who already have practical experience in business. These groups include MBA students, prospective entrepreneurs, and existing entrepreneurs. My success in communicating to this audience through this book was greatly enhanced by the help that I received from numerous people, including my secretary, Brenda McDaniel, who transcribed. I also owe a major debt of gratitude to the following Kellogg alums: Thane Gauthier, '05; Roza Makonnen, '97; Paul Smith, '07; Scott Whitaker, '97; and David Wildermuth, '01.

A year after purchasing my first business, I vividly remember returning from an early appointment and driving beside Lake Michigan on Lake Shore Drive. It was a gorgeous warm and sunny day, and I pulled off the road and got out of my car. There was no boss I had to call and no need to conjure up a reason for not returning to work. There was no manager to ask for an extended lunch break. I removed my socks and shoes, put my toes in the sand, and stayed there at the beach for the rest of the afternoon. Being an entrepreneur never felt so good.

Entrepreneurship is about getting your hands dirty *and* putting your toes in the sand. This book aims to help you get there. As Irving Berlin once advised a young songwriter by the name of George Gershwin, "Why the hell do you want to work for somebody else? Work for yourself!"

ENTREPRENEURIAL
FINANCE

CHAPTER 1

The Entrepreneurial Spectrum

INTRODUCTION

The 1990s could be called the original "entrepreneurship genera-tion."[1] Never before had the entrepreneurial spirit been as strong, in America and abroad, as it was during that decade. More than 600,000 new businesses were created at the beginning of the 1990s, with each subsequent year breaking the record of the previous one for start-ups.[2] By 1997, entrepreneurs were starting a record 885,000 new businesses a year—that's more than 2,400 a day. This astonish-ing increase in new companies was more than 4 times the number of firms created in the 1960s, and more than 16 times as many as during the 1950s, when 200,000 and 50,000, respectively, were being created each year.[3] This unprecedented growth in entrepreneurial activity was evidenced across all industries, including manufac-turing, retail, real estate, and various technology industries. This decade was also an "equal opportunity" time, as the entrepreneur-ial euphoria of the 1990s was shared by both genders and across all ethnicities and races. I've always believed that the beauty of entre-preneurship is that it is color-blind and gender-neutral.

New evidence indicates that this 1990s generation of entre-preneurs may actually be surpassed in upcoming years by the members of "Generation Y," or those born between the years 1977 and 1994. This should come as no surprise when one considers that this group grew up during entrepreneurship's golden age and later saw its parents laid off or downsized out of "lifetime" corporate jobs. Generation Y has also spent most of its life and virtually all of its postsecondary years in a digital age, where technology has significantly reduced the barriers of entry for start-ups. The members of Generation Y, who may have seen VHS tapes and record albums only at neighborhood garage sales or museums, are now enrolling in college entrepreneurship classes at a rate that is roughly seven times what it was just six years ago. Jeff Cornwall, the entrepreneurial chair at Belmont University in Nashville, characterizes Generation Y's increase in entrepreneurial interest well: "Forty percent or more of students who come into our undergraduate entrepreneurship program as freshmen already have a business. It's a whole new world."[4]

ENTREPRENEURIAL FINANCE

In a recent survey of business owners, the functional area they cited as being the one in which they had the weakest skill was the area of financial management—accounting, bookkeeping, the raising of capital, and the daily management of cash flow. Interestingly, these business owners also indicated that they spent most of their time on finance-related activities. Unfortunately, the findings of this survey are an accurate portrayal of most entrepreneurs—they are comfortable with the day-to-day operation of their businesses and with the marketing and sales of their products or services, but they are very uncomfortable with the financial management of their companies. Entrepreneurs cannot afford this discomfort. They must realize that financial management is not as difficult as it is made out to be. It must be used and embraced because it is one of the key factors for entrepreneurial success.

This book targets prospective and existing "high-growth" entrepreneurs who are not financial managers. Its objective is to be a user-friendly book that will provide these entrepreneurs with an understanding of the fundamentals of financial management and analysis that will enable them to better manage the financial resources of their business and create economic value. However, the book is not a course in corporate finance. Rather, entrepreneurial finance is more integrative, including the analysis of qualitative issues such as marketing, sales, personnel management, and strategic planning. The questions that will be answered will include:

What financial tools can be used to manage the cash flow of the business efficiently? Why is valuation important? What is the value of the company? Finally, how, where, and when can financial resources be acquired to finance the business?

Before we immerse ourselves in the financial aspects of entrepreneurship, let us look at the general subject of entrepreneurship.

TYPES OF ENTREPRENEURS

There are essentially two kinds of entrepreneurs: the "mom-and-pop" entrepreneur, a.k.a. the "lifestyle" entrepreneur, and the "high-growth" entrepreneur.[5]

The Lifestyle Entrepreneur

Lifestyle entrepreneurs are those entrepreneurs who are primarily looking for their business to provide them with a decent standard of living. They are not focused on growth; rather, they run their business almost haphazardly, with minimal or no systems in place. They do not necessarily have any strategic plans regarding the growth and future of their business and gladly accept whatever the business produces. Their objective is to manage the business so that it remains small and provides them with enough income to maintain a certain, typically middle-class, lifestyle. For example, Sue Yellin, a small-business consultant, says she is determined to remain a one-person show, earning just enough money to live comfortably and "feed my cat Fancy Feasts."[6]

While they may have started out as lifestyle entrepreneurs, some owners ultimately become, voluntarily or involuntarily, high-growth entrepreneurs because their business grows despite their original intention. For example, the *Inc.* magazine 500 is composed of 500 successful high-growth entrepreneurs. When a survey was taken of these entrepreneurs, their answers for the completion of the statement, "My original goals when I started the company . . ." suggest that almost 20 percent were originally lifestyle entrepreneurs, given the following responses:

- Company to grow as fast as possible: 50.9 percent.
- Company to grow slowly: 29.4 percent.

- Start small and stay small: 5.8 percent.
- No plan at all: 13.8 percent.[7]

Finally, one of the most prominent stories of a lifestyle entrepreneur turned high-growth entrepreneur is that of Ewing Marion Kauffman, who started his pharmaceutical company, Marion Laboratories, in 1957 with the objective of "just making a living" for his family. He ultimately grew the firm to over $5 billion in annual revenues by 1986, creating wealth for himself (he sold the company in 1989 for over $5 billion) and for 300 employees, who became millionaires.[8]

The High-Growth Entrepreneur

The high-growth entrepreneur, on the other hand, is proactively looking to grow annual revenues and profits exponentially. This type of entrepreneur has a plan that is reviewed and revised regularly, and the business is run according to this plan. Unlike the lifestyle entrepreneur, the high-growth entrepreneur runs the business with the expectation that it will grow exponentially, with the by-product being the creation of wealth for himself, his investors, and possibly his employees. One of the best stories of high-growth entrepreneurship is Google, which will be discussed in greater detail later. The high-growth entrepreneur understands that a successful business is one that has basic business systems—financial management, cash flow planning, strategic planning, marketing, and so on—in place. *Inc.* magazine surveyed a group of entrepreneurs who were identified as "changing the face of American Business" and found that these entrepreneurs were high-growth entrepreneurs, demonstrated by the fact that not only were they millionaires, but they grew their firms from median sales of $146,000 with 4.5 employees to median sales of $11 million with 219 employees. These data also show that these entrepreneurs grew their companies efficiently, since their sales per employee increased from $32,444 to $50,228, a 55 percent improvement.

Wilson Harrell, a former entrepreneur and current *Inc.* magazine columnist, did a fantastic job of describing the difference between these two types of entrepreneurs. The first description is that of a lifestyle entrepreneur:

Let's say a man buys a dry cleaning shop. He goes to work at 7 a.m. At 7 p.m. he comes home, kisses the wife, grabs the kids, and goes off to a school play. At his office you'll see plaques all over the walls: Chamber of Commerce, Rotary Club, the local Republican or Democratic club. He's a pillar of the community, and everybody loves him, even the bankers.

Change the scenario. After the man buys the dry cleaning shop, he goes home and tells his wife, "Dear, we're going to mortgage this house, borrow money from everyone we can, including your mother and maybe even your brother, and hock everything else, because I'm about to buy another dry cleaner. Then I'll hock the first to buy another, and then another, because I'm going to be the biggest dry cleaner in this city, this state, this nation!"[9]

The second scenario obviously describes the life of a high-growth entrepreneur who has the long-term plan of dominating the national dry cleaning industry by acquiring competitors, first locally and then nationally. His financing plan is to leverage the assets of the cleaners to obtain commercial debt from traditional sources such as banks, combined with "angel" financing from relatives.

Unfortunately, not all entrepreneurs who seek high growth can attain it. Sometimes circumstances outside of their control can hamper their growth plans. For example, one entrepreneur in Maine complained that he could not grow his business because of labor shortages in the region. He said, "I'm disgusted by the labor situation around here. People don't want to get ahead. It adds up to businesses staying small."[10]

THE ENTREPRENEURIAL SPECTRUM

When most people think of the term *entrepreneur*, they envision someone who starts a company from scratch. This is a major misconception. As the entrepreneurial spectrum in Figure 1-1 shows, the tent of entrepreneurship is broader and more inclusive. It includes not only those who start companies from scratch (i.e., start-up entrepreneurs), but also those people who acquired an established company through inheritance or a buyout (i.e., acquirers). The entrepreneurship tent also includes franchisors as well as franchisee. Finally, it also includes *intrapreneurs*, or corporate entrepreneurs. These are people who are gainfully employed at a Fortune 500 company and are proactively engaged in entrepreneurial activities in that setting. Chapter 13 is devoted to the topic of intrapreneurship. But be it via acquisition or start-up, each entrepreneurial process involves differing levels of business risk, as highlighted in Figure 1-1.

FIGURE   1-1

The Entrepreneurial Spectrum

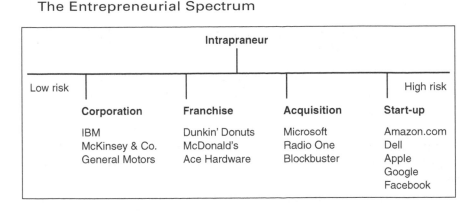

The Corporation

While the major Fortune 500 corporations, such as IBM, are not entrepreneurial ventures, IBM and others are included on the spectrum simply as a business point of reference. Until the early 1980s, IBM epitomized corporate America: a huge, bureaucratic, and conservative multibillion-dollar company where employees were practically guaranteed lifetime employment. Although IBM became less conservative under the leadership of Louis Gerstner, the first non-IBM-trained CEO of the company, it has always represented the antithesis of entrepreneurship, with its "Hail to IBM" corporate anthem, white shirts, dark suits, and policies forbidding smoking and drinking on the job and strongly discouraging them off the job.[11] In addition to the IBM profile, another great example of the antithesis of entrepreneurship was a statement made by a good friend, Lyle Logan, an executive at Northern Trust Corporation, a Fortune 500 company, who proudly said, "Steve, I have never attempted to pass myself off as an entrepreneur. I do not have a single entrepreneurial bone in my body. I am very happy as a corporate executive." As can be seen, the business risk associated with an established company like IBM is low. Such companies have a long history of profitable success and, more importantly, have extremely large cash reserves on hand.

The Franchise

Franchising accounts for 40 percent of all retail sales in the United States, employs over 18 million people and accounts for roughly $1.5 trillion in economic output.[12] Like a big, sturdy tree that continues to grow branches, a well-run franchise can spawn hundreds of entrepreneurs. The founder of a franchise—the franchisor—is a start-up entrepreneur, such as Bill Rosenberg, who founded Dunkin' Donuts in the 1950s and now has approximately 7,400 stores in 30 countries.[13] These guys sell enough donuts in a year to circle the globe . . . twice! Rosenberg's franchisees (more than 5,500 in the United States alone[14]), who own and operate individual franchises, are also entrepreneurs. They take risks, operate their businesses expecting to gain a profit, and, like other entrepreneurs, can have cash flow problems. The country's first franchisees were a network of salesmen who in the 1850s paid the Singer Sewing Machine Company for the right to sell the newly patented machine in different regions of the country. The franchise system ultimately became popular as franchisees began operating in the auto, oil, and food industries. Today, it's estimated that a new franchise outlet opens somewhere in the United States every 8 minutes.[15]

Franchisees are business owners who put their capital at risk and can go out of business if they do not generate enough profits to remain solvent.[16] By one estimate, there are over 750,000 individual franchise business units in America,[17] of which 10,000 are home-based. The average initial investment in a franchise, not including real estate, is approximately $250,000.[18] Examples include Mel Farr, the owner of five auto dealerships. Farr's auto group is just 1 of 15 subsidiaries in his business empire—valued at more than $573 million. Another such entrepreneur is Valerie Daniels-Carter, the founder of a holding company that manages 70 Pizza Hut and 36 Burger King restaurants that total over $85 million in combined annual revenue.[19] Additional data from the International Franchise Association and the U.S. Department of Commerce, given in

TABLE 1-1

Growth in Franchises in the United States (Selected Years)

Year	Number of Franchises	Annual Revenues of Franchises (Billions of Dollars)
1970	396,000	120
1980	442,000	336
1990	533,000	716
1992	558,000	803
2001	767,483	
2005	909,253	

Source: U.S. Department of Commerce; International Franchise Association.

Table 1-1, shows that the number of franchised establishments is continually and rapidly growing and has more than doubled since 1970.

Because a franchise is typically a turnkey operation, its business risk is significantly lower than that of a start-up. The success rate of franchisees is between 80 and 97 percent, according to research by Arthur Andersen and Co., which found that only 3 percent of franchises had gone out of business five years after starting their business. Another study undertaken by Arthur Andersen found that of all franchises opened between 1987 and 1997, 85 percent still operated with their original owner, 11 percent had new owners, and 4 percent had closed. The International Franchise Association reports that 70 percent of franchisors charge an initial fee of $30,000 or less.[20]

Max Cooper is one of the largest McDonald's franchisees in North America, with 45 restaurants in Alabama. He stated his reasoning for becoming a franchisee entrepreneur as follows:

> You buy into a franchise because it's successful. The basics have been developed and you're buying the reputation. As with any company, to be a success in franchising, you have to have that burning desire. If you don't have it, don't do it. It isn't easy.[21]

The Acquisition

An acquirer is an entrepreneur who inherits or buys an existing business. This list includes Howard Schultz, who acquired Starbucks

Coffee in 1987 for approximately $4 million when it had only 6 stores. Today, more than 40 million customers a week line up for their caffe mochas, cappuccinos, and caramel macchiatos in 12,400 Starbucks locations in 37 countries. Annual revenues top $7.8 billion, and, according to the company's SEC filings, the ownership team opened 2,199 new Starbucks outlets in the year 2006 alone![22]

The list of successful acquirers also includes folks like Jim McCann, who purchased the almost bankrupt 1–800-Flowers in 1983, turned it around, and grew annual revenues to $782 million by 2006.[23] Another successful entrepreneur who falls into this category is Cathy Hughes, who over the past 27 years has purchased 71 radio stations that presently generate $371 million in annual revenues, making her broadcasting company, Radio One (NYSE), the seventh largest in the nation. The 51 stations have a combined value of $2 billion.[24]

One of the most prominent entrepreneurs who fall into this category is Wayne Huizenga, *Inc.* magazine's 1996 Entrepreneur of the Year and Ernst & Young's 2005 World Entrepreneur of the Year. His reputation as a great entrepreneur comes partially from the fact that he is one of the few people in the United States to have ever owned three multibillion-dollar businesses. Like Richard Dreyfuss's character in the movie *Down and Out in Beverly Hills*, a millionaire who owned a clothes hanger–manufacturing company, Wayne Huizenga is living proof that an entrepreneur does not have to be in a glamorous industry to be successful. His success came from buying businesses in the low- or no-tech, unglamorous industries of garbage, burglar alarms, videos, sports, hotels, and used cars.

He has never started a business from scratch. His strategy has been to dominate an industry by buying as many of the companies in the industry as he could as quickly as possible and consolidating them. This strategy is known as the "roll-up," "platform," or "poof" strategy—starting and growing a company through industry consolidation. (While the term *roll-up* is self-explanatory, the other two terms may need brief explanations. The term *platform* comes from the act of buying a large company in an industry to serve as the platform for adding other companies. The term *poof* comes from the idea that as an acquirer, one day the entrepreneur has no businesses and the next, "poof"—like magic—he or she purchases a company and is in business. Then "poof" again, and the

company grows exponentially via additional acquisitions.) As Jim
Blosser, one of Huizenga's executives, noted, "Wayne doesn't like
start-ups. Let someone else do the R&D. He'd prefer to pay a little
more for a concept that has demonstrated some success and may
just need help in capital and management."[25]

Huizenga's entrepreneurial career began in 1961 when he purchased his first company, Southern Sanitation Company, in Florida.
The company's assets were a garbage truck and a $500-a-month
truck route, which he worked personally, rising at 2:30 a.m. every
day. This company ultimately became the multibillion-dollar Waste
Management Inc., which Huizenga had grown nationally through
aggressive acquisitions. In one nine-month period, Waste Management bought 100 smaller companies across the country. In ten years
the company grew from $5 million a year to annual profits of
$106.5 million on nearly $1 billion in revenues. In four more years,
revenue doubled again.[26]

Huizenga then exited this business and went into the video
rental business by purchasing the entire Blockbuster Video franchise for $32 million in 1984, after having been unable to purchase
the Blockbuster franchise for the state of Florida because the state's
territorial rights had already been sold to other entrepreneurs
before Huizenga made his offer. When he acquired Blockbuster
Video, it had 8 corporate and 11 franchise stores nationally.
The franchisor was generating $7 million annually through direct
rentals from the 8 stores, plus franchise fees and royalties from the
11 franchised stores.[27] Under Huizenga, who didn't even own a
VCR at the time, Blockbuster flourished. For the next seven years,
through internal growth and acquisitions, Blockbuster averaged a
new store opening every 17 hours, resulting in its becoming larger
than its next 550 competitors combined. Over this period of time,
the price of its stock increased 4,100 percent: someone who had
invested $25,000 in Blockbuster stock in 1984 would have found
that seven years later that investment would be worth $1.1 million,
and an investment of $1 million in 1984 would have turned into $41
million during this time period. In January 1994, Huizenga sold
Blockbuster Video, which had grown to 4,300 stores in 23 countries,
to Viacom for $8.5 billion.

Huizenga has pursued the same roll-up strategy in the auto
business by rapidly buying as many dealerships as he possibly can

and bundling them together under the AutoNation brand. By 2001, AutoNation was the largest automobile retailer in the United States, a title it still holds in 2008. By the way, if you ever find yourself behind the wheel of a National or Alamo rental car, you're also driving one of Wayne's vehicles—both companies are among his holdings. What Huizenga eventually hopes to do is to have an entire life cycle for a car. In other words, he buys cars from the manufacturer, sells some of them as new, leases or rents the balance, and later sells the rented cars as used.

Huizenga also owns or previously owned practically every professional sports franchise in Florida, including the National Football League's Miami Dolphins, the National Hockey League's Florida Panthers, and Major League Baseball's Florida Marlins. He never owned the National Basketball League's Miami Heat; his cousin did.

Now, here's your bonus points question—the one I always ask my Kellogg students. What's the common theme among all of Huizenga's various businesses—videos, waste, sports, and automobiles? Each one of them involves the rental of products, generating significant, predictable, and, perhaps most importantly, *recurring* revenues. The video business rents the same video over and over again, and the car rental business rents the same car a multitude of times. In waste management, he rented the trash containers. But what's being rented in the sports business? He rents the seats in the stadiums and arenas that he owns. Other businesses that are in the seat rental business are airlines, movie theaters, public transportation, and universities!

Another example of an acquirer is Bill Gates, the founder of Microsoft. The company's initial success came from an operating system called MS-DOS, which was originally owned by a company called Seattle Computer Products. In 1980, IBM was looking for an operating system. After hearing about Bill Gates, who had dropped out of Harvard to start Microsoft in 1975 with his friend Paul Allen, the IBM representatives went to Albuquerque, New Mexico, where Gates and Allen were, to see if Gates could provide them with the operating system they needed. At the time, Microsoft's product was a version of the programming language BASIC for the Altair 8800, arguably the world's first personal computer. BASIC had been invented in 1964 by John Kenney and Thomas Kurtz.[28] As he did not have an operating system, Gates recommended that IBM contact another company called Digital Research. Gary Kildall, the owner of Digital Research, was absent when the IBM representatives visited, and his staff refused to sign a nondisclosure statement with IBM without his consent, so the representatives went back to Gates to see if he could recommend someone else. True opportunistic entrepreneur that he is, Gates told them that he had an operating system to provide to them and finalized a deal with IBM. Once he had done so, he went out and bought the operating system, Q-DOS, from Seattle Computer Products for $50,000 and customized it for IBM's first PC, which was introduced in August 1981. The rest is entrepreneurial history. So Bill Gates, one of the world's wealthiest people, with a personal net worth in excess of $50 billion, achieved his initial entrepreneurial success as an acquirer and has continued on this path ever since. Despite its court battles, Microsoft continues to grow, investing hundreds of millions of dollars each year to acquire technologies and companies. Over the last three years, Microsoft has spent more than $3 billion on acquisitions.[29] Don't worry, however—there's still some spare change in the Microsoft couch. In June 2007, Microsoft had $23.4 billion in cash on its books.[30] In October 2007, Microsoft paid $240 million for 1.6 percent of the online social network Facebook, which was founded three years earlier.

The Start-Up

Creating a company from nothing other than an idea for a product or service is the most difficult and risky way to be a successful entrepreneur. Two great examples of start-up entrepreneurs are Steve Wozniak, a college dropout, and Steve Jobs of Apple Computer. As an engineer at Hewlett-Packard, Wozniak approached the company with an idea for a small personal computer. The company did not take him seriously and rejected his idea; this decision turned out to be one of the greatest intrapraneurial blunders in history. With $1,300 of his own money, Wozniak and his friend Steve Jobs launched Apple Computer from his parents' garage.

The Apple Computer start-up is a great example of a start-up that was successful because of the revolutionary technological innovation created by the technology genius Wozniak. Other entrepreneurial firms that were successful as a result of technological innovations include Amazon.com, founded by Jeff Bezos; Google, with Harry Page and Sergey Brin; and Facebook, with Mark Zuckerberg.

But entrepreneurial start-up opportunities in the technology industry do not have to be limited to those who create new technology. For example, Dell Computer, one of the largest computer systems companies in the world, with $61 billion in annual revenues in 2008,[31] is not now, and never has been, a research and development–driven company, unlike the companies previously mentioned. Michael Dell, the founder, got his entrepreneurial opportunity from the implementation of the simple idea that he could "out-execute" his competitors. He has always built computers to customer orders and sold them directly to consumers at prices lower than those of his competitors. As he explained, "I saw that you'd buy a PC for about $3000 and inside that PC was about $600 worth of parts. IBM would buy most of these parts from other companies, assemble them, and sell the computer to a dealer for $2000. Then the dealer, who knew very little about selling or supporting computers, would sell it for $3000, which was even more outrageous."[32]

Michael Dell, who dropped out of the University of Texas and founded his company in 1984 with a $1,000 loan from his parents, went on to become in 1992, at age 27, the youngest CEO of a Fortune 500 company. Less than 10 years later, Dell had revenues of more than $15 billion in just the first six months of 2001, and its founder topped the *Forbes* "40 richest under 40" list. Today, Dell is ranked number 43 on the Forbes list of the world's billionaires, with a net worth in excess of $16 billion.[33]

Entrepreneurial start-ups have not been limited to technology companies. In 1993, Kate Spade quit her job as the accessories editor for *Mademoiselle* and, with her husband, Andy, started her own women's handbag company called Kate Spade, Inc. Her bags, a combination of whimsy and function, have scored big returns on the initial $35,000 investment from Andy's 401(k). In 1999, sales had doubled to $50 million. Neiman Marcus purchased a 56 percent stake in February 1999 for $33.6 million.[34] And in 2006, revenues reached $84 million.

Finally, there are also numerous successful start-ups that began from an idea other than the entrepreneur's. For example, Mario and Cheryl Tricoci are the owners of a $40 million international day spa company headquartered in Chicago called Mario Tricoci's. In 1986, after returning from a vacation at a premier spa outside the United States, they noticed that there were virtually no day spas in the country, only those with weeklong stay requirements. Therefore, they started their day spa company, based on the ideas and styles they had seen during their international travels.[35]

NOTES

1. Michie P. Slaughter, "Entrepreneurship: Economic Impact and Public Policy Implications," Center for Entrepreneurial Leadership Inc., Ewing Marion Kauffman Foundation, March 1996; Mike Hermann, Kauffman Foundation, 1997.
2. Wendy M. Beech, "Business Profiles: And the Winners Are . . . , " *Black Enterprise*; Carolyn M. Brown and Tonia L. Shakespeare, "A Call to Arms for Black Business," *Black Enterprise*, November 1996, pp. 79–80.
3. Office of Economic Research, Small Business Administration.
4. Donna Fena, "The Making of an Entrepreneurial Generation," *Inc.*, July 2007.
5. Raymond W. Smilor, "Vital Speeches and Articles of Interest, Entrepreneurship and Philanthropy," prepared for the Fifth Annual Kellogg-Kauffman Aspen Seminar on Philanthropy, September 1996.
6. *New York Times*, September 23, 1998.
7. "1995 Inc. 500 Almanac," *Inc.*, 1995.
8. Anne Morgan, *Prescription for Success: The Life and Values of Ewing Marion Kauffman*, 1995.
9. Wilson Harrell, *Inc.*
10. David H. Freedman, "The Money Trail," *Inc.*, December 1998.
11. John Greenwald, "Master of the Mainframe: Thomas Watson Jr.," *Time*, December 7, 1998.
12. Kerry Pipes, "History of Franchising: This Business Model Is an Original—and a Winner," Franchising.com Web site, posted on March 25, 2007.
13. Dunkin' Donuts Franchising Web site, http://www.dunkinfranchising.com/aboutus/franchise/franchise-overview.html.

14. Ibid.

15. Pipes, "History of Franchising."

16. "Answers to the 21 Most Commonly Asked Questions about Franchising," International Franchise Association home page, October 22, 2001, http://www.franchise.org/resourcectr/faq/faq.asp.

17. Pipes, "History of Franchising."

18. Gerda D. Gallop, "15 Franchises You Can Run from Home," *Black Enterprise*, September 9, 1998.

19. *QSR Magazine*, June 2006.

20. "The Profile of Franchising," International Franchise Association Educational Foundation Inc., 2001.

21. Kristen Dunlop Godsey, "Market like Mad: How One Man Built a McDonald's Franchise Empire," *Success*, February 1997.

22. Starbucks, 2006 Annual Report, Starbucks home page, www.starbucks.com.

23. 1–800-Flowers.com Inc., 2006 Annual Report, 1–800-Flowers.com Inc. home page, www.1800flowers.com.

24. Radio One, Inc., 2005 Annual Report, Radio One home page, www.radio-one.com.

25. Duncan Maxwell Andersen and Michael Warshaw, with Mari-Alyssa Mulvihill, "The 1 Entrepreneur in America: Blockbuster Video's Wayne Huizenga," *Success*, March 1995, p. 36.

26. Ibid.

27. "Wayne Huizenga," video, University of Southern California.

28. David Gelernter, "Software Strongman: Bill Gates," *Time*, December 7, 1998, p. 131.

29. *BusinessWeek*, January 1997.

30. Microsoft, Inc., 2007 Annual Report, Microsoft home page, www.microsoft.com.

31. Dell Inc., 2008 Annual Report, Dell home page, www.dell.com.

32. Richard Murphy, "Michael Dell," *Success*, January 1999.

33. "World's Billionaires List," *Forbes*, March 2008.

34. "Top Entrepreneurs of 1999," *BusinessWeek*, January 2000, http://www.businessweek.co/smallbiz/content/jan2000/ep3663075.htm.

35. Terri Roberson, "The Partners behind the Day Spa Explosion," *Today's Chicago Woman*, December 1998.

CHAPTER 2

The Entrepreneur

INTRODUCTION

Faced with a white-knuckle crisis on the *Apollo 13* mission, legendary NASA flight director Gene Kranz rallied his troops with the now famous and stirring battle cry, "Failure is not an option." Unfortunately, a few million entrepreneurs beg to differ.

SUCCESS RATES OF ENTREPRENEURS

It takes a certain amount of guts, nerve, chutzpah—whatever you want to call it—to cut the safety net and go out on your own and start a business. No one who does it, including me, has the end goal of burning through his life savings, failing miserably, and dying alone and penniless! In reality, the deck is stacked against the entrepreneur. In Appendix C you will find a ranking of the riskiest and safest small businesses as determined by the percentage of those businesses that make or lose money. The failure rate of companies, particularly start-ups, is staggering. A study by the Small Business Administration (SBA) showed the following failure rates for small businesses:

- 34 percent within two years after starting up
- 56 percent after four years[1]

Another study done by Dun & Bradstreet shows that 63 percent of businesses with less than 20 employees fail within four years and a whopping 91 percent fail within ten.[2] Failure rates for start-up companies are also high in foreign markets. For example, in New Zealand, research shows that 53 percent of small and medium-sized businesses fail within three years.[3] Statistics Canada indicated that 145,000 new businesses start up each year in Canada, and 137,000 go bankrupt there.[4] Every year, 470,000 new businesses open in Brazil, but 43 percent of these businesses will close their doors before their third anniversary.[4a]

Table 2-1 provides data on the total number of business terminations (failures) in the United States from 1990 to 2006. While the data show that the number of failed businesses declined substantially in 2006 from a peak of over 586,000 companies in 2002, this is still higher than the 534,000 firm failures per year average over the period.

TABLE 2-1

Business Failures in the United States

Year	Business Terminations	Percent Change
2006	564,900	3.90
2005	543,700	0.49
2004	541,047	0.07
2003	540,658	−7.88
2002	586,890	6.07
2001	553,291	1.93
2000	542,831	−0.30
1999	544,487	0.72
1998	540,601	2.00
1997	530,003	3.43
1996	512,402	3.05
1995	497,246	−1.25
1994	503,563	2.21
1993	492,651	−5.55
1992	521,606	−4.56
1991	546,518	2.84
1990	531,400	N/A

Source: Small Business Administration, December 2007.

Failure rates climbed significantly in 2001 and 2002, when the "dot-bomb" era claimed thousands of casualties, turned Nasdaq darlings into duds, and foreshadowed a broader economic slowdown. True entrepreneurs have remarkable resilience, however, and the statistics suggest that they need it. The average entrepreneur fails 3.8 times before succeeding.[4a] One such entrepreneur is Steve Perlman, the cofounder of Web TV Networks, which he sold to Microsoft in 1997 for $425 million. Before his success with Web TV, he had been involved in three start-up failures in a 10-year period.

Despite these odds, people are still pursuing the entrepreneurial dream. And this is taking place not only in the United States, but overseas as well. For example, in Taiwan, 1,373 electronics companies were started in 1997. By the end of the year, 1,147 of these companies, or 84 percent, had gone out of business.[5] Despite this high failure rate, the entrepreneurial spirit was alive and well in Taiwan at that time, as evidenced by the fact that the venture capital industry in Taiwan, which had a compound annual growth rate (CAGR) of less than 16 percent from 1990 to 1995 and never exceeded US$600 million in total investments during that period, grew over 67 percent from 1996 to 1997 and over 36 percent from 1997 to 1998, ending at $2.2 billion in total investments in 1998.[6] In 2005, the Taiwanese venture capital industry invested over $5.7 billion. [6a]

One of the obvious reasons for the high rate of entrepreneurial failure is that it is tough to have a successful product, let alone an entire company. A recent Nielsen BASES and Ernst & Young study found that about 95 percent of new consumer products in the United States fail.[7] Kevin Clancy and Peter Krieg of Copernicus Marketing Consulting estimated that no more than 10 percent of all new products or services are successful.[8] Google's vice president for search products and user experience estimates that up to 60 to 80 percent of Google's products may eventually crash and burn.[9]

Another reason for failure is that people are starting companies and then learning about cash flow management, marketing, human resource development, and other such areas on the job. Too many people are learning about what to do when you have cash flow problems when they actually have those problems, rather than in a classroom setting or as an intern with an entrepreneurial firm. This type of training is costly, because the mistakes that are made have an impact on the sustainability of a company. A study of unsuccessful entrepreneurs found that most of them attributed their lack of success to inadequate training.[10] The area in which they lacked the most training was cash flow management.[11]

Now let's look at Table 2-2, which shows the number of business bankruptcies from 1990 to 2006. While the data show that the number of failed businesses declined substantially in 2006, 71,000 companies per year in 1991, the data for 2006 are very likely skewed as a result of significant changes in the U.S. consumer bankruptcy laws that occurred in 2005, which also made it more difficult for some businesses to file bankruptcy. On average, more than 47,000 businesses went belly-up and filed for bankruptcy every year during this period. Again, this is often a case of an entrepreneur who lacks the expertise to manage inventory and cash flow.

T A B L E   2-2

Business Bankruptcies in the United States

Year	Number of Bankruptcies	Percent Change
2006*	19,695	−49.8
2005	39,201	14.2
2004	34,317	−2.1
2003	35,037	−9.1
2002	38,540	−3.9
2001	40,099	13.0
2000	35,472	−6.4
1999	37,884	−14.6
1998	44,367	−17.9
1997	54,027	0.9
1996	53,549	3.1
1995	51,959	−0.8
1994	52,374	−15.9
1993	62,304	−11.8
1992	70,643	−1.3
1991	71,549	10.3
1990	64,853	N/A

Source: Small Business Administration, December 2007.

* There was a change in U.S. bankruptcy laws in 2005.

What we see in the tables is that the business bankruptcy trends in Table 2-2 and the trends for business starts and failures cited in Table 2-1 can be mapped to specific macroeconomic situations occurring in the country. Specifically, we see that the number of bankruptcies peaked in 1991, when the United States was mired in a recession, and the number of business failures peaked in 2002 following the dot-bomb period described previously. Thus, during tough economic times, the number of business failures will increase because owners cannot pay the bills. At the same time, the number of entrepreneurial start-ups will also generally increase during these periods because people get downsized.

There's an important lesson here. All entrepreneurs, prospective and existing, should easily and readily be able to answer the question, what happens to my business during a recession? Businesses respond to recessions differently. For example, one type of business that does well during recessions is auto parts and service because people tend to repair old cars rather than buy new ones. The alcoholic beverages industry also does well during recessions because people tend to drink more when they are depressed or unhappy. Businesses that do not fare as well include restaurants (people eat at home more), the vacation industry, and any businesses that sell luxury items, such as boats.

But just because a business does not fare well during a recession does not mean that a business should not be started at the beginning of or during a recession. It simply means that the entrepreneur should plan wisely, keeping costs under control and maintaining adequate working capital through lines of credit and fast collection of receivables. As an example, *BusinessWeek* magazine began six weeks after the onset of the Great Depression. On a personal note, about a year after I bought my first business, a lampshade-manufacturing firm, the country went into a recession. The Gulf War started, and people stopped shopping and sat home in front of their televisions watching events unfold. I needed them in department stores buying my lampshades! I remember sitting at my desk at work, holding my head in my hands, when my secretary, Angela, interrupted the silence with a gentle knock on my door. "Are you crying?" she asked. "No," I answered. "But I should be! I've had this business less than a year, I've got all this debt, and I've got to figure out how to pay it off." Prior to purchasing the business, I had laid out a specific plan for dealing with a downturn, and we did manage to make it through. But in the spirit of candor, I have to admit that I underestimated how tight business would be. It was ugly.

Years ago, former heavyweight champion Mike Tyson was preparing to fight Michael Spinks. A reporter doing a prefight interview with Tyson told him that Spinks had a carefully laid-out plan for beating the champ. Tyson replied, "Everyone has a plan 'till they get punched in the mouth." I couldn't say it better myself. Do yourself a huge favor: be brutally honest with yourself and any investors, and paint the ugliest damn picture you can imagine. Imagine how the economy, competitors, or other conditions could "punch you in the mouth." Now, tell everyone how your business is going to survive, thrive, and live to ring the cash register another day.

Finally, before starting a business and preparing for a recession, the prospective entrepreneur should be able to answer these questions: Where is the recession? Is it yet to come, has it passed, or are we currently in one? While the 2008 economy is bad, the country is not in a recession. The official definition of a recession is "two consecutive quarters of no GDP growth." The last recession in the United States began in March 2001 and ended in November 2001. The country's economy typically goes through a recession every five to seven years. During the Reagan administration, the country went 92 consecutive months, or 7.7 years, before going through a recession. The second-longest period that the country has gone without a recession was during the Vietnam War, with 106 consecutive months (8.8 years).[12] And the entrepreneurship decade of the 1990s holds the record for the longest period that the country has not been in a recession. As of March 2001, the country had gone 133 consecutive months without a recession.

But as noted earlier, failing does not exclude one from becoming an entrepreneur. There are many notable examples of entrepreneurs who have succeeded despite initial failures. For example, Fred Smith had an unsuccessful company before he succeeded with Federal Express. Berry Gordy, the founder of Motown Records, started a jazz record shop that went bankrupt. Following this bankruptcy, he went to work for Ford Motor Company on the assembly line to get his personal finances in order, then left that job to start Motown Records. Henry Ford went bankrupt twice before Ford Motor Company succeeded. And as Henry Ford said, "Failure is the chance to begin again more intelligently. It is just a resting place."[13]

Therefore, all prospective entrepreneurs should take heed of the fact that entrepreneurial success is more the exception than the rule. In all likelihood, one will not succeed. But one must simply realize that failure is merely an entrepreneurial rite of passage. It happens to almost everyone, and financiers will typically give the entrepreneur another chance as long as the failure was not the result of lying, cheating, stealing, or laziness. They would rather invest in someone who has failed and learned from the experience than in an inexperienced person. Venture capitalists in Silicon Valley deem failure not only inevitable but also valuable. Michael Moritz, a partner at Sequoia Capital, who invested $500,000 in Apple Computer in 1978 and turned that investment into a $120 million investment three years later when the company went public, noted that entrepreneurs who have suffered a setback could be better bets than those who have enjoyed only success.[14]

Warren Packard, managing director at the Silicon Valley venture capital firm Draper Fisher Jurvetson, is quoted as saying:

> Failure is just a word for learning experience. When we meet an entrepreneur who has not been successful, we ask ourselves, "Did he learn from past mistakes or is he just crazy?" As long as an entrepreneur is honest about his abilities, his past doesn't matter. He has learned some very important lessons on someone else's dollar.[15]

Renowned venture capitalist John Doerr of Kleiner Perkins Caufield & Byers (KPCB), the Silicon Valley fund that successfully invested in dozens of Internet-related companies, including Netscape and Amazon.com, said:

> Great people are so hard to find that even if one particular start-up fails, you're not tainted for life.[16]

And finally, Thomas G. Stemberg, founder and CEO of Staples, Inc., noted:

> How you recover is more important than the mistakes you make.[17]

WHY BECOME AN ENTREPRENEUR?

A Harris Interactive study found that 47 percent of Americans who do not currently own their own business have dreamed of starting their own business.[18] Now, why do people want to become entrepreneurs? Why has entrepreneurship become so popular? Everyone has a different reason for wanting to start a business.

Inc. magazine surveyed the owners listed in the *Inc.* magazine 500 and found that the number one reason these entrepreneurs gave for starting their own company was to gain the independence to be able to control their schedule and workload. In fact, 40 percent of the respondents indicated that they started their own companies to "be my own boss."[19]

Many people become entrepreneurs because they loathe working for others. As one person said, he became an entrepreneur because having a job was worse than being in prison:

In prison:	You spend the majority of your time in an 8×10 cell.
At work:	You spend most of your time in a 6×8 cubicle.
In prison:	You get three free meals a day.
At work:	You only get a break for one meal and you have to pay for it.
In prison:	You can watch TV and play games.
At work:	You get fired for watching TV and playing games.
In prison:	You get your own toilet.
At work:	You have to share.
In prison:	You spend most of your life looking through bars from the inside wanting to get out.
At work:	You spend most of your time wanting to get out and go inside bars!
In prison:	There are wardens who are often sadistic.
At work:	They are called MANAGERS![20]

The second most cited reason for becoming an entrepreneur is the sense of accomplishment people achieve when they prove that they can start or own a successful company. Seth Godin, who founded Yoyodyne, an interactive direct-marketing company bought by Yahoo! in late 1998, and is currently CEO of an online venture called Squidoo, a tool that lets users build Web pages, explains the desire: "Most people can't understand why someone who made $10 million would do it again. That's because most people don't like working, and they think it's irrational to keep working."[21] Joseph Schumpeter, the originator of the famous "creative destruction" moniker for capitalism, described it well. "Entrepreneurs, he insisted . . . feel the will to conquer: the impulse to fight, to prove oneself superior to others, to succeed for the sake, not fruits of success, but of success itself. . . . There is the joy of creating, of getting things done, or simply of exercising one's energy and ingenuity."[22]

Interestingly, most people, young or old, do not become entrepreneurs to become rich. This was the case with the 2005 *Inc.* Entrepreneur of the Year, Ping Fu. Ms. Fu was deported in 1981 by the Chinese government after releasing a research report on infanticide. She came to America and, after she learned English, became adept at computer programming. The owner of her company offered her 5 percent equity in the business where she worked and an opportunity to become a millionaire. Fu turned him down. Why? Because for her it was about creating something of value, not getting rich. She is now CEO of Geomagic, a digital shape sampling and processing company with $30 million per year in revenue.[23] In another example, in a survey of high school teens undertaken by the Gallup Organization, 71 percent of the respondents said that they were interested in starting their own businesses. However, only 26 percent cited earning a lot of money as their primary motivation for starting a business.[24] In the *Inc.* magazine survey mentioned earlier, "making a lot of money" was only the third most popular reason why entrepreneurs started their own companies. Finally, a 2006 survey conducted by the University of Nebraska indicated that only 6 percent of business owners believe that the major reason to start a business is to "earn lots of money."[25]

What is evident is that for most people, making a lot of money is not necessarily the driving force for becoming an entrepreneur. However, despite this fact, the majority of wealthy people in the United States became rich as a result of being an entrepreneur. The by-product of entrepreneurship is wealth creation. In the United

States, there are approximately 371 billionaires, 1 million decamillionaires, and over 9 million millionaires.[26] In *The Millionaire Next Door*, the authors found that 80 percent of these people gained their wealth by becoming entrepreneurs or as a result of being part of an entrepreneurial venture. For example, one of the country's wealthiest people, Bill Gates, achieved his wealth by founding Microsoft. Besides Gates, Microsoft has produced an additional 10,000 millionaires.[27] Many of these wealthy people are young men and women who were very ambitious, smart, and talented.

To further support the wealth creation–entrepreneurship relationship, *Forbes* reported that three out of five of the *Forbes* 400 richest Americans were first-generation entrepreneurs.[28] But this wealth creation–entrepreneurship relationship is not new. John D. Rockefeller cofounded Standard Oil, the first major U.S. multinational corporation, in 1870. In 1913, his personal net worth was $900 million, which was equivalent to more than 2 percent of the country's gross national product. Today, 2 percent of the country's gross national product would be approximately $273 billion, more than five times Bill Gates's net worth.

As mentioned earlier, for some people, becoming an entrepreneur was not a choice; rather, they took this route when they were laid off from their jobs. Others started companies with the objective of creating jobs for others. One entrepreneur who has been selected by *Inc.* magazine as one of the company builders who is "changing the face of American businesses" is quoted as saying, "I have a business that has the highest integrity in town. . . . People respect me and I support 72 families."[29] For some entrepreneurs, their business is an outlet for their creative talent. Others feel the need to leave behind a legacy that embodies their values. Still others have community or societal concerns that they feel can best be addressed through their company.[30]

For some people, becoming an entrepreneur is the natural thing to do. They either are the offspring of an entrepreneur or have developed an interest in being an entrepreneur because they were exposed to the business world at an early age. Successful high-growth entrepreneurs who were offspring of entrepreneurs include Berry Gordy of Motown Records; Wayne Huizenga of Waste Management, Blockbuster Video, and AutoNation;

Josephine Esther Mentzer of Estée Lauder; Ted Turner of TBS and CNN television stations; and Akio Morita, who left the sake business that his family owned for 14 generations to start Sony. Donald Trump is also included in this group; ironically, in contrast to Donald and his high-income real estate clients, his father owned real estate that he rented to low-income and working-class families in New York.

Another high-growth entrepreneur who belongs in this category is John Rogers, Jr., the founder of Ariel Capital—a financial management firm that manages billions of dollars. Financial management is in Rogers's blood. To encourage his son's interest in business, every birthday and Christmas, John's father gave his young son stocks as gifts. John's parents, grandparents, and great-grandparents have always owned their own businesses. In fact, his great-grandfather, C. J. Stafford, was an attorney by training but also owned a hotel in Florida. It burned down in the early 1900s when he was falsely accused of starting a race riot. Instead of giving up, Stafford fled Florida and came to Chicago, where he started his own law firm.

Other entrepreneurs start companies to develop a new idea or invention. For example, as discussed earlier, Steve Wozniak, the cofounder of Apple Computer, became an entrepreneur by default. If Hewlett-Packard had not rejected his idea for a user-friendly small personal computer, he probably would not have resigned from the company to start his own business and launch a dramatic change in the computer hardware industry.

Another reason why people want to become entrepreneurs is because of the emergence of role models. Fifteen years ago, the main business role models were corporate executives such as Robert Goizueta, the legendary CEO of the Coca-Cola Corporation who died of cancer in 1997, and Jack Welch of General Electric. In the entrepreneurship decade of the 1990s, entrepreneurs became primary business role models, the people that everyone wanted to emulate. For example, Christian and Timbers, a consulting firm, identified the top CEOs who were mentioned the most often in major business publications in 1997. As Figure 2-1 shows, three of the CEOs who received the most mentions were founders of their companies [those names with an asterisk (*)].[31]

F I G U R E   2-1

The Most Mentioned CEOs

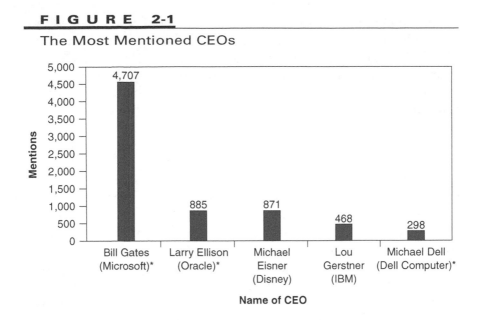

Name of CEO

In a speech titled, "Entrepreneurship, American Style," the American ambassador to Denmark highlighted the reverence that Americans have for entrepreneurs. He notes, "In America, Bill Gates of Microsoft, Steve Jobs of Apple, Fred Smith of Federal Express, and the self-made millionaire down the street, are all considered heroes. In just about every community there are entrepreneurs 'down the street' who have succeeded. In fact, it's the 'ordinary' millionaire down the street who is often the most celebrated, because people think 'hey, he's not half as smart as I am. If he can do it, then so can I.'" The ambassador continued with an anecdote from Kjeld Kirk Kristiansen, the legendary Danish entrepreneur and former CEO of the Lego Group, demonstrating his point: "He said that over the years fans and customers of Lego's products have created product conferences and tradeshows where adults, using Lego bricks, showcase their latest impressive creations. He described two recent such events. One in Berlin, and one in Washington, DC. In Berlin, he said, when he arrived at the conference [he was] treated as just another guest in the room. Nothing special, nothing unique. He contrasted that with the experience in Washington, where, upon his arrival, the 2000 adult customers who were gathered there treated him as a rock star, as a celebrity, as a hero; gathering around, taking photographs, seeking autographs. He says when he gets to go to America for a show like this, he knows how Elvis Presley must have felt."[32]

In 1997, *Inc.* magazine conducted a study aimed at assessing the impact of entrepreneurs and their companies on American businesses. A total of 500 entrepreneurs who had founded their companies between 1982 and 1996 and 200 upper- and middle-level Fortune 500 executives (vice presidents, directors, and managers) were surveyed and asked the same questions. When asked whether they agreed with the statement, "Entrepreneurs are the heroes of American business," 95 percent of the entrepreneurs and 68 percent of the corporate executives agreed. These results were starkly different from the responses given by these two groups 10 years earlier, when 74 percent of entrepreneurs and 49 percent of executives had agreed with this statement. Interestingly, 37 percent of the corporate executives noted that if they could live their lives over, they would choose to run their own companies.[33]

While annual corporate venture capital investments of $1.3 billion in 2005 are down from the stratospheric $17 billion invested in 2000, many of America's most profitable companies continue to devote resources to spurring entrepreneurial activity.[34] Several companies have, in fact, demonstrated this support by creating programs that encourage and assist employees who want to become entrepreneurs. Boeing's Chairman's Innovation Initiative, a $200 million in-house venture capital fund, provides employees the opportunities to develop new business ideas from company-developed ideas. Procter & Gamble pushes "open innovation," encouraging managers to seek new business ideas outside as well as inside the company.[35] Other firms, such as Intel, have internal venture capital arms that search for the next breakthrough technologies. Intel has invested more than $4 billion in about 1,000 companies since the early 1990s, maintaining a consistent investment pace through two major recessions. Adobe functions as a sole limited partner in a venture capital fund that it outsources to Granite Ventures in an effort to maintain relationships with the start-up community.[36]

Finally, as shown in Figure 2-2, a Coca-Cola Company announcement to all the company's employees provides an example of corporations supporting entrepreneurship.

FIGURE   2-2

Coca-Cola Corporation's Fizzion Announcement

To: All Employees Worldwide

Subject: Fizzion, L.L.C.

We recently renewed our company's commitment to benefit and refresh everyone who is touched by our business. Today, I am proud to announce a new endeavor to help The Coca-Cola Company gain access to innovations that will spur our growth as we press forward into a new century. Reflecting the creative energy that it will generate, this new initiative is called "Fizzion," a wholly owned subsidiary of The Coca-Cola Company where new ideas and technologies can grow into successful businesses. Located across the street from our main complex in The Learning Center, Fizzion will provide a host of powerful benefits to entrepreneurs from around the world. Entrepreneurs who become a member and reside at Fizzion will have access to world-class sales and marketing expertise, business management experience, office space and other basic infrastructure. In return, Fizzion member companies will be chosen based on their ability to positively impact the company's volume, revenues or profits when their applications are used in our business.

Fizzion is just one of the projects we are implementing to spur innovation in our business. Fizzion will augment our other partnerships with Ideas.com, Ideashare, and our new Think Tank, which are already underway. In making services available to Fizzion entrepreneurs, opportunities will be created for employees to work with startups in various functional areas. I encourage you to avail yourself of these opportunities as they present themselves in the future.

Source: Coca-Cola Corporation.

Corporate Downsizing

While the 1990s will be known as the entrepreneurship decade, the past 15 years will also be noted for corporate America's continuous downsizing. This corporate downsizing was so pervasive that it became an intrinsic part of the story line for Bill Cosby's television sitcom *Cosby*, which debuted in 1996. In the show, Hilton Lucas, played by Cosby, deals with the travails of being laid off from his job at a major airline. It accurately characterizes the plight of many who have lost their jobs. When he was laid off, Lucas had hoped to be called back, but three years later he was still waiting to hear from his former company.[37] Ironically, CBS eventually downsized the show itself—canceling it.

From January 1995 to October 2001, over 68 percent of all insurance companies, 66 percent of manufacturing companies, and 69 percent of banking and financial institutions laid off employees.

Layoffs have become a fact of life for American workers, and in 2001, the corporate carnage set new records. The numbers were so significant that *Forbes* magazine began to post a daily body count on its Web site. Major corporations trimming their ranks included Lucent (40,000 workers), Ford (5,000 white-collar workers), Agilent (4,000 workers), and Gateway (5,000 workers). By September 2001, more than 1.1 million employees had gotten the ax—an 83 percent jump from the previous year's tally and far above any annual total in the last 12 years.[38] The terrorist attack on the World Trade Center in September 2001 added even more casualties, with virtually all of the nation's airlines announcing major layoffs, more than 100,000 workers, in the weeks that followed. Others in the travel industry followed suit, with Starwood Hotels and Resorts laying off 10,000 workers. American workers have plenty of company overseas: more than 2 million workers in Japan and Southeast Asia lost their jobs in 2001.[39]

In 2008, the pace of corporate layoffs has started to increase again. The U.S. Department of Labor reports that from January 2008 to May 2008, there were 7,615 different layoff events of at least 50 people in the United States, resulting in almost 784,000 new claims for unemployment benefits. This is up substantially from the 6,325 events and 650,000 new claimants of just one year earlier.[40] Some of the business layoffs announced during that period included AOL (2,000), Morgan Stanley (5,000), Merrill Lynch (4,000), and Yahoo! (2,000).[41]

While many furloughed workers will eventually return to other corporate jobs, it's likely that others will follow in the footsteps of previous pink-slip recipients. Many workers who lost their jobs during the corporate cutbacks of the 1980s and 1990s either chose or were forced to pursue the entrepreneurial route rather than employment in the corporate arena. A survey of the founders of the 1996 *Inc.* 500—a list of the 500 fastest-growing small companies—found that 40 percent of these founders started their businesses after a company reshuffling.[42]

The Council on Competiveness, an organization devoted to driving U.S. competiveness in world markets, explains, "Economic growth is not an orderly process of incremental improvements—it happens because new firms are created and older firms are destroyed. . . . And entrepreneurs are the moving force behind this

churn that underpins the dynamism of the U.S. economy."
Economist Joseph Schumpeter refers to this process as "creative
destruction." A result of this creative destruction is that employees
are laid off as firms downsize or go out of business. This unemployment generates new entrepreneurial ventures.[43]

An example of an entrepreneur who chose to start his own
business after being downsized is Patrick Kelly, who started a company called Physicians Sales and Services, which now has over $1.6
billion in revenue and is the nation's largest supplier of medical supplies to physicians' offices. When asked why he became an entrepreneur, he said, "I didn't choose to become an entrepreneur. I got
fired and started a company in order to earn a living. I had to learn
to be a CEO. I'll tell you right now, I stole every idea I have. There is
not an original thought in my head. I stole everything and you
should too." Another happy story regarding a downsized employee
is the story of Bill Rasmussen, who was laid off from his public rela-
tions job in 1979. He went on to start the Entertainment Sports
Programming Network (ESPN) in Connecticut, which is now jointly
owned by Disney and the Hearst family and has over $4 billion in
annual revenues through four domestic cable networks, the nation's
largest sports radio network, and the most visited sports Web site on
the Internet.[44]

Academic Training

In 1970, only 16 American universities provided training in entrepreneurship. Today, more than 2,000 universities throughout the
country (roughly two-thirds of all institutions) have at least one
class, and many more classes are being taught in universities all
over the world. In 1980, there were 18 entrepreneurship endowed
chairs at business schools; today, there are more than 270.[45,46] In
fact, entrepreneurship has become an academic discipline in virtually all of the top business schools across the country. Another indicator of academia's commitment to this field is the fact that
business schools offer not only classes, but also minors and majors
in the field of entrepreneurship. The number of entrepreneurship
majors in undergraduate and MBA programs has risen from as few
as 175 in 1990 to more than 500 today.[47] A major contributor to the
growth of entrepreneurship on campus is the Kauffman Campus

Initiative, which is directing $100 million to the creation of entrepreneurial education programs.

Does entrepreneurial training work? While concrete research is difficult to gather and entrepreneurs such as Steve Jobs of Apple and Bill Gates of Microsoft have certainly succeeded without such education, a 2002 study by the University of Arizona showed that five years after graduation, the average annual income for entrepreneurship majors and MBAs who concentrated in entrepreneurship at school was 27 percent higher than that for students with other business majors and students with standard MBA's.[48] In addition, according to a study by the Kauffman Foundation, 32 percent of successful entrepreneurs had taken at least five business classes, while only 18 percent of unsuccessful entrepreneurs had taken these kinds of courses.

Anecdotal evidence is plentiful. Mark Cuban, who sold his start-up, Broadcast.com, to Yahoo! for $6 billion in 1999 and is the current owner of the Dallas Mavericks and HDNet, swears by his entrepreneurship training. He notes, "One of the best classes I ever took was entrepreneurship in my freshman year at Indiana University. It really motivated me. There is so much more to starting a business than just understanding finance, accounting, and marketing. Teaching kids what has worked with startup companies and learning about experiences that others have had could really make a difference. I know it did for me."[49]

Tatiana Saribekian, a Russian immigrant, believes that San Diego State University's MBA program helped her master the art of the deal. After failing with her first U.S.-based lumber venture, she decided to get an MBA, and concentrated in entrepreneurship. She has recently started over as a builder and reflects on her MBA in entrepreneurship: "My classes opened my eyes to how business works here in America. It is completely different from Russia. I think this time I will have a better chance at success."[50]

Finally, the growth in entrepreneurship will be forever linked with America's technological revolution, which began in the early 1980s. Companies such as Microsoft, Apple, Lotus, and Dell, to name a few, gave birth to the present $600 billion technology industry. Advances in technology have led to the proliferation of new products and services fostering the creation of companies in new areas, such as Internet-based businesses. For example, in 1999, a new computer product was developed every 7 seconds, and a new Internet-related company was established every 48 hours.[51] The years 1995 and 1996 were heady times for Internet pioneers. Table 2-3 shows the growth of Internet services companies during the 1990s as the new sector's growth began to explode.

T A B L E   2-3

Fastest-Growing Businesses, 1995–1996

Business	Number of Firms in 1995	Number of Firms in 1996	Growth
Internet services	24	2,298	9,475%
PC networking services	4,539	6,573	45%
Pager services	1,636	2,148	31%
Bagel shops	2,522	3,291	31%
Cellular phone services	4,037	5,253	30%
Tattoo parlors	2,156	2,569	19%

Source: *USA Today*, March 26, 1997.

This spur in entrepreneurial activity resulted in unprecedented job and wealth creation. In 1997, for example, in Silicon Valley (which is 50 miles long, crossing 30 different city lines), 11 new companies were created each week, resulting in the creation of 62 new millionaires every day.[52] This Internet bubble peaked on March 19, 2000, when the Nasdaq Composite reached 5,048, or twice its value just a year earlier. Of course, many of those millionaires saw their "paper fortunes" disappear in the coming years. More than seven years later, in the summer of 2007, the Nasdaq index was still 40 percent below its March 2000 peak. While much has been made of the losses stemming from the dot-bomb era, technology entrepreneurship has come roaring back. Venture capital funding has risen from $3.8 billion in 2002 to over $27 and $30 billion in 2005 and 2006, respectively. In 2005, the software and telecommunications industry accounted for over $14 billion in revenues.[53]

One of the most prominent entrepreneurial technology firms of the 1990s was Yahoo!. It was started in 1995 and went public in 1996 at an astonishing valuation of $850 million, despite the fact that its profits in 1996 were only $81,000 on revenues of $400,000. In 2001, the company lost 90 percent of its market capitalization, forced out its CEO, announced not one but two series of layoffs, and was struggling to regain its footing. Like the technology industry itself, however, Yahoo! has rebounded. Between April 2, 2001, and April 2, 2007, Yahoo!'s share price has risen from $7 per share to over $31 per share. This is a return of more than 440 percent.

Technology still remains a huge driver of entrepreneurship today. In fact, around 2005, Internet start-ups began to see a resurgence, due in part to the development of the next wave of Internet applications, commonly dubbed "Web 2.0" and most popularly characterized by Facebook.com. While this Web 2.0 period has seen an increase in the number of firms getting funded, an increase in valuations, and an increase in prominent acquisitions, fortunately, it appears that some of the craziness seen in the 1990s has been tempered. Bill Burnham, a former partner at Mobius Venture Capital, describes this new mentality well: "The bubble generation is much more attuned to the fact that things can get really out of hand. There's a level of caution that has been ingrained."[54]

TRAITS OF AN ENTREPRENEUR

Building a successful, sustainable business requires courage, patience, and resilience. It demands a level of commitment that few people are capable of making. Membership in the "entrepreneurs club," while not exclusive, does seem to attract a certain type of individual. What, if any, are the common attributes of successful high-growth entrepreneurs?

While it is impossible to identify all the traits that are common to all entrepreneurs, it is possible to describe certain characteristics that are exhibited by most successful entrepreneurs. A survey of 400 entrepreneurs undertaken by an executive development consultant, Richard Hagberg, identified the top 10 characteristics that define entrepreneurs. These characteristics are

- Focused, steadfast, and undeviating
- Positive outlook
- Opinionated and judges quickly
- Impatient

- Prefers simple solutions
- Autonomous and independent
- Aggressive
- Risk taker
- Acts without deliberation and reactive
- Emotionally aloof [55]

While this list is thorough, the addition of a few more traits would make it more complete:

- Opportunist
- Sacrificer
- Visionary
- Problem solver
- Comfortable with ambiguity or uncertainty

Some of these traits are worth discussing in more detail.

Focused, Steadfast, and Undeviating

Successful entrepreneurs are focused on their mission and committed to getting it accomplished despite the enormous odds against them. They are tenacious in nature—they persevere. They are not quitters. If you want to join the club of entrepreneurship and you have never done anything to its completion in your life, this may not be the club for you, because it is one where you will be required to hang tough even when times get rough. And in all likelihood, especially in the first three to five years of a new business, there will be more bad times than good, no matter how successful the venture is.

An example of an entrepreneur who was focused on her goals is Josephine Esther Mentzer, the founder of the Estée Lauder Cosmetic Company, who is described as a person who "simply outworked everyone else in the cosmetics industry. She stalked the bosses of New York City department stores until she got some counter space at Saks Fifth Avenue in 1948."[56] Her company, which presently controls 8 percent of the cosmetics market in U.S. department stores and had $6.4 billion in revenues in 2006 from 130 countries throughout the world, pioneered the practice, which is common today, of giving a free gift to customers with a purchase.

Positive Outlook and Optimistic

Entrepreneurs are confident optimists, especially when it comes to their ideas and their ability to successfully achieve their goals. They are people who view the future in a positive light, seeing obstacles as challenges to be overcome, not as stumbling blocks. They visualize themselves as owners of businesses, employers, and change agents. The rough-and-tumble world of entrepreneurship is not a good fit for someone who is not an optimist.

Bryant Gumbel, the former *Today* show host and CBS morning show anchor, once told a story that illustrates this point well:

> It is Christmas morning and two kids—one a pessimist, the other an optimist—open their presents. The pessimist gets a brand new bike decked out with details and accessories in the latest style. "It looks great," he says. "But it will probably break soon." The second kid, an optimist and future entrepreneur, opens a huge package, finds it filled with horse manure and jumps with glee, exclaiming, "There must be a pony in there somewhere!"[57]

Prefers Simple Solutions

Ross Perot, the founder of EDS, and Ted Turner, the founder of CNN, are two successful entrepreneurs who have a prototypical knack for always describing the simplicity of their entrepreneurial endeavors. One of their favorite quotes, stated with their respective comforting southern accents, is, "It's real simple." One can easily envision one of them being the entrepreneur described in the following story of a chemist, a physicist, an engineer, and an entrepreneur. Each of them was asked how he or she would measure the height of a light tower with the use of a barometer. The chemist explained that she would measure the barometric pressure at the base of the tower and at the top of the tower. Because barometric pressure is related to altitude, she would determine the height of the tower from the difference in pressures. The physicist said that he would drop the barometer from the top of the tower and time how long it took to fall to the ground. From this time and the law of gravity, he could determine the tower's height. The engineer said that she would lower the barometer from the top of the tower on a string and then measure the length of the string. Finally, the entrepreneur said that he would go to the keeper of the tower, who probably knows every detail about the tower, and say, "Look, if you tell me the height of the tower, I'll give you this new shiny barometer."[58]

Autonomous and Independent

Entrepreneurs are known to be primarily driven by the desire to be independent of bosses and bureaucratic rules. Essentially, they march to their own beat. As one observer who was experienced in training entrepreneurs noted, "Entrepreneurs don't march left, right, left. They march left, left, right, right, left, hop, and skip."[59]

Risk Taker

A study by Wayne Stewart, a management professor at Clemson University, investigated common traits among serial entrepreneurs, whom he defined as people owning and operating three or more businesses over their lifetime. He found that the 12 percent of all entrepreneurs who fit the "serial entrepreneur" bill had a higher propensity for risk, innovation, and achievement than their counterparts. In essence, they were less scared of failure.[60]

The most common misconception people have of entrepreneurs is that they are blind risk takers. Most people think that entrepreneurs are no more than wild gamblers who start businesses with the same attitude and preparation that they would undertake if they were going to Las Vegas to roll the dice, hoping for something positive to happen. This perception could not be further from the truth. Successful entrepreneurs are, without doubt, risk takers—they have to be if they are going to seize upon new opportunities and act decisively in ambiguous situations—but for the most part they are "educated" risk takers. They weigh the opportunity and its associated risks before they take action. They research the market or business opportunity, prepare solid business plans prior to taking action, and afterward diligently "work" the plan. They also recognize that risk taking does not—despite the fact that this is a calculated risk—always guarantee success. There are always exceptions to the rule, however. Fred Smith, the founder and CEO of Federal Express, did roll the dice, so to speak, 20 years ago when his start-up was low on capital. Despondent after being unsuccessful at raising capital during a trip to Chicago, he boarded a plane to Las Vegas at O'Hare Airport instead of to his home in Memphis and played blackjack, winning $30,000, which he used to save his company.

Entrepreneurs are risk takers because failure does not scare them. As John Henry Peterman, the founder of the Kentucky-based J. Peterman catalog, commonly known as the company that employed Elaine Benis on the hit television series *Seinfeld*, said, "There is a great fear of failure in most people. I never had that. If failing at something destroys you, then you really have failed. But if failing leads you to a new understanding, new knowledge, you have not. If you don't make any mistakes, you're not doing it right."[61]

Opportunist

Entrepreneurs are proactive by nature. The difference between an entrepreneur and a nonentrepreneur is that the former does not hesitate to seize upon opportunities. When entrepreneurs see an opportunity, they execute a plan to take advantage of it. That disposition is in stark contrast to nonentrepreneurs, who may see something glittering at the bottom of a stream and say, "Isn't that gold?" But instead of stopping and mining the gold, they simply keep paddling their boat.[62] An example of this type of opportunism is the story of Henry Kwahar, who owned a hot dog stand on the south side of Chicago in the early 1970s. During one of the hottest days of August 1973, a refrigerated truck filled with frozen fish broke down in front of Henry's stand. Rather than let the fish spoil, Henry, who had never sold fish before, offered to buy the entire stock at a very sharp discount. The truck driver agreed, and that is how Dock's Great Fish Fast Food Restaurant began. Henry named the restaurants after his father, Dock. There are presently 27 Dock's restaurants in Chicago and Cleveland.

Sacrificer

Every successful entrepreneur will acknowledge that success does not come without sacrifice. The most common sacrifice that an entrepreneur makes is in terms of personal income, particularly during the initial stages of a company. Almost all entrepreneurs must be willing to give up some amount of personal income to get a business started, either by committing their own resources or by taking a cut in pay. One of Jeff Bezos's early investors said that the most convincing factor was that Bezos had given up a job at D. E. Shaw with a seven-figure annual salary to start Amazon.com. The investor quoted, "The fact that Bezos had left that kind of situation overwhelmed me. It gave me a very, very powerful urge to get involved with this guy."[63] In fact, capital providers, such as bankers and venture capitalists, want to see an entrepreneur earning a salary that is enough to live comfortably, but not too comfortably, during the buildup stage of the business. Specifically, the entrepreneur's expected salary should be enough to cover her personal bills (e.g., home mortgage, car payment, and so on), but not enough to permit personal savings of any significant magnitude. This indicates to potential financial backers both the entrepreneur's level of commitment to the venture and her realism about the challenges that lie ahead.

A case in point: In 1996, a venture capitalist received a business plan from a team of three prospective entrepreneurs who wanted to start a national daily newspaper targeting middle-class minorities. The idea seemed sound—such a newspaper did not exist to meet the demands of a rapidly growing segment of the U.S. population. The request for start-up capital was rejected, however, as it was evident to the venture capitalist, upon reading the business plan, that the team did not understand this key notion of sacrificing personal income. The three of them included in their projections starting salaries of nearly $400,000 each, comparable to the corporate salaries they were earning at the time! Such salaries put them in the top 1 percent of the highest-salaried people in the country. The venture capitalist viewed this as a sure sign that these three businesspeople were not sincere entrepreneurs. Business owners in general earn much less than what these three prospective entrepreneurs expected. Even 10 years after those entrepreneurs proposed combined compensation of over $1.2 million, according to Salary.com's survey of small businesses in 2006, the average base salary for CEOs of small businesses was $258,000 (see Table 2-4).[64] For entrepreneurs in information technology and health sciences, industries in which venture capital is prominent, the average compensation is $238,000 for founder CEOs and $290,000 for non-founder CEOs.[65] According to the SEC, Bill Gates's 2001 annual salary, excluding bonuses, was only $616,677.

T A B L E   2-4

Average Total Cash Compensation for CEOs of Companies with Fewer than 500 Employees

Region	Average Salary
Northeast	$545,000
South	$411,000
West Coast	$430,000
Midwest	$243,000
Mountain States	$109,000

Source: Salary.com, 2006.

Another difficult sacrifice that successful entrepreneurs sometimes make is spending less time with their families. For example, entrepreneur Alan Robbins, the owner of a 50-employee firm called Plastic Lumber Company, once said that he regretted not spending more time with his children during the beginning of his business, but he considered it a trade-off he had to make. He argued, "When you start a business like this . . . you have to deny your family a certain level of attention."[66] The demands of owning or building a business put considerable strains on an entrepreneur's time.

However, this doesn't mean that the entrepreneur must *completely* neglect his family or friends in order to run a successful business. To do so in the name of entrepreneurship is called "entremanureship"! When I owned my businesses, I didn't miss the nightly dinner with my family. I didn't miss my kids' birthday parties or baseball games—I worked around them. My two daughters are older now—one in graduate business school at Harvard and the other recently graduating from Princeton—but when I started my businesses they were ages eight and four. I coached my younger daughter's Little League baseball team and her flag football team. I would have coached the older one, too, but she'd decided that perhaps it would be best for me to simply cheer from the stands. I've seen more of my kids' games and events than any other parent I know.

Of course you're going to work long hours in the first couple of years to get your business going. But one of the beautiful things about being your own boss is that, by and large, you're the one who determines *which* hours to work. In addition to sitting on several boards of billion-dollar companies, I'm also a director for several start-ups. I tell these entrepreneurs, "Go home, have dinner with the family, and read the kids a bedtime story. Then get your butt back to work." When Staples surveyed small-business owners (those with under 20 employees), 33 percent reported working while they eat dinner, 73 percent said that they worked during their last vacation, and over 75 percent reported working more than a 40-hour workweek.[67] The MasterCard Global Business Survey of 4,000 small-business owners found that the average U.S. business manager works 52 hours per week. This figure actually rises to 54 hours per week if you include all eight countries surveyed.[68] When *Inc.* magazine surveyed the CEOs of its 500 fastest-growing companies, 66 percent of them remember working at least 70 hours per week when they started their company, and 40 percent reported working more than 80 hours per week.[69] Ken Ryan, CEO of Airmax, told *Inc.*, "There were times when I slept on the floor by the phone so as not to miss a call." The good news is that only 13 percent say that they *now* log more than 70 hours. Trust me, it gets better. You *can* make time to take your kids to the park, but nobody said starting a business was a walk in one.

Visionary

Webster's Collegiate Dictionary defines a visionary as someone who is "marked by foresight." This is an appropriate characterization of most successful entrepreneurs. They are able to anticipate future trends, identify opportunities, and visualize the actions needed to accomplish a desired goal. They must then sell this vision to potential customers, financiers, and employees. A couple of entrepreneurs who were great visionaries and made an impact on almost everyone's daily lives include

Ray Kroc, Founder—McDonald's Corporation

Ray Kroc was an acquirer; he purchased McDonald's restaurants in 1961 for $2.7 million from the two brothers who founded the chain, Dick and Mac McDonald. After concluding that Americans were becoming people who increasingly liked to "eat and run" rather than dining traditionally at a restaurant or eating at home, his vision was to build the quick-service, limited-menu restaurants throughout the country. McDonald's, with operations in 118 countries, is now the largest restaurant company in the world. By the way, for the graying dreamers reading this book, Kroc was a 52-year-old salesman when he bought McDonald's.

Akio Morita, Cofounder—Sony Corporation

Akio Morita cofounded Sony—the company that a Harris survey ranked as the number one consumer brand in America for the seventh consecutive year in 2006. The company, which was started in 1942 under the name Tokyo Telecommunications Engineering Inc. and went on to become the first Japanese firm on the NYSE in 1970, succeeded by using Akio's vision to market the company throughout the world so that the name would immediately communicate high product quality. While this is a marketing concept that is commonly used today, it was not so 40 years ago, especially in Japan. In fact, most Japanese manufacturers produced products under somebody else's name, including Pentax for Honeywell, Ricoh for Savin, and Sanyo for Sears. Sony successfully introduced the small pocket-sized transistor radio in 1957. Six years later, in 1963, with the vision of making Sony an international company, Morita moved his entire family to New York so that he could personally get to know the interests, needs, and culture of Americans and the American market.[70]

All successful entrepreneurs are visionaries at one time or another. They have to constantly reinvent their strategy, look for new opportunities, and go after new products and new ideas if they are to survive. However, this does not mean that they have this ability all the time. Visionaries can become nonvisionaries. In fact, as Cognetics Consulting points out, sometimes "the most astute masters of the present are often the least able to see the future."[71] Examples of some famous nonvisionaries include:

Heavier than air flying machines are impossible.

—*Lord Kelvin*
President of the Royal Society, in 1895[72]

Everything that can be invented has been invented.
—*Charles H. Duell*
Commissioner, U.S. Office of Patents, in 1899[73]

I think there is a world market for maybe five computers.
—*Thomas Watson*
Chairman, IBM, in 1943[74]

We don't like their music, we don't like their sound, and guitar music is on the way out.
—*Decca Recording Company*,
rejecting the Beatles in 1962[75]

There is no reason anyone would want a computer in their home.
—*Ken Olsen*
Founder and Chairman, Digital Equipment Corp., in 1977[76]

Problem Solver

Anyone working in today's competitive and ever-changing business environment knows that the survival of a company, be it large or small, depends on its ability to quickly identify problems and find solutions. Successful entrepreneurs are comfortable with and adept at identifying and solving problems facing their businesses. Risk takers by nature, they are willing to try new ways to solve the problems facing their companies and are capable of learning from their own and others' mistakes or failures. The successful entrepreneur is one who says, "I failed here, but this is what I learned." Successful entrepreneurs are always capable of extracting some positive lesson from any experience.

An example of someone who exhibits this characteristic is Norm Brodsky, a former owner of six companies and presently a writer for *Inc.* magazine. In an article, he says, "I prefer chaos. Deep down I like having problems. It's hard to admit it, but I enjoy the excitement of working in a crisis atmosphere. That's one of the reasons I get so much pleasure out of starting businesses. You have nothing but problems when you are starting out."[77]

Comfortable with Ambiguity or Uncertainty

The ability to function in an environment of continual uncertainty is a common trait found among successful entrepreneurs. Often, they will be required to make decisions, such as determining market demand for a newly developed product or service, without having adequate or complete information. Other important traits that successful entrepreneurs have in common are that they are hard-working people who possess numerous skills, as they are required to play multiple roles as owners of businesses. They are good leaders. They have the ability to sell, whether it is a product, an idea, or a vision. One of the most infamous sales pitches used by an entrepreneur was when Steven Jobs, the cofounder of Apple Computer, was closing his recruiting speech to PepsiCo.'s John Sculley, whom he wanted to become Apple's CEO. To sell John on the opportunity, Jobs asked him, "Do you want to spend the rest of your life selling sugared water or do you want a chance to change the world?"[78]

IMPACT ON THE ECONOMY

Entrepreneurs with small and medium-sized growth businesses are playing an increasingly crucial role in the success of the U.S. economy.[79] Not only are they providing economic opportunities to a diverse segment of the population, but they are also providing employment to an increasingly large segment of the U.S. population. The Fortune 500 companies are no longer the major source of employment; rather, entrepreneurs are creating jobs and therefore are doing "good for society by doing well." As one employee of a 400-employee firm said about his company's owner, "To everybody else she's an entrepreneur. But to me she is a Godsend."[80]

In the 1960s, 1 out of every 4 persons in the United States worked for a Fortune 500 company. Today, only 1 out of every 14 people works for one of these companies. Companies with fewer than 500 workers employ 51 percent of all employees. Approximately 42 million people work at companies with 20 to 49 employees, a workforce second only to that of companies with at least 5,000 employees.[81]

Small businesses have long been recognized as a primary engine of growth and innovation. The SBA reports that new businesses create between 60 and 80 percent of all new jobs every year. In 2003, as the United States emerged from a recession, firms with fewer than 500 employees created almost 1 million net jobs. Recent data even within small business segments show that the smaller the firm, the more jobs it creates. Between 2002 and 2003, firms with fewer than 20 employees added 4 times as many jobs (1.6 million) as firms with 20 to 499 employees. Small businesses produce 13 to 14 times more patents than do large firms.[82]

Finally, entrepreneurial firms are also important participants in U.S. international trade. Data from the Department of Commerce show that in 2002, companies with fewer than 500 employees represented 97 percent of all U.S. exporters and contributed approximately 26 percent of the $599.8 billion in exports that year.[83]

As the data in Table 2-5 show, entrepreneurial firms created almost all of the net new jobs from 1998 through 2003.

T A B L E   2-5

Job Creation by Industry and Size of Firm, 1998–2003

Industry	Firm Size (by Number of Employees)								
Industry	1–19	%	20–99	%	100–499	%	500+	%	Total
All industries	6,494,443	122.95	451,455	8.55	14,510	0.27	−1,678,180	−31.77	5,282,228
Manufacturing	156,738		−386,461		−532,122		−2,136,555		−2,898,400
Retail trade	440,504		−56,808		−20,381		528,099		891,414
Services	857,132		332,601		234,302		204,635		1,628,670
Other	5,040,069		562,123		332,711		−274,359		5,660,544

Source: Small Business Administration.

The findings of a study undertaken by Cognetics Consulting, a company specializing in small businesses, reinforces the data provided in Table 2-5. As you can see in Table 2-6, from 2000 through 2005, employment increased mainly in small companies, while it decreased in larger ones.

T A B L E   2-6

Employment Growth by Firm Size, 2000–2005

Number of Employees	Employment Growth, 2000–2005
1–19	3.4%
20–499	2.2%
Over 500	1.3%

Source: Small Business Association.

Contrary to popular belief, small businesses are not the exception in the American economy; they are the norm. This fact was highlighted when *Crain's Chicago Business* weekly business newspaper advertised its new small-business publication by taking out a full-page advertisement that read:

THERE WAS A

TIME WHEN 90% OF

CHICAGO AREA

BUSINESSES HAD

REVENUES OF

UNDER $5 MILLION.

(YESTERDAY).[84]

On the national level, the same holds true. Out of the approximately 23 million businesses in the United States, only about 5.2 percent have annual revenues greater than $1 million, and approximately 15,000 companies have sales of $100 million or more.[85] Figure 2-3 provides data on the ownership category of all businesses in 2000.

FIGURE 2-3

Business Ownership, 2000

5.8 million nonfarm employer firms

9.9 million self-employed

17.9 million sole proprietorships

2 million partnerships

5.5 million corporations

Source: SBA Office of Advocacy, August 2001.

In terms of firm size, again Chicago is an excellent example of the national situation. Data from the U.S. Census Bureau show that 95.3 percent of businesses in Chicago have fewer than 100 employees.[86] As stated earlier, the national situation is the same: only 103,585 companies have more than 100 employees, and only 17,047 employ more than 500 employees. In fact, of the 5.88 million companies with at least 1 employee, more than 60 percent employ fewer than 5 people, while 89 percent employ fewer than 20.[87] Clearly, large companies are the exception.

The dominance of small businesses as major employers holds true on the international level as well, particularly in Asia. In Japan, for example, 70 percent of the workforce is employed at companies with 300 or fewer workers[88]; in South Korea, 87 percent of the workforce is employed in companies with less than 200 employees.[89] In Taiwan, 78 percent of the labor force is employed by companies with fewer than 200 employees.[90] Small companies are also very dominant in the United Kingdom, where 99.3 percent of all businesses had fewer than 49 employees and 58.5 percent of all employment came from firms with fewer than 250 employees.[91]

Thus, small-business owners should not be ashamed or embarrassed by their size, but should rather be proud that they are major contributors to the success of the U.S. and the global economy. They are, in fact, economic "heroes and sheroes."

IMPACT ON GENDER AND RACE

The entrepreneurial phenomenon has been widespread and inclusive, affecting both genders and all races and nationalities in the United States. One group that has benefited is female entrepreneurs. In the 1960s, there were fewer than 1 million women-owned businesses employing less than 1 million people. By the 1970s, women owned less than 5 percent of all businesses in the United States. In the 1980s, they owned about 3 million businesses, approximately 20 percent of all businesses, generating $40 billion in annual revenues.

Things have changed tremendously. Recent statistics from the Center for Women's Business Research showed that in 2006, privately held women-owned businesses in the United States totaled 7.7 million, employed 7.1 million people, and generated $1.1 trillion in revenues. This report defines women-owned businesses as privately held firms in which women own 51 percent or more of the firm. When firms that are 50 percent owned by women are considered, an additional 2.7 million firms come into play, raising the total number of firms to 41 percent of all privately held firms in the country. Between 1997 and 2006, the number of majority women-owned firms increased 42.3 percent—nearly twice the rate of all other firms (excluding publicly held companies). Also, at 4.4 percent growth, revenues for these firms increased faster than the national average, which was actually a decline of 1.2 percent for the same period.[92] Finally, not surprisingly, contrary to much of what is said in the popular press, women are not starting businesses out of need. Forte Foundation research reports that women start businesses for the same reasons as men: because they are driven to achieve and want control over their achievement.[93]

The entrepreneurship revolution has also included virtually all of the country's minority groups. Minority-owned firms grew three times faster than the national average between 1997 and 2002, increasing from 3.1 million to about 4.1 million firms. The number of African –American–owned businesses jumped 45 percent to 1.2 million over the same five-year period, and the number of Asian-owned businesses jumped 24 percent to 1.1 million. Hispanic enterprises also saw a significant increase, moving up 31 percent to 1.6 million.[94] Finally, for minority women, the data are also strong. The number of businesses owned by women of color grew at six times the rate of all privately held firms in the United States and generated $147 billion in annual sales.

NOTES

1. Small Business Administration, Office of Advocacy, "Frequently Asked Questions," June 2006.
2. "Some of the Reasons Why Businesses Fail and How to Avoid Them," *Entrepreneur Weekly*, Issue 36, March 10, 1996.
3. Statistics New Zealand, 2003.
4. The Brazilian Micro and Small Business Support Service(SEBRAE), August 2004.
4a. *Black Enterprise*, December 1997.
5. Jonathan Moore, Pete Engardio, and Moon Ihlwan, "The Taiwan Touch," *BusinessWeek*, May 25, 1998.
6. AnnaLee Saxenian, "Taiwan's Hsinchu Region: Imitator and Partner for Silicon Valley," Stanford Institute for Policy Research, June 16, 2001.

6a. Taiwan Private Equity and Venture Capital Association, 2008.

7. "Failure Rate of New Products Is 65%,"*International Manufacturing Review,* July 1, 1999.

8. Kevin J. Clancey and Peter C. Krieg, "Surviving Innovation," *Marketing Management,* March/April 2003.

9. "So Much Fanfare, So Few Hits," *BusinessWeek,* July 10, 2006.

10. Hisrish and Brush survey, 1988.

11. Dun & Bradstreet, *Crain's Small Business,* February 1997.

12. Del Jones, "Optimism about Economy Astounds Experts," *USA Today,* March 24, 1998.

13. Steve Mariotti, *The Young Entrepreneur's Guide to Starting and Running a Business* (New York: Times Books, 2000).

14. Otis Port, "Starting Up Again—and Again and Again," *BusinessWeek,* August 25, 1997.

15. *New York Times,* September 23, 1998.

16. *Fast Company,* February–March 1998.

17. *Success,* May 27, 1998.

18. Harris Survey, 2002.

19. Robert A. Mamis, *Inc.,* March 1997, p. 73.

20. Jack Bishop, Jr., Ph.D.

21. "The Secrets of Serial Success," *Wall Street Journal,* August 20, 2007, p. R1.

22. "Mapping the Entrepreneurial Psyche," *Inc.,* August 2007, p. 73.

23. "Entrepreneur of the Year: The Dimensions of Ping Yu," *Inc.,* July 19, 2007.

24. Junior Achievement Poll on Teens and Entrepreneurship, August 2006.

25. William Walsted, "Entrepreneurship in Nebraska: Findings from a Gallup Survey," University of Nebraska–Lincoln, 2006.

26. Spectrem Group, 2006.

27. "The Microsoft Millionaires Come of Age," *New York Times,* May 29, 2005.

28. Paul Maidment, *Forbes,* September 27, 2005.

29. Roper Starch Worldwide, "Risk and Reward: A Study of the Company Builders Who Are Changing the Face of American Business," *Inc.,* 1997, p. 5.

30. *Harvard Business Review,* November–December 1996, p. 122.

31. Anne R. Carey and Dave Merrill, "CEOs Who Are Household Names," *USA Today,* July 22, 1998.

32. James P. Cain, U.S. ambassador to Denmark, Speech to Børsen Executive Club, September 28, 2006.

33. Roper Starch Worldwide, "Risk and Reward."

34. National Venture Capital Association, "Venture Capital, Without the Risk," March 28, 2005.

35. Council on Competitiveness, "Where America Stands: Entrepreneurship," February 2007.

36. National Venture Capital Association, "Venture Capital, Without the Risk."

37. *USA Today*, December 7, 1998.

38. Gene Koretz, "Downsized in a Down Economy," *BusinessWeek*, September 17, 2001.

39. "Layoff Tracker," Forbes.com, September 25, 2001.

40. Bureau of Labor Statistics, May 2008.

41. "The Language of Loss for the Jobless," *New York Times*, May 18, 2008.

42. *Inc.*, March 1997.

43. Council on Competitiveness, "Where America Stands."

44. Walt Disney Company, 2006 Annual Report.

45. Ethan Bronner, "Students at B-Schools Flock to the E-Courses," *New York Times*, September 23, 1998, p. 6.

46. Donald Kuratko, "The Emergence of Entrepreneurship Education," September 2005.

47. *USA Today*, July 18, 2007.

48. "Can Entrepreneurship Be Taught?" *Fortune Small Business*, March 10, 2006.

49. Ibid.

50. Ibid.

51. Cynthia Hanson, "Working Smart," *Chicago Tribune*, October 8, 1995.

52. *Forbes*, November 15, 1998.

53. National Venture Capital Association, "2005–2006 Year in Review."

54. "It Feels Like 1998 All Over Again," *BusinessWeek*, May 22, 2006.

55. I. Jeanne Dugan, ed., "Portrait of an Entrepreneur," *BusinessWeek/Enterprise*.

56. Grace Mirabella, "Beauty Queen: Estee Lauder," *Time*, December 7, 1998.

57. Tom Stemberg, *Staples for Success*.

58. Morton I. Kamien, "Entrepreneurship: What Is It?" *BusinessWeek* Executive Briefing Service, 1994.

59. Paul Verrochi, "The Quotable Entrepreneur," *Inc.*, December 1998.
60. "The Secrets of Serial Success," *Wall Street Journal*, August 20, 2007.
61. *USA Today*, April 23, 1997.
62. *Inc.*, December 1998.
63. *Business 2.0*, April 2000, p. 261.
64. Salary.com, "2006 Small Business Executive Compensation Survey."
65. WilmerHale, "2006 Compensation and Entrepreneurship Report in Life Sciences."
66. Timothy Aeppel, "Losing Faith: Personnel Disorders Sap a Factory Owner of His Early Idealism," *Wall Street Journal*, September 27, 1996, p. A13.
67. Staples Survey.
68. KRC Research, MasterCard Global Small Business Survey, December 2006.
69. Anne Murphy, "Analysis of the 2000 *Inc.* 500," Inc.com.
70. Kenichi Ottmae, "Guru of Gadgets: Akio Morita," *Time*, December 7, 1998.
71. Cognetics Consulting, October 17, 1997.
72. Ibid.
73. Ibid.
74. Ibid.
75. Ibid.
76. Ibid.
77. Norm Brodsky with Bo Burningham, "Necessary Losses," *Inc.*, December 1997, p. 120.
78. Philip Elmer DeWitt, "Steve Jobs: Apple's Anti-Gates," *Time*, December 7, 1998, p. 133.
79. Unless otherwise stated, small businesses are defined as firms with fewer than 500 employees.
80. "Owning the Airwaves," *Essence*, October 1998.
81. U.S. Census Bureau, 2002.
82. Small Business Administration, June 2006.
83. Ibid.
84. *Crain's Chicago Business*, January 24, 1994.
85. Small Business Administration, June 2006.
86. U.S. Census Bureau, 2002.
87. Small Business Administration, June 2006.
88. Japan Small and Medium Enterprise Agency.

89. Korea Small and Medium Business Administration, 2004.

90. Taiwan Small and Medium Enterprise Administration, 2004.

91. U.K. Small Business Service, 2004.

92. Center for Women's Business Research, "Women-Owned Businesses in the United States, 2006."

93. Nan Langowitz, "The Myths and Realities about Women Entrepreneurs," *Babson Alumni Magazine*, Winter 2004; *LA Times*, June 2, 2001.

94. U.S. Census Bureau, 2002.

CHAPTER 3

The Business Plan

INTRODUCTION

Starting a new business or growing an already established one requires careful planning. An entrepreneur is faced with the challenge of making decisions in an ever-changing business environment that is affected by external factors, many of them beyond the entrepreneur's direct control. The emergence of new competitors, technological advances, and changes in the macroeconomic and regulatory environments are just a few of the factors with which an entrepreneur needs to deal.

In order to build a successful and sustainable business, entrepreneurs must be forward-looking and determine what lies ahead for their company, what their future objectives and strategies are, and how they plan to achieve their goals and manage their risks. This is done through a business plan, which, unfortunately, many entrepreneurs never write. As Thomas Doherty, the senior vice president of a commercial bank, said, "Most small business owners have the plan in their head, but we would like to see a larger number who actually put it down on paper and think through some of the details—financing, competition, strengths and weaknesses, the whole strategic plan."[1] Essentially, the business plan is the evidence that the entrepreneur respects the "seven Ps of business": proper prior preparation prevents piss-poor performance.[2]

THE DUAL-PURPOSE DOCUMENT

For the entrepreneur, the business plan serves a dual purpose. First, it should be used as an internal document to help define a company's strategies and objectives and provide a plan for the future growth of the company. It is basically the company's "road map," laying out the planned entrepreneurial journey. The plan should not be written and filed away. It must become a living, breathing document. To be successful and experience high growth, the entrepreneur must "work the plan" by using it as a proactive tool. The business plan is an evolving, rather than an immutable, document. The entrepreneur should update and revise it at least once a year, preferably at the end of each year in preparation for the next year's operations.

In addition, an entrepreneur must always present the business plan to a potential investor(s) when raising capital. It should be noted that business plans are not always capital-raising documents. Some entrepreneurs mistakenly believe that having a business plan is synonymous with raising capital. There is an endless number of stories about business plans sent to potential investors that never provide key information, such as how much capital the entrepreneur wants, what the capital is going to be used for, and what the investor will get in terms of targeted returns. A well-articulated business plan—one in which a company's vision, strategies, financing needs, and goals are clearly outlined—will not only help an entrepreneur keep his business on track, but also make it easier for him to raise capital.

Investors are inundated with business plans but are willing to finance only a few. The old axiom "you get only one chance to make a good first impression" is especially true when you are procuring capital for your business. Typically, that one chance is through the business plan. For example, John Doerr, of the venture capital firm of Kleiner Perkins Caufield & Byers (KPCB), said, "We receive 2,500 plans per year, meet with at least 100 of those who submitted the plans and invest in about 25."[3] To the investor, the business plan in most cases is the first, and often the only, representation of an entrepreneur. Therefore, it is important to have a well-written, original, and thorough business plan. A well-written business plan is one that is free of grammatical errors, concise, and simple to understand; it clearly describes the company's product or service and tells the reader the amount of capital being sought and the way it will be repaid. A business plan with all these elements will be well received by potential investors.

BUSINESS PLAN DEVELOPMENT AND ADVICE

One venture capitalist suggests that the business plan be written or edited by the entrepreneurial team member who is the best writer and the most articulate.[4] The result should be a document that can be understood by the average 14-year-old. In fact, after writing the plan, the entrepreneur should give it to a teenager and ask her to read it and verbally explain what the proposed product or service is, how it is going to be made available to the marketplace, how much capital is being requested, and if the management team is experienced or inexperienced, old or young. There is nothing more frustrating for a potential investor than expending valuable time reading a plan that is difficult to understand because of complicated and/or vague descriptions, poor writing, misspellings, and grammatical errors. In response to criticism that the business plan could not be understood, many entrepreneurs will say, "I know. Let me meet with you to explain it." No! The business plan should be a viable and adequate communication tool on its own, in the absence of the entrepreneur.

Another option for getting the business plan written that is available to the entrepreneur is to approach a graduate business school. Many of these schools allow their students to get academic credit for working on business projects, including writing business plans for local entrepreneurs, under the supervision of an entrepreneurship professor. Such graduate schools include New York University's Stern School of Business and Northwestern University's Kellogg School of Management. There are also numerous Web sites (e.g., Garage.com) and books (e.g., *Business Plans for Dummies*) that can help with basic templates. More sources are noted at the end of this chapter, in Figure 3-1.

Investors are primarily interested in knowing what they will get in return for risking their capital and whether the entrepreneur has the ability to successfully execute the plan that will deliver this return. A well-written plan provides all the necessary information about the company and the business opportunity to enable investors to assess whether the venture is worth financing. What is the proper length of a business plan? While there is no "right" length, shorter plans tend to be better received. At the maximum, a business plan should be no longer than 30 pages.

The information contained in a business plan will vary depending on the investor(s) being solicited for financing and the type of company seeking funding. Is the financing for an acquisition or a start-up? For instance, a start-up company with a new product or service should provide data that substantiate the existence of market demand for the product or service. Also, priority should be placed on ensuring that investors are convinced that the management team has the experience and the skills necessary to launch and manage a new business venture. Bill Sutter, former general partner at Mesirow Capital, says that the three most important things he looks for in a business plan are (1) management, (2) management, and (3) cash flow.[5]

Concerning the targeted audience, if the business plan is to be presented to someone who is familiar with the industry, the company, or the management team, it may not be necessary to provide as much detailed information as it would if the plan were being presented to potential investors who had no such knowledge.

The greatest examples of this fact are the plans submitted by Intel and Sun Microsystems to Kleiner Perkins Caufield & Byers. The Intel business plan was one page, and the Sun Microsystems business plan was three pages. KPCB financed both companies.

THE BUSINESS PLAN

The development of a business plan can be a difficult, time-consuming process, but it must be done. While the general format of a business plan is standard, it should be written in a way that highlights the uniqueness of the company. The business plan should:

- Tell a complete story about the company: its management team, product or service, financing needs, and strategies, and the financial and nonfinancial goals the company expects to achieve.

- Be a balanced document, highlighting both the positive and negative aspects of the business opportunity.
- Be a forward-looking document with a time frame of at least three years.
- Be clear, concise, and organized.
- Be simple to understand.
- Provide realistic data to substantiate its claims.
- Propose the deal to the investors—what the expected returns on their investment are, and what the exit or liquidation options available to investors are.
- Provide historical and projected financial statements.

The contents of the business plan will vary depending on the type of business. For example, a research and development section should be included if the company's product is in the research and development stage or if the company has undertaken substantial research and development to get the product to market, e.g., a new drug or new technology. On the other hand, this section would not be required in a plan for a restaurant, for example. The research and development section should include a summary of the major findings, while the details should be included in the appendixes. In general, a business plan contains the following sections.

Executive Summary

In most instances, given the large number of business plans that they receive, the only section that potential investors will read thoroughly is the executive summary. This section may be the only opportunity for an entrepreneur to make a good first impression on a potential financier. Therefore, it is *the* most important section of the business plan. It has to capture all the main issues contained in the detailed business plan. It should be concise (i.e., no longer than two pages), be clear and simple to understand, and present a good summary of the most relevant information needed by potential investors.

In support of the point just stated, Barbara Kamm, while an executive at Silicon Valley Bank, said, "When bankers review a business plan, they want to see a well-written executive summary. The executive summary is the key—it's where you distill the essence of your business."[6] In addition to a summary of the main issues of the business plan, a good executive summary must include the following items, which are often missing from executive summaries (and sometimes even the full business plans) written by novices:

- Return on investment (ROI). This is the amount earned on an investor's capital, expressed as a percentage. For example, for an investment of $1 million that returns $5 million, the ROI is 400 percent.
- Internal rate of return (IRR). This is the return on investment taking into consideration the length of the investment. Using the previous example, if five years is the length of time of the investment, then the IRR is 38 percent.
- Current and potential risks.

The Company

The objective of this section is to provide information on the background of the company. The following questions should be answered:

- When was the company established, and by whom?
- Is it a start-up or a going concern?
- What type of industry is it in? Service, retail, or manufacturing?
- What market area(s) does it serve or intend to serve?
- What is the business's legal structure—sole proprietorship, corporation, or limited partnership?
- Who are the company's principals, and what are their ownership stakes? What experience and skills do they bring, and what is their involvement in the day-to-day operations of the company?
- What is the total number of employees?
- What is the revenue size of the company?
- What is the historical growth rate of the company?

Information related to the legal structure of the company should also be provided. There are advantages and disadvantages of different legal structures, as detailed here.

Sole Proprietorship

Advantages

- There is no legal expense for setting up a formal structure.
- It is easy to set up, and therefore is the most typical way small businesses start.
- All income is reported on Schedule C of the owner's personal income tax return.
- All legitimate expenses can be deducted from business income or income earned at another job.

Disadvantages

- There is unlimited personal liability for business debts.
- The business can't have employees unless you get an employer ID number to file payroll tax returns.
- You are unable to take certain kinds of business deductions.

General and Limited Partnerships

Advantages

- You save money on accounting and legal fees.
- Business income or losses go to the partners, who report it on their personal income returns.
- Business expenses and other deductions flow to the partners.
- Limited partners are not personally liable for business debts, and only in some instances are they liable for the full amount of their original investment.
- Regardless of ownership percentages, all operational decisions are made only by the general partners.

Disadvantages

- General partners are personally liable for business obligations and can be personally sued.
- Limited partners cannot participate in any decisions or they will jeopardize their liability status.

C Corporation
Advantages

- You get protection from personal liability for business debts.
- There is no limit on the number of shareholders or on stock classes or voting arrangements.
- It can provide qualified stock option and employee stock purchase plans to employees as incentives.
- There is no need to restructure prior to an IPO.

Disadvantages

- Costs of incorporation can be significant.
- The corporation is taxed as a separate entity.
- Dividend income is taxed at both the corporate and the shareholder level (double taxation).
- The corporate tax rate may be higher than the personal tax rate.

S Corporation
Advantages

- It has the same limited liability as a C corporation has.
- Profits are passed through to shareholders and taxed on an individual's return, similar to a partnership.
- Deduction of losses on a personal tax return is allowed up to the amount of the individual's cost of the company's stock, plus any loans made to the company.

Disadvantages

- The corporation can't have more than 35 shareholders.
- It can have only one class of stock, limiting the flexibility to add future investors and restrict their share of profits.
- It can't have foreigners, trusts, or other corporations as shareholders.

- It can't offer certain benefits that a C corporation can, such as medical reimbursement plans.

LLC (Limited Liability Corporation)

Advantages

- It has the ownership flexibility of a C corporation.
- There is no limit to the number of shareholders.
- You can create several classes of shareholders (founders can be entitled to a greater share of profits or of the stock's future value if it is sold to the public).
- There is no double taxation because profits are taxed only at the shareholder level.
- There is no limit to the deductibility of losses for shareholders.

Disadvantages

- If you convert a current corporation to an LLC, you might have to liquidate first and owe a big tax.
- You cannot transfer the business of your old corporation to a new LLC.

Each state has its own laws regarding how businesses must be structured and operated. Be sure to check the laws of your state or speak with a lawyer, if necessary, since many states have significant penalties for failing to register businesses properly, and many require out-of-state entities that do business within their borders to pay income or other taxes, especially if those entities have employees in the state or own property there. It is generally a good idea to incorporate in the state in which your place of business will be, but many companies also choose to incorporate in a state like Delaware, which has a well-developed body of corporate law and is generally considered more business-friendly than some other states.[7] There are many online resources, such as www.legalzoom.com and www.incorporate.com, that will assist you in choosing a legal entity for your company, provide sample incorporation documents, and actually manage the incorporation process for you in whatever state you choose—for a fee, of course.

The Industry

It is necessary to provide the context in which the business will operate. Macroeconomic as well as industry-specific data should be presented to provide a better understanding of the overall environment in which the company will operate. This information should include:

- Macroeconomic data, such as the unemployment rate, inflation rates, interest rates, and so on, that have or will have an impact on the industry and, more specifically, on the company's operations.
- Information on regulatory changes that might have an impact on the industry or the company.
- A description of the industry—e.g., major participants, competition, and so on.
- The size of the industry—e.g., historical, current, and future trends.
- Characteristics of the industry—e.g., is it seasonal, cyclical, or countercyclical?
- Trends taking place in the industry that have an impact on the business—e.g., consolidation or deregulation.
- The key drivers in the industry—e.g., R&D, marketing, price, quick delivery, or relationships.
- Industry growth rates—past and future.
- Customer payment practices—for example, are there slow payers, such as the government or insurance companies?

The Market

This section should provide a description of the target market(s)—both primary and secondary. It's important to be specific when identifying the markets to be targeted. If the product or service is new, market research data should be included to provide information on initial and future markets. Research can be done by paying a consulting firm or by getting the information free, or at a substantially lower cost, by going to a local business school and asking the marketing department to assign students to do it as a project for academic credit. Questions to be answered include the following:

- What are the key customer market segments? What is their size?
- Where are these market segments located? Are they regional, national, or international?
- What are the past growth rates in the market and anticipated trends?
- What are the market characteristics—seasonal, cyclical, and so on?
- Are there any anticipated changes within the primary market?
- How will each customer market segment be reached?
- How are purchasing decisions made? By whom? What are the factors that influence purchasing decisions?
- How do customers buy products—through competitive bidding, contracts, unit purchases, or some other way?
- Is there a possibility to create new customer bases? If so, how?

Product or Service Description

Investors need to know the type of product or service the company will offer to customers. They will need the following information:

- A detailed description of the product or service to be developed and marketed, including:
  - The benefits of the product or service
  - The stage of the product or service—is it an idea, a prototype, or at some other stage?
- Key product characteristics—performance, quality, durability, price, service, and so on.
- What is your differentiation strategy?
- What is your positioning strategy?
- What is your pricing strategy? Why?
- What are the chances of product obsolescence?

- Are there legal issues relating to the product or service that provide legal protection, e.g., obtained or pending patents, copyrights, trademarks, royalties, and so on?
- Other legal and regulatory issues that relate to the product or service.

Competition

Competition is a reality for every business. You should not underestimate a competitor's capabilities or overestimate your capacity to deal with them. Investors prefer to go with entrepreneurs who have a realistic assessment of their competitors and, accordingly, make a realistic plan for dealing with this competition. In this section, key competitors—direct and indirect—should be identified, and an explanation of how the company will successfully compete should be provided. Questions to be answered include the following:

- Who are the key competitors, both direct and indirect? Are they mom-and-pop or high-growth entrepreneurs? What are their strengths and weaknesses?
- Where do they operate? Are they local or national players?
- What is the market share of each?
- What are the key competitive factors—pricing, quality, performance, or something else? How does your company fare in this regard?
- What are the competitors' present market shares? What are their expected market shares? How will your company gain market share?
- Are there any barriers to entry into the market—e.g., is this a capital-intensive industry?
- What do you plan to do to mitigate this competition?

Marketing and Sales

The main question to answer here is how the product or service is going to be made available in the marketplace.

- What is your marketing strategy?
- How is your product or service going to be advertised and promoted?

- How important is marketing to the industry?
- What is the expected return on resources spent on marketing?
- What is the sales growth—historical, current, and expected in three years?
- What is the sales strategy to achieve these sales levels? At a regional or national level?
- What is the product distribution strategy? Will there be an in-house sales force or outside manufacturers' representatives? What is the sales compensation plan?
- What are the sales per employee—historical, present, future, and for the industry as a whole?

Facilities

Information provided in this section should include:

- A description of plants and their operations—size, location (e.g., rural or urban), age, and condition of plants
- Ownership or lease
- Cost estimates to run facilities
- Capital equipment required
- Condition of equipment and property
- Sales per square foot
- Insurance—coverage and name of provider(s)
- Access to public transportation
- Utilities
- Available parking for customers and employees

Operating Plan

Information should be provided to explain the day-to-day operations of the company, including the following:

Business Operations

- Days of operation and hours
- Shutdown periods
- Number of shifts

Production

- Production plans
- Key quality-control issues
- Capacity
- Utilization
- Bottlenecks
- Automation: technology versus manual
- Build to order versus build to inventory

Purchasing

- Purchasing plans
- Material resource systems
- Inventory plan
- Suppliers—local or national, proximity, single or multiple
- Product delivery
- Office: invoicing, payables, collecting
- Receiving and shipping

Labor Force

- Number of employees
- Skill levels
- Gender
- Age range
- Union versus nonunion status
- Years of service
- Compensation and salary plan
- Hourly versus exempt
- Payroll—weekly versus monthly
- Benefits
- Safety concerns
- Insurance
- Source of labor
- Productivity per employee
- Projections for labor force changes in the future

Management Team

One of the most important elements that investors look for when assessing the viability of a business venture is the strength of the management team. In this section, it is important to provide background information on the people who will be involved in the day-to-day operations of the company. From this information, the investor will try to determine whether the management team can implement the plan successfully. The ideal management team has complementary skills and expertise. Information should include:

- Names and titles of the key management personnel
- Experience, skill levels, and functional responsibilities of the key management personnel
- Anticipated changes in the management team
- Names of the principal owners
- Names of the members of the board of directors
- Names and affiliation(s) of advisors—both external and internal
- Compensation plan for key members of the management team
- Life insurance policy for the CEO or president of the company
- Succession plan
- Investments

Appendixes and Tables

Information in this section may include:

- Résumés and biographies
- Union contracts
- Leases
- Customer contracts
- Research findings

References

References should include both financial (i.e., personal and business) and character references. The idea is to make the investor as comfortable and knowledgeable as possible about the company and the entrepreneurial team. For example, when seeking bank financing, Tom and Cherry Householder, the founders of Staffing Resources, a prominent regional temporary staffing company in Illinois, submitted more than 15 letters of reference from their local police chief, from politicians, and even from competitors of their bank. It worked. They got the $135,000 line of credit they needed to start their business.[8]

Potential Risks

An assessment of the risks currently facing the company, as well as future risks and how the company intends to mitigate these risks, needs to be presented. Some risks, such as "acts of God" (e.g., weather, major disasters, unexpected death, and so on), may not be exclusive to the company and therefore cannot be dealt with by the company. The objective is to assure the investor that the entrepreneur (1) has a realistic view of the business opportunities and the risks associated with pursuing those opportunities, and (2) has proactively thought through how to manage and mitigate those risks that can be dealt with by the company. Potential risks to consider include:

- The advent of a recession.
- The unanticipated demise or removal of the CEO.
- Unanticipated changes in key management personnel.
- Appropriateness of insurance coverage and amount required.
- The loss of a major customer(s). This issue is particularly relevant if the company's revenues are dependent on one or a few major customers.
- Problems with suppliers.
- A potential strike or labor stoppage.
- A capital or financing shortfall.

Financial Statements and Pro Formas

Projecting the future is challenging, but it must be done. Debt and equity investors know that financial projections that go out three to five years into the future are at best guesstimates—they have to be, as no one can predict the future (unless, of course, guaranteed future contracts have been signed). Potential investors are looking for projections grounded in defensible logic. When asked how financiers know when pro formas are correct, a venture capitalist responded, "We don't know. In all likelihood, they will be ultimately wrong. In a start-up, it is rare for pro formas to ever match reality. We are looking for logical, defensible reasoning behind the numbers versus B.S.—'Blue Sky'—projections simply pulled out of the air."

DEVELOPMENT OF PRO FORMAS

Entrepreneurs should develop pro forma financial statements for all new entrepreneurial opportunities, including either a start-up or an existing company that is being purchased. Any pro forma should have figures for at least three years and three scenarios—a best-case, worst-case, and most-likely-case scenario. If only one scenario is provided, then the automatic assumption is that it is the best case because most people always put their best, not their worst, foot forward. The historical performance of a company drives the financial projections for the future of that company, unless there is other information that indicates that past performance is not a good indicator of future performance.

For example, if a new contract has been signed with a new customer, then this could be used to adjust the financial projections. Otherwise, historical numbers must be used.

For instance, Livent Inc. created major musicals such as *Joseph and the Amazing Technicolor Dreamcoat* and *Ragtime*. In 1998, the company added Chicago's Oriental Theatre to the three other company-owned theaters in New York, Toronto, and Vancouver. Livent's pro formas for the newly renovated Oriental Theatre were allegedly based on its success with *Joseph*, which it had staged two years earlier at the Chicago theater and in similar venues throughout the country. Livent's projections were as follows:

Oriental Theatre
- 80 percent capacity
- 52 weeks per year
- $40 million annual gross revenues

Before the end of 1998, Livent Inc. experienced major financial difficulties and filed for Chapter 11 bankruptcy. In bankruptcy court, an attorney for the city of Chicago, which filed a condemnation case, challenged the legitimacy of the pro formas. He argued that the $40 million annual projected gross revenues was out of line with reality and intentionally fraudulent, given the fact that "in a recent year, a similar theater located in downtown Chicago and similar in size, reported an annual gross of just $20,455,000!"[9]

When there are no historical data, financial projections for a start-up company can be determined in one of the following ways:

- Conduct an industry analysis and select a company within the same industry that can be used as a comparable. Where possible, review the sales figures of this company to determine its sales history from Year 1 as well as its sales growth in the past few years. Extrapolate from these figures and use the data to determine sales growth for your company. Cost figures may be determined from cost data obtained through research on, for example, a publicly owned company in the same industry.

- If sales commitments have already been secured, use these commitments to calculate the worst-case scenario. Use larger amounts to calculate the best-case and most-likely-case scenarios.

- If the product or service is completely new, market research can be undertaken to determine the overall market demand for this new product or service. Identify the size of the market and assume that the company will get a specific percentage of the total market, depending on the total number of competitors. Also, identify the potential customers and estimate the number of units that can be sold to each. It is critical that whenever possible this market research be based on both secondary research (third party market reports and/or articles from credible sources) and also primary research (direct conversations and/or surveys with potential customers in the targeted segment). This ensures that the projections are based on reliable, defensible information sources and are not just "back of the envelope" guesses.

- Alternatively, you can use specific figures for your projections, based on your own assumptions or expectations. It is important to state what these assumptions are and to justify why you believe them to be realistic.

An important issue for a start-up company to consider is to make sure that all the necessary equipment financing needs are included.

Before closing this section on pro forma development, a major warning must be given. It is important that the worst-case-scenario pro formas show that the cash flow can service the company's debt. Otherwise, procuring financing, particularly debt, may prove to be virtually impossible. This does not mean that the pro formas should be developed by working backward and "plugging" numbers. For example, if the principal payments on debt obligations are $7,000 per month, it would be wrong to forecast the monthly revenue size, gross margins, and so on such that at least $7,000 would be generated in after-tax cash flow to service this obligation.

No, pro formas should be developed from the top down; forecasting defensible revenues and legitimate variable costs, including labor and materials, and market-rate fixed costs such as rent. If, after developing the pro formas in this manner, it is shown that debt cannot be serviced, the action that needs to be taken is not to plug numbers, but rather to

- Reduce the amount of the debt.
- Lower the interest rates on the debt.
- Extend the terms of your loan.

All of these actions are designed to free up cash flow to service short-term debt.

Even if the entrepreneur is successful in raising capital using pro formas filled with plugged numbers, she will ultimately experience difficulties when the company's performance proves to be lower than the projections and the cash flow is not sufficient to meet debt obligations. Finally, experienced business investors such as bankers and venture capitalists can easily detect pro formas filled with plugged numbers because typically the projections are such that all the company's debt can be serviced, with maybe a little cash left over. Therefore, do not plug numbers. A pro forma development case study for Clark Company is included at the end of Chapter 5.

CHECKLIST OF FINANCIAL INFORMATION

To enable investors to better understand the information presented in this section, it is best to provide a summary of financial data and then present the detailed financial tables. Data should include:

- Historical financial statements (i.e., three to five years):
  - Cash flow statement
  - Income statement
  - Balance sheet
- Pro formas (i.e., three to five years). Financial projections (as described previously) should be provided under three scenarios—best, worst, and most-likely cases—where each scenario is based upon a different set of assumptions. For example, the worst-case scenario may assume no growth from Year 1 to Year 2, the best-case scenario may assume 5 percent growth, and the most-likely-case scenario may assume a 2 percent growth rate. A summary of the assumptions should also be provided.
- Detailed description of banking relationships for business accounts and payroll.
- The terms and rates of loans and their amortization period.
- The proposed financing plan, including:
  - The amount being requested.
  - Sources and uses of funds. [*Note:* This information is important for several reasons. First, financiers need to know how their funds are going to be used. Second, identifying other investors who are willing to provide you with resources (sources) will encourage potential investors to make a similar commitment—people find it easier to invest once they know that others have already done so. Third, value-added investors may be able to help you find alternative ways of getting resources.]
  - Payback and collateral.
  - Proposed strategy for the liquidation of investors' positions.
- Financing plan for the immediate term, short term, and long term.

- Working capital needs.
- Line of credit.
- Cash flow from operations—outside investors, sell debt, or IPO.

MOST IMPORTANT BUSINESS PLAN SECTIONS

By now, you realize that your business plan had better be compelling if your venture hopes to receive funding. Here's one more review of the "must haves" of any good business plan.

The Executive Summary

As stated earlier, the executive summary is probably the most important section of the business plan. Most potential investors don't have the time to read through a detailed plan, and therefore they read through the summary quickly to assess whether or not a venture is worth pursuing. It is extremely important to make sure that this summary is clear and explicitly highlights the factors differentiating the company that is seeking capital from its competitors. For example, the 20-page Amazon.com business plan was very successful at highlighting the fact that the book retailing industry averaged 2.7 inventory turns a year, while Amazon.com planned annual inventory turns of 70.

The Management Team

Jeff Bezos's first investors said, "We didn't invest in Amazon.com, we invested in Jeff."[10] This is a perfect confirmation of the old axiom, "The investment is in the jockey, not the horse." In other words, the investment is in the team, not necessarily in the idea, product, or service. Experience has shown that having the right management team can usually be the deciding factor in the success or failure of a business venture. Remember, the venture capitalist Bill Sutter gave management as two of the three most important things that he looks for. The scarcest resource for venture capitalists today is good management. A good management team can take a mediocre idea and make it successful. Conversely, a bad management team can take an outstanding idea and ruin it. One venture capitalist said, "In the world today, there's plenty of technology, plenty of money, plenty of venture capital. What is in short supply are great teams."

Investors look carefully to see who the members of the management team are, particularly if the venture is a start-up company. Do they have complementary skills, or are they a homogeneous group? Do they have relevant industry, market, or product experience? How was the leader selected? Do the team members have experience working with one another? Do they have contacts in the industry that can be leveraged? What are their track records in management, leadership, and execution?

Great teams are made up of smart people with complementary skills and styles—not everyone can deal with "in-your-face" managers—and the commonality of passion for the business, commitment to growing it rapidly and exponentially, and the experience and drive to execute quickly without quitting.

Financial Projections

Investors understand the difficulty of preparing projections of future revenues and profits. They do not expect the financial projections to be "correct"; rather, they want to see whether the entrepreneur used realistic assumptions in preparing these projections. They look at whether the analysis is logical and defensible, given the realities of the marketplace. They not only look at whether the projected cash flow can service the debt, but also ask whether the cash flow projections justify the value placed on the firm today and in the future, and also whether the company is the size they are interested in. For example, some financiers want to do business only with companies that will have at least $200 million in revenue by Year 3. It is important to make sure that all relevant information is provided in this section and to make all the assumptions used clear.

BUSINESS PLAN DEVELOPMENT SOURCES

There are numerous books available that provide detailed information on the preparation of a business plan; you can find them in the small-business section of most major bookstores. In addition, various companies provide consulting services on business plan development to entrepreneurs, albeit sometimes at a considerable cost. Local small-business development centers are also a good source of information and assistance. In addition, as mentioned earlier, business schools can be good sources of talented, and in most instances free, assistance. Alternatively, Figure 3-1 shows several online sources that provide detailed information on business plan development, available for free.

FIGURE 3-1

Business Plan Development Sources

Small Business British Columbia (Canada)
www.sb.gov.bc.ca
This site provides online small-business seminars, in addition to other information on business plan preparation.

Entrepreneur Magazine Online
www.entrepreneur.com
The "Starting a Business" section provides a number of business plan tips and templates for a variety of business types.

Kauffman eVenturing Entrepreneur's Resource Center
eventuring.kauffman.org
The "Business Models and Plans" section provides original articles and an aggregation of some of the best articles on business plans.

Small Business Administration
www.sba.gov
The "Small Business Planner" section, in addition to providing a business plan template, provides other relevant information, including financing and management tips for small businesses.

Business Plan Software and Free Sample Business Plans
www.bplans.com
This site provides business plan templates and software for free and for purchase.

Venture Capital Resource Library
www.vfinance.com
This online library features free business plan templates and evaluations of business plans.

AFTER THE BUSINESS PLAN IS WRITTEN

It is very important to choose potential investors carefully—you will be establishing an important long-term relationship with them. Do your research on a potential investor(s) before sending your business plan to ensure a better rate of acceptance. Find out what types of deals the investor pursues. What is the firm's investment strategy, and what are its selection criteria? What is its success rate? How have the investors reacted during critical situations, such as a financial crisis? Do the investors just bail out, or are they in for the long haul? One good source of information in this regard is other companies that have received backing from that particular investor. Will the investors be "value-added" investors (discussed in more detail in Chapter 8), providing useful advice and contacts, or will they provide only financial resources?

It is extremely important that you know your audience so that you can limit your search to those who have an affinity for doing business with you. If your company is a start-up, then you should send the plan to those who provide "seed" or start-up capital rather than later-stage financing. For example, it would be a waste of time to send a business plan for the acquisition of a grocery store to a technology-focused lender, such as the Silicon Valley Bank. This issue will be discussed in more detail in Chapter 8, "Raising Capital."

It is always advisable to get what Bill Sutter calls "an endorsed recommendation," preferably from someone who has had previous business dealings with the investor, before submitting your business plan. John Doerr at KPCB stated, "I can't recall ever having invested in a business on the basis of an unsolicited business plan."[11] This endorsement will guarantee that your business plan will be considered more carefully and seriously. If a recommendation is not possible, then an introduction by someone who knows the investor will be helpful. In most instances, unsolicited business plans submitted to venture capital firms without a referral have a lower chance of getting funding than those submitted with one. If you are submitting an unsolicited business plan, it is important that you write it to be consistent with the investment strategy of the investor.

A good example of someone who did it correctly is Mitch Kapor, the founder of Lotus Development Corporation, who, in 1981, sent his business plan to only one venture capital firm.

Recognizing that his business plan was somewhat different—it included a statement that said he wasn't motivated by profit—he knew himself and his company well enough to know that not all venture capitalists would take him seriously. He carefully selected one firm—Sevin and Rosen. Why? Because this firm was used to doing business with his "type"—namely, computer programmers. They knew him personally, and they also knew the industry. It was a good decision. He got the financing he sought, even though he had a poorly organized, nontraditional plan. The way to find debt and equity providers who have a proclivity for certain types of deals will be discussed in Chapter 8.

NOTES

1. Martha Russis, "Loans Will Flow, but Less Freely than during 1998," *Crain's Chicago Business/Small Business Report*, December 14, 1998, p. SB4.
2. *Black Enterprise.*
3. *Fast Company*, February–March 1998.
4. Ibid.
5. Bill Sutter, classroom presentation at Kellogg School of Management, March 10, 1999.
6. *Chicago Sun-Times*, April 4, 1996.
7. Constance Bagley and Craig Dauchy, *The Entrepreneur's Guide to Business Law*, 2nd ed. (1993), pp. 76–77.
8. *Inc.*, December 1998.
9. Laurie Cohen and Andrew Martin, "Theater Plan Not Living Up to Billing," *Chicago Tribune*, January 15, 1999.
10. *Business 2.0*, April 2000, p. 259.
11. *The New Yorker*, August 11, 1997.

CHAPTER 4

Financial Statements

INTRODUCTION

As stated earlier, one of the most important sections of the business plan is the one that details the firm's financial statements. Therefore, the discussion in this chapter is intended as an overview of the main issues of relevance regarding key financial statements. The objective is to teach the purpose of the different statements, their components, and their significance to entrepreneurs who are not financial managers. This is the final step toward making financial statement analysis, which will be the focus of the next chapter, simple and user-friendly.

Financial statements are important because they provide valuable information that is typically used by business managers and investors. However, it is not necessary for the entrepreneur to be able to personally develop financial statements.

In this chapter, we will focus on three financial statements: the income statement, the balance sheet, and the statement of cash flows. Each of these statements, in one way or another, describes a company's financial health. For example, the income statement describes a company's profitability. It is a measurement of the company's financial performance over time. Is the company making or losing money? On the other hand, the balance sheet describes the financial condition of a company at a particular time. Does it own more than it owes? Can it remain in business?

THE INCOME STATEMENT

The income statement, also known as the profit and loss (P&L) statement, is a scoreboard for a business and is usually prepared in accordance with generally accepted accounting principles (GAAP). It records the flow of resources over time by stating the financial condition of a business over the course of a period, usually a month, quarter, or year. It shows the revenues (i.e., sales) achieved by a company during that particular period and the expenses (i.e., costs) associated with generating these revenues. That is the reason why the income statement, in addition to being known as the P&L statement, is also referred to as the statement of revenues and expenses.

The difference between a company's total revenues and total expenses is its net income. When the revenues are greater than the costs, the company has earned a profit. When the costs are greater than the revenues gained, the company has incurred a loss.

The income statement is used to calculate a company's cash flow, which is also known as EBITDA: earnings (i.e., net income or profit) before interest (i.e., the cost of debt), taxes (i.e., the payments to the government based on a company's profit), depreciation (i.e., noncash expenditures for the decline in value of tangible assets), and amortization (i.e., noncash expenditures for the decline in value of intangible assets such as patents or goodwill). To determine a company's EBITDA for any period—that is, the cash being generated by the company after paying all the expenses directly related to its operations, and therefore the cash available to pay for nonoperational expenses such as taxes and principal and interest payments on debt—one must utilize the income statement. A sample income statement is provided in Figure 4-1.

The income statement is divided into two sections: "Revenues," a measure of the resources generated from the sales of products and services, and "Expenses," a measure of the costs associated with the selling of these products or services. The accounting equation to remember is Equation 4-1.

E Q U A T I O N   4-1

Net Income

Revenues − expenses = net income

F I G U R E   4-1

Bruce Company Income Statement, Year Ended 12/31/07

Revenues	$8,000
Expenses	
Cost of Goods Sold	$2,000
Gross profit	**$6,000**
Operating expenses	
Wages	$1,000
Rent	300
Selling expense	400
Depreciation	500
Amortization	300
Total operating expense	$2,500
Operating profit or profit before interest and taxes	**$3,500**
Interest expense	200
Profit before taxes	**$3,300**
Income tax expense	$1,320
Net income	**$1,980**

Using the information contained in Figure 4-1, we can calculate EBITDA at the end of the year for the Bruce Company as shown in Figure 4-2. As you can see, we added back "noncash" expenses, i.e., those for which no cash is actually disbursed, such as depreciation and amortization, to determine the company's true cash position—EBITDA.

F I G U R E   4-2

Sample EBITDA Calculation

Net income	$1,980
+ Interest expense	200
+ Taxes	1,320
+ Depreciation	500
+ Amortization	300
EBITDA	**$4,300**

Let us define and analyze each revenue and expense item on the typical income statement:

Revenues
- Receipts from the sale of products and services
- Returns on investments, such as interest earned on a company's marketable securities, including stocks and bonds
- Franchising fees paid by franchisees
- Rental property income

Expenses
- Cost of goods sold
- Operating expenses
- Financing expenses
- Tax expenses

Cost of Goods Sold
The cost of goods sold (known as the COGS) or the cost of services rendered is the cost of the raw materials and direct labor required to produce the product or service that generated the revenue. The COGS does *not* include any overhead, such as utilities or management costs. The difference between revenues and the COGS is gross profit, a.k.a. gross margin. The proper way to calculate the gross profit is simply to subtract the COGS, as defined earlier, from the revenues produced by the sale of the company's goods or services. Other income, such as interest earned on investments, should not be included.

The reason for this is that in the world of finance, internal comparisons of a company's year-to-year performance, and also external comparisons of a company's performance to that of another company or an entire industry, are quite common. These kinds of comparisons are called *internal and external benchmarking*. Therefore, in order to make "apples-to-apples" comparisons that are not skewed by, for example, Company A's revenues being stronger than Company B's because the former is getting higher interest payments on investments, only the revenues from operations are used.

To determine gross profit from total revenues, regardless of the source, would be to ignore the obvious definition of the COGS, which is the cost of *only* the goods sold to generate revenues.

Operating Expenses

Operating expenses, also known as selling, general, and administrative expenses (SG&A), are all of the other tangible and intangible (e.g., depreciation and amortization) expenses required to carry on the day-to-day activities of a company. Included in this category are fixed costs (i.e., those costs that do not vary with the volume of business), such as insurance, rent, and management salaries, and variable costs (i.e., the costs that vary depending upon the volume produced), such as utilities (e.g., electricity and water) and invoice documents. For example, in the Bruce income statement in Figure 4-1, the rent is $300 per year—an amount that remains the same whether 200 or 2,000 widgets per year were produced.

Another simple way to think about fixed versus variable costs is to determine the expenses that would be affected by, for example, closing the company for a month. The rent would still be due to the landlord, and interest payments on bank loans would still be due to the bank. These are the fixed costs. On the other hand, since the company is closed and is not producing or shipping for a month, there would be no need to buy invoice documents, and utility bills would decrease dramatically, since electricity and water were not being used.

Excluded from this category are interest expenses, which are not operating expenses, but rather financing expenses. Therefore, revenues minus the sum of the COGS and operating expenses equals operating income, or EBIT (earnings before interest and taxes). The operating income is then used to make any interest payments on debt. The balance is called earnings before taxes (EBT), and these funds are then used to pay taxes on the company's EBT figure.

As stated earlier, "intangible, noncash" expenses—expenses that do not require actual cash disbursements, such as depreciation and amortization—are also included in the operating expense category. Every company, under GAAP, is allowed to "write off" (i.e., expense) a portion of its tangible assets each year over the life of the asset. The theory behind this practice is that the value of all assets typically depreciates over time as a result of natural deterioration and regular use. Therefore, the depreciation of an asset is a cost to the company because the value of the asset is declining. As we will see in the discussion of the balance sheet later in this chapter, the depreciated value of the asset is recognized on the balance sheet, and the amount it depreciates each year is presented on the income statement.

The amount to be depreciated each year is determined by the accounting method that the company selects to recognize depreciation. The most common methods are straight-line (i.e., an equal percentage of the asset's cost minus salvage value is recognized each year for the predetermined number of useful years) and accelerated (i.e., double-declining-balance or sum-of-the-years' digits, which recognize a larger portion of the depreciation in the early years).

The method used to calculate depreciation can have a significant impact on the timing of reported income. Using the straight-line depreciation method rather than one of the two accelerated methods, double-declining-balance or sum-of-the-years'-digits, will result in a higher net income in the early periods and lower net income in the later years of an asset's estimated useful life. Also, the change in net income from one period to the next is greater under the double-declining balance method than it is under the sum-of-the-years'-digits method. This makes the former method the most extreme form of depreciation. Finally, the two accelerated methods produce low levels of net income in the early periods that increase rapidly over the asset's life.[1]

While depreciation is the expensing of tangible assets, amortization is the expensing of intangible assets. Intangible assets include such items as goodwill (i.e., the surplus paid over an asset's book value), franchise rights, patents, trademarks, exploration rights, copyrights, and noncompete agreements. These items must be amortized, generally in equal annual amounts, over 15 years.

Other Expenses

Found on the income statement, financing expenses are basically the interest payments paid on loans to the business. And finally, tax expenses are the taxes due on the company's profits. There are also other taxes that a company incurs, including unemployment and real estate taxes, but these fall into the operating expenses category.

If a company has a negative profit before taxes—in other words, a loss—then corporate taxes are not due to the government. In fact, not only will taxes not be due, but also the company's losses can be used to reduce tax obligations on future positive profits. This is called a *tax-loss carryforward*, where a company's previous losses can be carried forward against future profits. Interestingly, a company with a history of annual losses can be more valuable to a prospective buyer than a company that regularly has a breakeven or profitable financial history. Since tax-loss carryforwards are transferable from seller to buyer, they are attractive to a prospective buyer because they are assets for companies that are trying to shield future profits.

At the end of the year, if a company's net income after taxes is positive, it is retained in the form of retained earnings, reflected on the next year's beginning balance sheet, or distributed to investors as dividends, as shown in Equation 4-2.

E Q U A T I O N   4-2

Retained Earnings and Shareholders' Dividends

Revenues − expenses = net income
→ Retained earnings and shareholders' dividends

Before closing the discussion of the income statement, it is imperative that we clear up a few terms that are commonly used interchangeably. These include:

- Revenues and sales
- Margins, profits, earnings, and income

The three different kinds of margins, profits, earnings, and income—in the order of their appearance on the income statement—are as follows:

- *Gross*. The difference between revenues and COGS
- *Operating*. Revenues − (COGS + operating expenses)
- *Net*. The difference between revenues and *all* of the company's costs

Cash versus Accrual Accounting

A final point to be made about the income statement is that it can be affected by the accounting method selected by the entrepreneur. The options for the entrepreneur are cash or accrual accounting. Typically, a company will select the accounting method that provides the greatest immediate tax benefit. It must also be noted that a company can, in its lifetime, change from one method to another only once, and this change must be approved by the Internal Revenue Service (IRS). The IRS usually approves a requested switch from cash to accrual accounting and usually rejects a request to change from accrual to cash accounting. What is the main difference between cash and accrual accounting? Simply stated, it is the time at which a company recognizes its revenues and expenses. Table 4-1 clearly shows the difference.

T A B L E 4-1

Cash versus Accrual Accounting

Accounting Method	Revenues Recognized	Expenses Recognized
Cash	When actual cash is received from the customer	When actual cash is paid to the supplier
Accrual	When the product is shipped and the invoice is mailed	When the invoice is received from the supplier

The accrual accounting method gives the reader of the income statement a richer and more complete depiction of the business's financial condition, since all revenues generated by the business and all expenses incurred are included, regardless of whether actual cash has been received or disbursed. Because this method recognizes items immediately, many business owners try to use it to their advantage. For example, prior to the end of the year, many owners will increase their inventories dramatically. The result is an increase in expenses and therefore a reduction in profits and taxes.

For publicly owned companies, where the markets reward revenue and profit growth with an increasing stock price, many owners prefer to use the accrual method because it helps them achieve the aforementioned increases. Unlike many privately owned companies, which seek to minimize taxes by reducing their reported EBT, public companies seek to show the highest possible EBT, as well as revenue growth. Given this objective, it is not unheard of for a company's owner to get too aggressive and some-times even act unethically with regard to growth.

For example, Premiere Laser Systems Inc., a spin-off from Pfizer, won FDA approval for a new laser device that promised to make drilling cavities painless. The publicly owned company, trad-ing on the Nasdaq market, shipped and recognized revenues of $2.5 million in products to Henry Schein, Inc., the powerhouse dis-tributor in the dental business, in December 1997. The only prob-lem was that Henry Schein claimed that it had never ordered the products, refused to pay, and alleged that the products had been shipped to it so that Premiere could show current and future stock-holders an increase in revenues. Obviously, the supplier used the accrual method, which allowed it to recognize the revenue imme-diately upon shipment. Had its accounting method been cash, the revenue would have never been recognized because the recipient company had refused to pay.[2] Premiere settled a number of class action suits; it also cooperated with a securities investigation and replaced its CEO. The company eventually filed for Chapter 11 in March 2000.[3]

Another "fishy numbers" case involved Sunbeam Corporation, which conceded that while under the leadership of Al Dunlap, a.k.a. "Chainsaw Al," its "1997 financial statements audited by Arthur Andersen LLP may not be accurate and should not be relied upon."[4] Sunbeam filed for Chapter 11 bankruptcy protection in 2001 after three years of trying to turn around its fortunes. The company was saddled with a debt load of $2.6 billion.[5]

Private-practice physicians usually operate some of the most profitable small businesses in the country. Typically, doctors use the cash accounting method, which gives the reader a more limited pic-ture of the company's financial condition. Physicians and others who use this method do so primarily because their revenues come from notoriously slow payers, such as insurance companies and the government, also known as third-party payers. Therefore, instead of recognizing this unpaid revenue and paying taxes immediately on the profits it helps to generate, the users of the cash method prefer to delay revenue recognition until the cash is actually received, thereby reducing the company's profit before taxes and consequently the taxes paid. Using this method does not result in tax avoidance or elimination, however; it simply delays tax payments into future years.

Not all companies are allowed to use the cash method, including the following:

- Companies with average annual revenues of $5 million or more
- Companies where inventories are a heavy part of their business, such as auto dealerships and grocery wholesalers

Let's look at Figure 4-3, which shows an end-of-the-year income statement using both methods. The company has sold and invoiced $1 million worth of merchandise and has received payment for $600,000. The merchandise cost was $500,000, an amount for which the company has been billed. The company has paid its suppliers $400,000.

F I G U R E   4-3

Cash versus Accrual Accounting Example

	Cash Method	Accrual Method
Revenues	$600,000	$1,000,000
Cost	$400,000	$ 500,000
Profit before taxes	$200,000	$ 500,000
Taxes (50% rate)	$100,000	$ 250,000
Profit after taxes	$100,000	$ 250,000

As is obvious from this simple example, the accounting method that a company uses can affect not only the taxes owed but also the three profit categories mentioned earlier. All three would be lower as a percentage of revenues under the cash method than under the accrual method. Therefore, it is imperative that when comparing income statement items against those of other companies, the comparison be made with those using the same accounting method.

As mentioned earlier, a company can change its accounting method with the approval of the IRS. To see the impact of these changes, examine Figure 4-4.

F I G U R E   4-4

Income Statement for the Bruce Company

	Cash Business with No Receivables	Business with Receivables
Cash to accrual	• Revenues remain the same. • Expenses increase • Profit before taxes decreases. • Taxes decrease. • Net income decreases.	• Revenues increase. • Expenses increase • Profit before taxes increases. • Taxes increase. • Net income increases.
Accrual to cash	• Revenues remain the same. • Expenses decrease. • Profit before taxes increases. • Taxes increase. • Net income increases.	• Revenues decrease. • Expenses decrease. • Profit before taxes decreases. • Taxes decrease. • Net income decreases.

Why would someone in a business with receivables want to switch from the cash method to the accrual accounting method when the result can be an increase in taxes? There could be several legitimate business reasons, including the following:

- For better comparison purposes, the company may want to use the same accounting method used by its competitors.
- The entrepreneur may be preparing the company to go public or to be sold. The accrual method would show the company to be bigger and more profitable than it would appear using the cash method.

Before ending the discussion on accounting methods, it should be pointed out that in December 1999, the IRS issued new rules regarding this topic. Specifically, the IRS said that companies carrying no inventory and having annual revenues between $1 million and $5 million could no longer choose the cash method. They must use the accrual method. The result of this change has been quite significant for the cash flow of businesses in this revenue range. They now pay more taxes sooner. The beneficiary has been the U.S. Treasury, which was expected to collect an additional $1.8 billion by 2005 as a result of accelerated tax payments.[6]

THE BALANCE SHEET

An example of a balance sheet is shown in Figure 4-5.

FIGURE 4-5

Bruce Company Balance Sheet, Year End 12/31/07

Assets	
Current assets	
Cash	$300
Accounts receivable	300
Less: Uncollectibles	(10)
Inventory	600
Total current assets	**$1,190**
Property, plant, and equipment	
Property	$5,000
Buildings	4,000
Less: Accumulated depreciation	(1,000)
Equipment	3,000
Less: Accumulated depreciation	(1,000)
Total property, plant, and equipment	**$10,000**
Other assets	
Automobiles	$4,500
Patents	1,000
Total other assets	**$5,500**
Total assets	**$16,690**

continued on next page

F I G U R E   4-5

Bruce Company Balance Sheet, Year End 12/31/07 (continued.)

Liabilities and shareholders' equity	
Current liabilities	
Accounts payable	$500
Wages	700
Short-term debt	900
Total current liabilities	**$2,100**
Long-term liabilities	
Bank loans	$4,000
Mortgages	5,000
Total long-term liabilities	**$7,000**
Shareholders' equity	
Contributed capital	$5,000
Retained earnings	2,590
Total shareholders' equity	**$7,590**
Total liabilities and shareholders' equity	**$16,690**

The information contained on the balance sheet is also often presented in the format shown in Figure 4-6. The balance sheet is a financial snapshot of a company's assets, liabilities, and stockholders' equity at a particular time. Bankers have historically relied on analysis of ratios of various assets and liabilities on the balance sheet to determine a company's creditworthiness and solvency position.

F I G U R E   4-6

Balance Sheet Information

Assets	Liabilities
▪ Current	▪ Current
▪ Long-term	▪ Long-term
▪ Tangible	
▪ Intangible	**Equity**
	▪ Stock—common, preferred, etc.
	▪ Retained earnings

A company's assets on the balance sheet are separated into current and long-term categories. Current assets are those items that can be converted into cash within one year, including a company's cash balance, the dollar amount due to the company from customers (i.e., accounts receivable), inventory, marketable securities, and prepaid expenses.

Long-term assets, tangible and intangible, are the remaining assets. They are recorded at their original cost, not their present market value, minus the accumulated depreciation from each year's depreciation expense, which is found on the income statement. The assets that fall into this category include buildings, land, equipment, furnaces, automobiles, trucks, and lighting fixtures.

As stated earlier in this chapter, all long-term assets , except land, can be depreciated over time. This is permissible under GAAP despite the fact that some assets, in fact, appreciate over time. An example is real estate, which usually tends to appreciate over time, but the balance sheet does not reflect this fact. Therefore, it is commonly known that the balance sheet often undervalues a company's assets, especially when real estate is owned. This fact was highlighted in the mid-1980s during the leveraged-buyout, hostile-takeover craze. Corporate raiders, as the hostile-takeover artists were known, would forcibly buy a company at an exorbitant price because they believed that the company had "hidden value" in excess of what the financial statements showed. One of the primary items they were concerned with was the real estate owned by the company, which was recorded on the balance sheet at cost minus accumulated depreciation. The raiders would take over the company, financing the purchase primarily with debt. Then they would sell the real estate at market prices, using the proceeds to reduce their debt obligations, and lease the property from the new owners.

The other components of the balance sheet belongs to the liabilities and shareholders' (stockholders') equity sections. A company's liabilities consist of the amounts owed by the company to creditors, secured and unsecured. The liabilities section of the balance sheet, like the assets section, is divided into current and long-term. Current liabilities are those that must be paid within 12 months. Included in this category is the current portion of any principal payments due on loans for which the company is responsible—remember, the current interest payments on the loan are on the income statement—and accounts payable, which is very simply money owed to suppliers. Long-term liabilities are all of the company's other obligations. For example, if the company owns real estate and has a mortgage, the total balance due on that mortgage minus the current portion would be reflected in the long-term liabilities category.

Stockholders' equity is the difference between total assets and total liabilities. It is the net worth of the company, including the stock issued by the company and the accumulated earnings that the company has retained each year. Remember, the retained earnings are an accumulation of the profits from the income statement. Note that the company's net worth is not necessarily the company's value or what it would sell for. A company with a negative net worth, where total liabilities exceed total assets, may sell for quite a bit of money without any problems. As we will see in Chapter 7, the net worth of a company typically has no bearing on its valuation. A few important equations to remember are shown in Equation 4-3.

E Q U A T I O N   4-3

Shareholders' Equity

Total assets − total liabilities = shareholders' equity

Net worth = total assets − total liabilities

Therefore   Net worth = shareholders' equity

Finally, the items on the balance sheet are also used to compute a company's working capital and working capital needs. Net working capital is simply a measure of the company's ability to pay its bills—in other words, the company's short-term financial strength. A company's net working capital is measured as shown in Equation 4-4.

E Q U A T I O N   4-4

Net Working Capital

Net working capital = current assets − current liabilities

The fact that two companies have the exact same level of working capital does not mean that they have equal short-term financial strength. Look, for example, at Figure 4-7. While both companies have the same amount of working capital, a banker would prefer to lend to Cheers Company because Cheers has greater financial strength. Specifically, for every dollar that Cheers owes, it has $6 in potentially liquid assets, whereas Hill Company has only $2 in assets for every dollar owed.

F I G U R E   4-7

Working Capital Comparison

	Hill Company	Cheers Company
Current assets	$1,000,000	$600,000
Current liabilities	500,000	100,000
Working capital	$ 500,000	$500,000

Now look at the example in Figure 4-8. It shows that a company with greater working capital than another is again not necessarily stronger. With a 10-to-1 asset-to-liability ratio, Jardine is obviously financially stronger than Webb, with a 2-to-1 ratio, despite the fact that Webb has more working capital.

F I G U R E   4-8

Working Capital Comparison

	Jardine Company	Webb Company
Current assets	$10,000,000	$20,000,000
Current liabilities	1,000,000	10,000,000
Working capital	$ 9,000,000	$10,000,000

The entrepreneur must recognize that potential investors use the company's working capital situation to determine whether they will provide financing. In addition, loan covenants may establish a working capital level that the company must always maintain or risk technical loan default, resulting in the entire loan being called for immediate payment.

The balance sheet assumes greater importance for manufacturing companies than for service companies, primarily because the former tend to have tangible assets, such as machinery and real estate, whereas the latter tend to have people as their primary assets.

THE STATEMENT OF CASH FLOWS

The statement of cash flows uses information from the two other financial statements, the balance sheet (B/S) and the income statement (I/S), to develop a statement that explains changes in cash flows resulting from operations, investing, and financing activities. Figure 4-9 provides an example of a cash flow statement.

F I G U R E 4-9

Richardson Company Cash Flow Statement, Year Ended 12/31/07

Cash flow from operations	
Net income	$400,000
Noncash expenditures	
Depreciation	110,000
Amortization	95,000
Net working capital	10,000
Cash available for investing and financing activities	**$615,000**
Cash flow from investing activities	
Equipment purchases	($140,000)
Automobile purchases	(50,000)
Sale of old equipment	70,000
Cash available for investing activities	**$495,000**
Cash flow from financing activities	
Dividends paid	($30,000)
Mortgage payments	(100,000)
Loan payments	(200,000)
Repurchase company stock	(65,000)
Net cash flow	**$100,000**

The relationship between the sources and uses of cash is shown in Equation 4-5.

EQUATION   4-5

Cash Flow

Cash sources − cash uses = net cash flow

→ Fund operations and return to investors

Cash Flow Ledgers and Planners

The cash flow ledger, regardless of accounting issues such as cash versus accrual methods or noncash expenses such as depreciation, provides a summary of the increases (inflows) and decreases (outflows) in actual cash over a period of time. It provides important information primarily to the entrepreneur, but also possibly to investors and creditors (such as banks), about the balance of the cash account, enabling them to assess a company's ability to meet its debt payments when they come due. A famous (but unnamed) economist once said, "Cash flow is more important than your mother"—well, maybe not *more* important, but it is essential because it is the lifeline of any business. Cash flow is different from profit and more important, as we will see later in this chapter.

The cash flow at the end of a period (for example, a month) is calculated as shown in Figure 4-10. And Figure 4-11 provides an example of a monthly cash flow ledger. It indicates, on a transaction basis, all cash received and disbursed during a month's period. As shown, the cash balance at the end of the month is equal to the total cash received less the total cash disbursed for the month.

FIGURE   4-10

Sample Cash Flow Calculation

	Cash on hand at the beginning of the month
plus	Monthly cash received from customer payments, etc.
equals	Total cash
minus	Monthly cash disbursements for fixed and variable costs
equals	**Cash available at the end of the month**

F I G U R E   4-11

Oscar's Business Ledger*

Date	Explanation	To/From	Received	Disbursed	Balance
6/30/05					$1,000
7/1/05	Silkscreen start-up supplies	Ace Arts		$ 250	750
7/2/05	Bought 4 doz. T-shirts	Joe		240	510
7/6/05	Monthly registration fee	Flea market		100	410
7/6/05	Business cards	Print shop		20	390
7/6/05	Flyers	Print shop		10	380
7/7/05	Sold 4 doz.@ $12	Flea market	$ 576		956
7/10/05	Bought 5 doz. T-shirts	Joe		300	656
7/14/05	Sold 4 doz.@ $12, 1 doz.@ $10	Flea market	696		1,352
7/16/05	Bought 5 doz. T-shirts	Joe		300	1,052
7/16/05	Silkscreen ink	Print shop		50	1,002
7/16/05	Flyers	Print shop		10	992
7/21/05	Sold 3 doz. @ $12 (rained)	Flea market	432		1,424
7/25/05	Bought 2 doz. T-shirts	Joe		120	1,304
7/26/05	Sold 4 doz. @ $12	Flea market	576		1,880
Totals			**$2,280**	**$1,400**	**$1,880**

* Adapted from Steve Mariotti, *The Young Entrepreneur's Guide to Starting and Running a Business.*

The successful entrepreneurs are those who know their company's actual cash position on any given day. Therefore, unlike the comparatively few number of times they need to reread the income statement and balance sheet, it is recommended that entrepreneurs, especially the inexperienced and those in the early stages of their ventures, review the cash flow ledger at least weekly.

Figure 4-12 provides a weekly cash flow projection summary, which every new and inexperienced entrepreneur should prepare immediately upon opening for business and each month thereafter. It indicates the anticipated cash inflow during the month and cash payments to be made. In the figure, the anticipated cash inflow—59—is less than the expected cash outflow—60—for the month; therefore, the cash balance for the month will be negative 1.

The projection in Figure 4-12 was prepared at the end of September for the following month. It anticipates the cash inflows during the month and the cash payments to be made. The "Cash in" section includes expected payments from specific customers

FIGURE   4-12

Sample Weekly Cash Flow Projections

Week of	Oct. 1	Oct. 8	Oct. 15	Oct. 22	Oct. 29	Oct.'s Total Cash Received
(Cash in)						
1. Beginning cash	10					10
2. Receivables						
Customer 1					5	5
Customer 2		3	3	3		9
Customer 3		8				8
Customer 4			12			12
3. Cash payments	5	3	1	1	5	15
	15	14	16	4	10	59
(Cash out)						
1. Payroll	3	3	3	3	3	15
2. Loan payments			6			6
3. Rent	5					5
4. Insurance						
Property	2					2
Health	3					3
5. Vendor payments						
Vendor 1	1	2	3	4	4	14
Vendor 2	1		3			4
Vendor 3		2	6			8
Vendor 4	1		2			3
	16	7	23	7	7	60

Source: Teri Lammers, "The Weekly Cash-Flow Planner," *Inc.*, June 1992, p. 99.

based on the terms of the invoices and the aging of the corresponding receivables. The terms were net 30, which means that the payment was due 30 days following the invoice date. But the
entrepreneur who completed this projection did not simply project
October 29 because that was 30 days after invoicing. To do this
would be too theoretical and quite frankly naïve on the entrepreneur's part. Instead, she used common sense and factored in the
extra 7 days that Customer 1 typically takes before paying the bills.
Thus, the product was invoiced on September 22, and the entrepreneur is forecasting the actual receipt of payment on October 29.

This section also includes the cash payments expected each week throughout the month. These are expected to be actual cash payments that customers make when they pick up their merchandise. In these cases, the entrepreneur is not supplying any credit to the customer.

By doing this kind of projection each month, the entrepreneur can schedule her payments to suppliers to match her expected cash receipts. This planner allows her to be proactive, as all entrepreneurs should be, with regard to the money owed to her suppliers. It enables her to let specific vendors know in advance that her payment will probably be late. The cash flow ledger and planner are simple and very useful tools that the entrepreneur should use to manage cash flow successfully.

N O T E S

1. Jamie Pratt, *Financial Accounting*, 2nd ed. (Cincinnati, Ohio: South-Western Publishing Co., 1994), pp. 396–397.
2. Kathleen Morris, "No Laughing Gas Matter—A Dental-Tech Startup May Have Hyped Its Numbers," *BusinessWeek*, June 9, 1998, p. 44.
3. Stanford Law School, Securities Class Action Clearinghouse, http://securities.stanford.edu/1012/PLSIA98/.
4. Martha Brannigan, "Sunbeam Concedes 1997 Statements May Be Off," *Wall Street Journal*, July 1, 1998, p. A4.
5. *U.S. Business Journal*, February 2001.
6. *Crain's Chicago Business*, July 10, 2000.

Financial Statement Analysis

INTRODUCTION

Sadly, it is common to hear entrepreneurs say, "I do not know any thing about finance, because I was never good with numbers. Therefore, I focus on my product and let someone else worry about the numbers." Someone with such an attitude can never achieve successful high-growth entrepreneurship. Financial statement analysis is not brain surgery! Everyone can understand it. In fact, no matter how distasteful or uncomfortable it might be to the high-growth entrepreneur, he must learn and use financial statement analysis. Finance is like medicine. No one likes it because it usually tastes awful, but everyone knows that it is good for you.

PROACTIVE ANALYSIS

Entrepreneurs must engage in proactive analysis of their financial statements to better manage their company and influence the business decisions of the company's managers, as well as attract capital from investors and creditors.[1]

Financial statements must be used as tangible management tools, not simply as reporting documents. While it is not required that the entrepreneur be able to develop these statements herself—a job that is done by the CFO—she must be able to completely understand every line item. The entrepreneur who cannot do this will have a much more difficult time growing the company and raising capital.

For example, one of the fundamentals of finance says that accounts receivable (A/R) and inventory should not grow at an annual rate faster than revenue growth. If they do, it is a sign that the company's working capital is being depleted because the accounts receivable and inventory represent a drag on a company's cash.

A case in point: The management team at Lucent Technologies failed to do a proactive analysis of this relationship. The result? The stock price declined 30 percent shortly after the company reported its 1999 financial results. The results showed that compared with the previous year, revenues grew an impressive 20 percent. Unfortunately, A/R and inventory grew 41 percent and 54 percent, respectively!

Another problem for entrepreneurs who do not analyze their financial statements proactively is that these entrepreneurs also risk being taken advantage of or exploited. There are numerous accounts of companies losing money to employees who were stealing products and cash. In many instances, the theft was not identified immediately because the owners excluded themselves from all financial statement analysis. Not surprisingly, many of the thieves are bookkeepers, accountants, accounts receivable and payable clerks, and CFOs. All of the aforementioned are positions intimately involved in the company's financings. There's a lesson here: thieves do not always look like scumbags! Heck, if they did, you would not have hired *that* person in the first place.

Automated Equipment Inc. is a family-run manufacturing business in Niles, Illinois. The company's bookkeeper was a friendly 35-year-old woman who was inflating payouts to vendors and then altering the names on the checks and depositing them in accounts under her control. It took the company four years to discover the embezzlement, and by then the woman had stolen nearly $610,000, leaving the company in near financial ruin. Among other things, the bookkeeper purchased a Cadillac sport-utility vehicle, expensive clothing, and fine meats. Oh, she also put a $30,000 addition on her home. The theft forced the company to lay off 4 of its 11 employees, including the owner's wife and a 27-year worker. By the way, the bookkeeper had a separate federal student loan conviction from her *previous* job.

Bette Wildermuth, a longtime business broker in Richmond, Virginia, has 25 years' worth of stories of business owners getting surprised by the people they trust. Often, she's the one who catches the shenanigans when poring over financials at the time of a sale. "I was asked by the owner of a fabrication company to come talk about the possibility of selling his company. He specifically asked me to come on a Wednesday afternoon because his bookkeeper would not be there. You see he didn't want to cause her any worry over a possible job loss. After all, she'd been with his company for 15 years." Wildermuth was left alone with the books and records to try and determine a valuation. After about two hours, she said, the owner returned and proudly asked, "Did you notice that our sales are up and we're continuing to make a profit?" Wildermuth had noticed and congratulated him. "I also told him that an astute buyer would notice that and more, and that both of us would have the same question. 'Bob,' I asked, 'Why are you paying your home mortgage from the business account?' He told me that that was impossible because his mortgage had been paid off years ago." It turned out that the sweet, Norman Rockwellesque woman who had handled his finances for 15 years was robbing him blind. She was also paying her personal Visa card from the company books. "When I told him what was going on," Wildermuth remembers, "he looked like he had been punched in the stomach."

Another great example to highlight this point is the story of Rae Puccini, who, by the time she was 55 years old, had been convicted eight times over two decades for stealing money from her employers. In July 2000, while facing another conviction for the same crime, she committed suicide. Her final crime was using her position as the office manager to steal $800,000 from her employer, Edelman, Combs & Latturner (ECL), a prominent Chicago-based law firm that hired her in 1996. The lawsuit against her stated,

> She forged signatures, cut herself "bonus" checks and transferred money from her bosses' bank account. She used the firm's American Express credit card to pay for a Caribbean cruise and a vacation at the Grand Hotel on Mackinac Island, Michigan. She also used the credit card to pay for a Mexico vacation with her boyfriend as well as groceries, flowers, furniture and liquor. Her 2000 Buick LeSabre was paid for by a $35,000 bonus that she paid herself. Her most expensive gift to herself was the $200,000 house that she purchased in the suburbs, using a $42,000 check that she cut from the firm.[2]

How did she pull off this incredible crime? First, she created a fake résumé to hide her prison record. Second, she earned her employers' trust easily. Third, she worked long hours to create an impression that she was very dedicated to the firm. As an attorney at another law firm, where she also stole money, stated, "She ostensibly was very loyal and trusted. She came in early and stayed late."[3] The final reason was that no one in the law firm was involved in the supervision and analysis of its financials. She was practically given carte blanche, without any checks and balances. She was finally caught when ECL partners asked her to show documentation explaining how the company's cash had been spent. When she hedged, the partners looked through her work area and found incriminating evidence.[4]

Approximately one month before her death, Puccini went to a funeral home, selected flowers, and paid for her body to be cremated. She donated many of her clothes to Goodwill and set up a postfuneral dinner at a Greek restaurant. Her final act was to type a confessional letter that included the statement, "No one knew what I was doing with the finances of ECL."[5] She was absolutely correct.

When the entrepreneur is involved in his company's finances, such sordid stories regarding losses of cash to theft can be practically eliminated because the entrepreneur's knowledge and participation serve as a deterrent.

To utilize the financial statements as management tools, the entrepreneur must have them prepared more than once a year. Monthly financial statements developed by an outside accounting firm can be expensive. In addition, monthly statements, by definition, are short-term-focused, and their analysis may encourage entrepreneurs to micromanage and overreact. The ideal is to produce quarterly statements, which should be completed, and be in the entrepreneur's hand for analysis, no later than 30 days following the close of a quarter.

In this chapter, we will learn that the data contained in financial statements can be analyzed to tell an interesting and compelling story about the financial condition of a business. Included in the financial statement analysis discussion will be a case study. We will examine the income statement of the Clark Company to determine what is taking place with its operations, despite the fact that we know nothing about the industry or the company's products or services. Using information provided in this statement, we will then prepare financial projections (i.e., pro formas) for the next year.

INCOME STATEMENT ANALYSIS

In terms of financial analysis, all items, including expenses and the three margins—gross, operating, and net—mentioned in Chapter 4, are analyzed in terms of percentage of revenues. As Figure 5-1 shows, the cost of goods sold (COGS) percent *plus* the gross profit percent should equal 100 percent. The COGS percent *plus* the total operating expense percent *plus* the interest expense percent *plus* the tax expense percent *plus* the net income percent should also equal 100 percent.

FIGURE 5-1

Income Statement Analysis

Total revenues	$8,000	100.00%
COGS	2,000	25.00%
Gross margins	**$6,000**	**75.00%**
Operating expenses		
Wages	$1,000	12.50%
Rent	300	3.75%
Selling expenses	400	5.00%
Depreciation	500	6.25%
Amortization	300	3.75%
Total operating expense	**$2,500**	31.25%
Operating profit	**$3,500**	**43.75%**
Interest expense	200	2.50%
Profit before taxes	**$3,300**	**41.25%**
Income tax expenses	1,320	16.50%
Net income	**$1,980**	**24.75%**

RATIO ANALYSIS

A ratio analysis, using two or more financial statement numbers, may be undertaken for several reasons. Entrepreneurs, along with bankers, creditors, and stockholders, typically use ratio analysis to objectively appraise the financial condition of a company and to identify its vulnerabilities and strengths. As we will discuss later, ratio analysis is probably the most important financial tool that the entrepreneur can use to proactively operate a company. Therefore, the entrepreneur should review the various ratios that we discuss in this section at least quarterly, along with the three key financial reports: income statement, balance sheet, and cash flow statement. There are six key ratio categories:

- Profitability ratios
- Liquidity ratios
- Leverage (capital structure) ratios
- Operating ratios
- Cash ratios
- Valuation ratios

Table 5-1 provides a description of selected financial ratios and the formulas used to calculate them.

T A B L E   5-1

Financial Accounting Ratios

Ratio	Description	Formula
Profitability ratios	**Measure earning potential.**	
Gross margin percentage	Measures the gross profit margin the company is achieving on sales—that is, the profit after COGS is deducted from revenues.	(Sales – COGS)/sales
Return on equity	Measures the return on invested capital. Shows how hard management is making the equity in the business work.	Net income/ stockholders' equity
Net operating income	Measures income generated from operations without regard to the company's financing and taxes.	Sales expenses (excluding interest)/sales
		Continued on next page

T A B L E 5-1

Financial Accounting Ratios (continued)

Ratio	Description	Formula
Net profit margin	Measures the net profit margin the company is achieving on sales.	Net profit/sales
Liquidity ratios	**Measure a company's ability to meet its short-term payments.**	
Current ratio	Measures whether current bills can be paid. A 2-to-1 ratio minimum should be targeted.	Current assets/current liabilities
Quick ratio (acid-test ratio)	Measures liquidity. Assesses whether current bills can be paid without selling inventory or other illiquid current assets. A 1-to-1 ratio minimum should be targeted.	(Current assets – inventory and other illiquid assets)/current liabilities
Leverage ratios	**Evaluate a company's capital structure and long-term potential solvency.**	
Debt/equity ratio	Measures the degree to which the company has leveraged itself. Ideally, the ratio should be as low as possible, giving greater flexibility to borrow.	Total liabilities/ stockholders' equity
Operating ratios	**Focus on the use of assets and the performance of management.**	
Days payable	Measures the speed at which the company is paying its bills. Ideally, one should wait to pay the bills as long as possible without negatively affecting product service or shipments from suppliers.	Accounts payable/(COGS/365)
Collection ratio ("days receivable")	Measures the quality of the accounts receivable. It shows the average number of days it takes to collect receivables. The ideal situation is to get paid as quickly as possible.	Accounts receivable/ (revenues/365)
Inventory turns	Measures the number of times inventory is sold and replenished during a time period. It measures the speed at which inventory is turned into sales.	COGS/average inventory outstanding

Continued on next page

T A B L E   5-1

Financial Accounting Ratios (continued)

Ratio	Description	Formula
Days inventory carried	Measures the average amount of daily inventory being carried.	Inventory/(COGS/365)
Cash flow ratios	**Measure a company's cash position.**	
Cash flow cycle	Measures the number of days it takes to convert inventory and receivables into cash.	(Receivables + inventory)/COGS
Cash flow debt coverage ratio	Measures whether a company can meet its debt service requirements. A 1.25-to-1 ratio minimum should be targeted.	EBITDA/(interest + principal due on debt)
Valuation ratios	**Measure returns to investors.**	
Price/earnings (P/E) ratio	Measures the price that investors are willing to pay for a company's stock for each dollar of the company's earnings. For example, a P/E ratio of 8 means that investors are willing to pay $8 for every dollar of a company's earnings.	Price of stock/earnings per share

A company's ratios cannot be examined in a vacuum, i.e., by looking at only one year for one company. To attempt to do so renders the ratios virtually meaningless. The greatest benefit of historical and present-day ratios derived from two analytical measurements—internal and external—is the ability to do annual internal comparisons. This type of analysis will show if there are any trends within a company across time. For example, a comparison can be made of selected income statement line items across a two-year, five-year, or ten-year period. This type of analysis will help to assess the soundness of a company's activities as well as identify important trends. Basically, it allows the entrepreneur to answer the question, is my internal performance better today than it was last year, five years ago, or ten years ago? If the answer is yes, then the next question is, how did it get better? If the answer is no, then the next question is, why didn't it get better? Deeper analysis should be undertaken to determine not only why things are getting worse but also what is making things better. If the entrepreneur knows and understands the detailed reasons why her ratios improved over time, then she can use that information for prescriptive elements of future strategic plans.

The entrepreneur should also do an external comparison of the company's ratios against those of the industry. This comparison should be against both the industry's averages and the best and worst performers within the industry. This will allow the entrepreneur to assess the company's operations, financial condition, and activities against comparable companies. (Table 5-2 shows a comparison of turnover ratios.) The successful entrepreneur knows that respecting and understanding the competition is a basic business requirement, and the first step to take toward that endeavor is to understand how you compare with the competition. Ratio analysis is one of the most objective ways to do such measurements.

T A B L E 5-2

Inventory Turnover Ratios

Store	Turnover
Wal-Mart	8.0
Target	6.6
Kohl's	4.0
Sears	3.8
J.C. Penney	3.5
Macy's	3.0

Source: 2007 company financial statements (as compiled by Reuters).

Many banks provide business loans on the condition that the company maintains certain minimum ratios, such as debt/equity, net worth, and acid test. These conditions are usually included in the covenant section of the loan agreement, and not maintaining the minimum ratios puts the company technically in default on the loan. Other investors, such as venture capitalists, may use ratio attainment as "milestones" for determining whether and when they will invest more capital. For example, they may tell the entrepreneur that his next round of financing will occur when the company attains 50 percent gross margins for four consecutive quarters.

In addition to performing historical and present ratio analyses internally and externally, the entrepreneur should also use ratios to drive the future of the business. For example, the entrepreneur's strategic plans may include growing revenues while decreasing inventory. Therefore, the days of inventory carried must be reduced while the inventory turnover ratio is increased to some targeted number. Simply stating these objectives is not enough. After determining the respective targeted numbers, a strategic plan must be developed and implemented to actually reduce the amount of inventory carried and to ship to customers new inventory that is received to customers quickly.

Such a relationship between the two ratios would look as shown in Table 5-3.

T A B L E   5-3

Inventory Ratio Comparison Example

	2003	2004	2005	2006	2007
Inventory turns	8	11	11	12	14
Days of inventory carried	43	34	33	30	28

As you can see in the table, the amount of average daily inventory being carried decreases from 43 days' worth of inventory to 28 over a projected five-year period. Now, if the entrepreneur's goal is also to increase revenues over this same period of time, then she must turn the smaller volume of daily inventory each year more frequently. And, as the table shows, that is in fact what the entrepreneur forecasts: to increase the inventory turns from 8 times a year to 14. The just-in-time inventory model, pioneered and perfected by companies such as Toyota and Dell, works only if a company's vendors and partners are highly synchronized.

Events outside the control of the company can also cause big problems. In the wake of the terrorist attacks in New York in September 2001, Cherry Automotive of Waukegan, Illinois, was forced to shut down three production lines while it waited for circuit boards to be flown in from Asia. The delay cost the company $40,000. To ensure that this didn't happen again, Cherry started carrying three weeks' worth of components inventory, compared with the two to three days' worth it carried prior to the attacks. Managers described the move as "going from just-in-time to just-in-case." Not that the owners took the decision lightly; by their estimates, that one change will cost the company $250,000 annually.[6] Appendix A offers a listing of national average inventory turnover ratios and amount of sales in ending inventory for selected retail and wholesale industries.

Another proactive way to use ratios is for the entrepreneur to set short-term, medium-term, and long-term objectives with regard to internal and external ratios. For example, the short-term plan covers the next 12 months to get the days receivables ratio back down to the best level in the company's 10-year history. The medium-term (i.e., 24 months) plan may be to get the company's days receivable down to at least the industry average. Finally, the long-term (i.e., 36 months) plan may be to make the company's days receivable the lowest in the industry, making it the market leader. Thus, ratios have immense value to the entrepreneur as analytical and proactive management tools. And successful entrepreneurs regularly compare their performance against historical highs, lows, and trends, as well as against the industry.

What are good and bad ratios? Well, it depends on which ratios are being examined and, more importantly, the specific industry. Regarding the first point, good days receivable are determined by a company's invoice terms. The standard invoice has the following terms: "2/10, net 30 days." This means that the payer can take a 2 percent discount if the invoice is paid within 10 days. After 10 days, the invoice's gross amount must be paid within the next 20 days. Thus, the customer is being given a total of 30 days following the date of the invoice to pay the bill. If the company does business under these terms, then days receivable of 45 days or greater are considered bad. The ideal target is to have days receivable no more than 10 days greater than the invoice.

The second factor that determines what are good and bad ratios is the industry (see Table 5-4 for good and bad key ratios for several industries). For example, if we analyze two different technology industries, we will see two distinctly different ideas of what is considered good operating margins. In the office equipment industry, the company with the strongest operating margin is Pitney Bowes at 16 percent.[7] That is significantly lower than that of GlaxoSmithKline, the pharmaceutical industry leader, which had an operating margin of 34 percent![8] As stated earlier, everything is relative. Both of these companies have significantly better operating margins than Amazon.com, whose operating margin was 3.7 percent in 2007.[9]

T A B L E   5-4

Key Ratios for Various Industries

Industry	Ratio	Best	Worst
Landscaping services	Current ratio	2.0	1.0
	Inventory turns	N/A	N/A
	Days receivable	8.0	55.0
Grocery stores	Current ratio	2.3	0.9
	Inventory turns	23.3	11.8
	Days receivable	0.0	3.0
Electronic computer manufacturing	Current ratio	2.9	1.2
	Inventory turns	21.0	3.3
	Days receivable	30.0	60.0
Colleges and universities	Current ratio	4.1	1.0
	Inventory turns	N/A	N/A
	Days receivable	8.0	38.0
Airlines	Current ratio	1.5	0.6
	Inventory turns	N/A	N/A
	Days receivable	1.0	30.0
Dress manufacturing	Current ratio	1.5	1.1
	Inventory turns	7.2	2.8
	Days receivable	39.0	63.0
Soft drink manufacturing	Current ratio	2.3	1.1
	Inventory turns	19.3	7.3
	Days receivable	19.0	34.0

Source: Annual Statement Studies: Financial Ratio Benchmarks, 2006-2007, Risk Management Association.

Typically, the financial ratios of successful firms are never lower than the industry average. For example, companies in the computer-manufacturing industry carry, on average, 75 days of inventory. That dramatically contrasts with Dell, which carries an average of 4 days of inventory.[10] This is one of the reasons why Dell has been so financially successful. As Kevin Rollins, CEO of Dell at the time, explained, "Our product is unique, in that it's like fresh fish. The longer you keep it, the more it loses value. In our industry, the product depreciates anywhere from a half to a full point a week. You can literally see the stuff rot. Cutting inventory is not just a nice thing to do, it's a financial imperative."[11]

There are some instances where it is perfectly acceptable for a company's ratios to be worse than the industry average. This occurs when the below-average ratios are part of the company's strategic plan. For example, inventory turns and days inventory carried that are slower and greater, respectively, than the industry average may not be signs of negative performance. It could be that the company's strategic plan requires it to carry levels of inventory greater than the industry average; as a result, inventory turns would be slower. For example, if a company promises overnight delivery, while competitors ship in 14 days, that company's inventory carried will be higher and turns will be slower. Ideally, the gross margins should be higher than the industry's because the company should be able to charge a premium for the faster deliveries. Given this fact, it is essential that the entrepreneur perform a comparison of industry averages when writing the business plan, when developing the projections, and, most importantly, before submitting the plan to prospective investors.

An example of a company that runs with higher expenses than its competitors is Commonwealth Worldwide Chauffeured Transportation. Dawson Rutter, the company's founder and CEO, dropped out of three universities before starting the company. Over a four-year period, Commonwealth grew its business from 40 customers to 4,000 and increased its revenues over 248 percent. Rutter has the philosophy of "building the church for Easter Sunday." He says, "We create infrastructure in anticipation of revenue. That ensures delivery will be impeccable 100 percent of the time. We can always handle 105 percent of our absolute busiest day. Is that a more expensive way of doing it? You bet. But the fact is we don't lose customers, which means we can afford to pay that premium."[12]

How can entrepreneurs find out industry averages for private companies? Figure 5-2 lists periodicals and other resources commonly used to compare an existing company's performance against the industry, as well as to determine if the pro formas in a business plan are in line with the industry being entered. As noted previously, you'll also find national averages for turnover ratios in Appendix A.

FIGURE 5-2

Industry Ratio Sources

Annual Statement Studies, Risk Management Association (formerly Robert Morris Associates)

Almanac of Business and Industrial Financial Ratios, Prentice Hall

Bizstats.com

Industry Norms and Key Business Ratios, Dun & Bradstreet

Risk Management Association eCompare2, online financial statement analysis tool

Value Line Investment Survey

BREAKEVEN ANALYSIS

The analysis of financial statements should also be used to determine a company's breakeven (BE) point. Successful entrepreneurs know how many widgets, meals, or hours of service they have to sell, serve, or provide, respectively, before they can take any real cash out of the company. Equation 5-1 shows the equation for calculating a company's BE point.

EQUATION 5-1

Breakeven Point

Fixed expenses ÷ gross margin = total breakeven sales

Total breakeven sales ÷ unit price = number of units to sell

Using the information contained in Figures 4-1 and 4-4 for the Bruce Company, one can prepare a selected set of financial ratios and BE for the company. Table 5-5 shows the financial ratios, BE, and an explanation of the numbers.

TABLE 5-5

Selected Financial Accounting Ratios for the Bruce Company

Ratio	Amount	Explanation
Gross margin percentage	75%	75 cents of every dollar of sales goes to gross profit. Or the product's labor and material costs were 25 cents.
Return on equity	26%	The company is getting a return of 26% on the capital invested in the company.
Net profit margin	24.75%	More than 24 cents of every dollar of sales goes to the bottom line.
Current ratio	0.57	The ratio is less than 1, which indicates that the company can't meet its short-term financial obligations.
Quick ratio (acid-test ratio)	0.28	The ratio is less than 1, which means that the company can't pay its debt.
Debt/equity ratio	1.2	The company owes $1.20 of debt for every dollar of equity.
Collection ratio	13 days	It takes 13 days on average to collect receivables.
Inventory turns	3.33	Inventory turns 3.33 times.
Cash flow cycle	0.45 day	It would take less than a day to convert inventory to cash.
Breakeven point		BE = $700 ÷ 0.75 = $933

MEASURING GROWTH

When measuring the growth of a company, the entrepreneur should be sure to do it completely. Many people use compounded annual growth rate (CAGR) analysis when measuring and discussing growth. In addition to CAGR, another means of measurement is simple growth. Before going any further, let's discuss the two. In finance, both terms are typically used to discuss the rate of growth of money over a certain period of time.

Simple interest is the rate of growth relative to only the initial investment or original revenues. This base number is the present value (PV). Future value (FV) is the sum of the initial investment and the amount earned from the interest calculation. Thus, the simple interest rate or the rate of growth of a company with revenues of $3,885,000 in Year 1 and $4,584,300 in Year 2 is 18 percent, because $699,300, the difference between revenues in Years 1 and 2, is 18 percent of Year 1 revenues. Using the simple interest rate of 18 percent, Year 3's revenues would be $5,283,600. This was determined by simply adding $699,300, or 18 percent of the initial number, $3,885,000, to Year 2's revenue number. Therefore, an 18 percent simple growth rate would add $699,300 to the previous year's revenue to determine the level of revenues for the next year. In conclusion, the formula to determine the simple growth rate is the equation shown in Equation 5-2.

EQUATION 5-2

Simple Growth Rate

$$\text{Simple growth rate} = \frac{\text{dollars of growth}}{\text{initial investment} \times \text{time}}$$

Using Equation 5-2, let's input the numbers to answer the question, at what simple interest rate must $3,885,000 grow in two years to equal $5,283,600? Another way to look at this question is, if you received a two-year loan of $3,885,000 at 18 percent simple interest, what would you owe in total principal and interest? The answer would be $5,283,600, as calculated in Figure 5-3.

FIGURE   5-3

Components of Dollar of Growth Calculation

Year 1 (present value)	=	$3,885,000
Year 3 (future value)	=	$5,283,600
Dollars of growth (or FV – PV)	=	$1,398,600
Time	=	2 years

The concept of compounding is commonly used by financial institutions such as banks, relative to both the money they lend and the deposits they receive. CAGR analysis—which is popular among professionals with graduate business school backgrounds, including consultants and commercial and investment bankers—simply shows the interest rate, compounded annually, that must be achieved to grow a company from revenues in Year 1 to revenues in a future year. That sounds similar to what we just said about simple interest. However, the word *compounded*, which is *not* included in the definition of simple interest, makes a huge difference. Compounding means that you earn interest not only on the initial investment (i.e., the PV), as was the case with simple growth, but also on the interest earned each year, or the actual dollars of growth. Therefore, unlike simple growth, the compounded rate of growth each year reflects the initial investment plus the earnings on reinvested earnings.

Let's use the same numbers from the simple growth rate discussions to illustrate the concept of CAGR. A company with an 18 percent CAGR and Year 1 revenues of $3,885,000 will have the future revenues shown in Figure 5-4.

F I G U R E 5-4

CAGR Example

Year 2: $4,584,300 (i.e., $3,885,000 × 1.18)
Year 3: $5,409,474 (i.e., $4,584,300 × 1.18)

In comparing simple annual growth with compounded annual growth, clearly the comparison in Table 5-6 shows the latter to be more advantageous to investors or entrepreneurs who want rapid growth.

T A B L E 5-6

Simple and Compounded Annual Growth Comparison

Revenues at 18% Rate	Simple Growth	Compounded Annually
Year 1	$3,885,000	$3,885,000
Year 2	$4,584,300	$4,584,300
Year 3	$5,283,600	$5,409,474
Year 4	$5,982,900	$6,383,179
Year 5	$6,682,200	$7,532,151

As you can see in Table 5-6, the first-year growth with compounding is the same as simple growth because the base is the same. The shortcoming with using CAGR is that it looks at only two years, the beginning year and the ending year, completely ignoring the years in between. Therefore, when used alone, this popular growth measurement tells an incomplete story that can be misleading.

For example, two companies with Year 1 revenues of $3,885,000 and Year 5 revenues of $7,532,151, as shown in Table 5-7, will show the same 18 percent CAGR despite the fact that the revenues in Years 2, 3, and 4 looked very different.

T A B L E   5-7

CAGR Comparison

	Company 1	Company 2
Year 1	$3,885,000	$3,885,000
Year 2	$4,584,300	$3,000,000
Year 3	$5,409,474	$2,900,000
Year 4	$6,383,179	$2,700,000
Year 5	$7,532,151	$7,532,151

The reason why both companies have the same CAGR is that both had the same revenues in Year 1 and Year 5. The formula for CAGR considers only these two data points. It ignores what happens in between because theoretically CAGR means that in any given year throughout the five-year period, the company's annual compounded growth in revenues was an even 18 percent based on the information given about Year 1 and Year 5 and based on how CAGR is calculated. That is to say, the growth followed a relatively linear progression. But as Table 5-7 shows, that is not always the case. Company 2's revenues declined in three consecutive years. So the major shortfall in using CAGR is that it does not take into account the actual growth rates from year to year over the five-year period. Therefore, a more complete analysis using CAGR must include the analysis of real annual growth rates to see if there are any trends.

Finally, if we want to determine the actual revenues in Year 5 (i.e., FV) of a company that had revenues of $3,885,000 in Year 1 (i.e., PV) and was growing at a compounded annual rate of 18 percent, the formula shown in Figure 5-5 could be used.

FIGURE 5-5

Sample Future Value Calculation

Future value = present value × (1 + Year 1 rate) × (1 + Year 2 rate) × (1 + Year 3 rate) × (1 + Year 4 rate)

Future value = $3,885,000 × (1.18) × (1.18) × (1.18) × (1.18)

Future value = $3,885,000 × (1.18)^4

Future value = $7,532,151

Note: 1 is added to each year's interest rate to show that for every dollar invested, 18% will be returned.

CASE STUDY—CLARK COMPANY

Figure 5-6 presents an income statement for the Clark Company for three years. There is no information regarding the company's industry, products, or services. This information is not needed. Numbers alone can tell a story, and every entrepreneur must get comfortable with being able to review financial statements, understand what is going on with the company, and recognize its strengths, weaknesses, and potential value. As we stated in Chapter 1, a successful entrepreneur must have the ability, willingness, and comfort to make decisions given ambiguous, imperfect, or incomplete information. The analysis of Figure 5-6 gives you the opportunity to demonstrate this trait. As you will see, it is an itty-bitty, tiny business. Nevertheless, the analysis would be exactly the same if each line item were multiplied by $1 million. The point being made is that the analysis of a small company's financials is the same as that of a large company's. The only difference is the number of zeros to the left of the decimal points. An appropriate analogy can be made to swimming. If you can swim in 4 feet of water, you can also swim in 10 feet of water and deeper.

FIGURE 5-6

Clark Company Income Statement (Selected Years)*

	2005	2006	2007
Revenues	137,367	134,352	113,456
Returns and allowances			588
Cost of goods sold	42,925	38,032	40,858
Gross profits	**94,442**	**96,320**	**72,010**
Operating expenses			
Advertising	3,685	3,405	2,904
Bad debts	150	50	130
Automobile expense	1,432	460	732
Depreciation	1,670	1,670	835
Employee benefits programs			
Insurance	2,470	2,914	1,915
Interest			
Mortgage			
Other	153		2,373
Legal and professional services	1,821	1,493	
Office expense	10,424	8,218	8,965
Rent	14,900	20,720	13,360
Repairs and maintenance	1,293	2,025	
Supplies	305	180	195
Taxes and licenses	11,473	5,790	1,062
Travel	730	1,125	
Meals and entertainment	108	220	192
Utilities	2,474	2,945	2,427
Wages	5,722	11,349	12,214
Other			
Freight	1,216	1,645	874
Sales tax			7,842
Total Expenses	**60,026**	**64,209**	**56,020**
Net profit or loss	**34,416**	**32,111**	**15,990**

* *Note:* The cash accounting method was used for 2005 and 2006. The accrual accounting method was used for 2007.

By examining the income statement, we will be able to better understand how management is handling the company's overall operations. Using financial ratio analysis, we will assess how well the company's resources are being managed. A good analysis will enable a potential buyer to assess, for example, whether the company is worth acquiring, based on its strengths and weaknesses, and to determine how much to pay for it.

When analyzing the numbers, it is important to (1) look at the numbers and compare them with historical performance or with a benchmark such as an industry average, to assess how the company is performing in that specific area, and (2) highlight any trends. The importance of trends as one looks at financial statements is that they are used to predict the future. One should always ask: Is there a trend in this line item? Is it an upward or downward trend? What is the main reason(s) for this trend? What does the trend mean for the future?

The following assumptions should be made in the analysis of the Clark Company case:

- This company is a cash business; there are no receivables.
- It is owner-operated.
- The numbers provided are correct.

An analysis of every line item could be made, but our analysis will focus on three of the most important items: revenue, gross profit, and net profit.

Revenue Analysis

The analysis of a company's historical annual revenue includes answers to the following questions: What are the sales growth rates for the past few years? What is the trend in sales growth? Is it declining or increasing? Why are revenues increasing or decreasing? Not only should you be concerned about whether or not revenues are increasing, but you should also ask whether the increase is consistent with what is taking place in the industry. Sales increasing for a short period may not be good enough. You need to compare a company's sales growth with the rate at which you want it to grow. The absolute minimum amount you want sales to grow, at an annual rate, is at the rate of inflation, which since 1774 has averaged approximately 4.1 percent per year.[13] Some industries have clearly outperformed this benchmark. For example, in the professional sports industry, since 2002, the average annual percentage increase in ticket prices for the four major sports leagues (i.e., the NBA, NFL,

NHL, and MLB) has been 14.5 percent.[14,15] The revenue at the largest 17 securities companies in 2006 rose a staggering 44 percent.[16] In 2006, Fortune 500 companies increased their revenues by 9 percent,[17] while inflation that year was 3 percent.

Revenue for the Clark Company has been declining. Revenues declined by 2 percent between 2005 and 2006 and by 16 percent between 2006 and 2007. This downward trend is a cause for concern. Some of the reasons for the decline in revenues may be:

- Price increases resulting from higher costs.
- The owner is despondent, and he is not managing his business properly, or he simply is not present at the company.
- Increased competition, as a result of the high gross margins, could be putting pressure on prices. One way to keep prices high is to have a patent on a product, which allows the owner to set the price fairly high. This assumes, of course, that there is a demand for the product or service. When the patent expires, the business will inevitably face competition.
- The product could be becoming obsolete.
- An unanticipated event or an act of God, known in the legal profession as a "force majeure," could be one reason for the decline in revenue. For example, there could have been a tornado or a severe rainstorm and the storage area where the entire inventory was kept could have been flooded, thereby damaging inventory and reducing the volume that was available for sale.
- There could have construction outside of the company's place of business that prevents easy access by customers.

So there are, in some instances, legitimate reasons why revenue could be decreasing that have nothing to do with the soundness of the business or its management. When undertaking financial analysis, it is important to consider all likely scenarios.

While strong revenue growth is typically viewed positively, it can also be a sign of bad tidings. The fundamentals of finance associate excellent revenue increases with at least corresponding increases in the company's net income. The best example of this point is Microsoft. From 1990, when Microsoft introduced its Windows 3.0 operating system, to 1999, its revenues grew 17 times, from $1.18 billion to $19.8 billion. During the same time period, its net income grew an astounding 28 times, from $279 million to $7.79 billion! On a larger scale, the Fortune 500 demonstrated this concept in historic fashion between 2000 and 2006. Aided by strong productivity gains and a growing economy, the largest American companies grew earnings an astonishing 80 percent while revenue growth grew 38 percent. During this period, posttax profit margins hit 7.9 percent, a 27 percent increase over the already impressive 6.2 percent margins in 2000.[18]

But if revenues are growing because prices have been lowered, then that means that the company is probably growing at the expense of margins. Therefore, the growth may not in fact be profitable. For example, during the period from 1991 to 1997, Hewlett-Packard's revenue from personal computers increased dramatically to approximately $9 billion in annual revenues. Also during this period, its market share increased from 1 to 4 percent. In 1998, with the support of price cuts, sales increased 13 percent. Despite all this good news, HP's personal computer business experienced a loss of in excess of $100 million.[19]

Another issue with regard to revenue growth that you should be aware of is that the growth may be occurring because competitors are conceding the market. Competitors may be leaving the market because the product will soon be obsolete; or perhaps they are leaving because the ever-increasing cost of doing business—things such as liability insurance—is driving them out of the market. Thus, it is just as important for the entrepreneur to know why he is experiencing excellent growth as it is to know the reasons for low or no growth. The successful entrepreneur knows that revenues should be grown strategically. It is well-managed growth that ultimately improves the profitability of the company.

Sometimes growing too fast can be just as damaging as no growth at all. A few problems common to rapid growth are poor quality, late deliveries, an overworked labor force, cash shortages, and brand dilution. Unmanaged growth is usually not profitable. For example, Michael Dell, the founder of Dell Computers, which grew 87 percent per year for the first eight years and 34 percent annually since 1992, said, "I've learned from experience that a company can grow too fast. You have to be careful about expanding too quickly because you won't have the experience or the infrastructure to succeed."[20] This comment was made after he experienced a $94 million charge against earnings in 1993 for, among other things, the failure of a line of poor-quality laptops.

The story of 180s, a sports apparel company, further demonstrates the dangers of growing too fast. At one point, the company was ranked number 32 on the prestigious *Inc.* 500 list of fastest-growing companies. The firm grew revenues from $1 million in 1999 to $50 million in 2004. However, by 2005, 180s was suffocating under too much debt and was taken over by a private equity firm. Lamenting its impending sale, Bernie Tenenbaum, a venture capitalist who had considered investing in 180s at one point, said, "I'd say they'd be lucky to get 10 cents on the dollar." Actually, he was optimistic—it turned out to be 8 cents on the dollar. Bill Besselman, a one-time partner with the co-owners of the firm, explains their failure: "In the end, they grew the top line, but they didn't manage the bottom line. They got sucked into the vortex."[21]

Even Starbucks, one of the greatest entrepreneurial stories of all time, has suffered unmanageable growth that has diluted its brand and caused it to fall behind Dunkin' Donuts in customer loyalty. Starbucks founder and chairman Howard Schultz explains how growing too fast caused this problem: "Over the past ten years, in order to achieve the growth, development, and scale necessary to go from less than 1,000 stores to 13,000 stores and beyond, we have had to make a series of decisions that, in retrospect, have led to the watering down of the Starbucks experience, and, what some might call the commoditization of our brand."[22] In 2008 Starbucks took steps to correct this problem by announcing the closing of 600 underperforming stores across the United States.

The Largest Customer

Inherent in the growth issue is a key question: how large is the company's largest customer? Ideally, an entrepreneur's largest customer should account for no more than 10 to 15 percent of the company's total revenues. The reasoning is that a company should be able to lose its largest customer and still remain in business. Of course, the ideal is often not the reality. One survey of 300 manufacturers in the apparel and home goods industries showed that over half of these firms receive more than 20 percent of their sales from their largest customer.[23] The goal should be to diversify your client base while maintaining the benefits of economies of scale. An example of a company that suffered as a result of not properly diversifying is Boston Communications Group, Inc. (BCGI). In 2004, Verizon Wireless, representing approximately 20 percent of BCGI sales, decided to end the relationship between the two companies.[24] BCGI's shares, which had traded as high as $22 in 2003, dropped 50 percent in one year. The company was unable to recover. In 2006, it laid off 21 percent of its workforce and fired two of its top officials. The company was finally purchased in 2007 by India-based Megasoft Ltd. for $3.60 per share, less than 20 percent of its 2003 value.[25]

Interestingly, many companies find that losing the customer that generates the largest amount of revenue actually results in more company profitability, because the largest customers are rarely the most profitable. The reason is that customers who purchase large volumes are often invoiced at lower prices. For example, Morse Industries, a private lamp manufacturer, was ecstatic to get Wal-Mart, the country's largest retailer, as a customer. The addition of Wal-Mart increased its revenue over 50 percent in one year. But after one year, the company decided to drop Wal-Mart as a customer. Why? The revenues of Morse Industries had grown enormously, but the gross, operating, and net margins had actually declined because the company charged Wal-Mart 25 percent less than it charged its other customers. Another reason for the decline was that Wal-Mart's orders were so large that Morse Industries' labor force could barely produce enough. The result was that orders placed by other consumers, who were not receiving a discount and therefore were generating higher margins, were being delayed or even canceled. Several of these long-term, excellent, paying customers quietly moved their business from Morse Industries to another supplier.

The founder of Morse solved the company's problem after he performed an analysis of his company's growth and found that it was not profitable. His analysis included using the matrix shown in Figure 5-7 to define each customer and the importance of that customer.

F I G U R E   5-7

Customer Analysis Matrix

High volume	High volume
Low margin	High margin
Low volume	Low volume
low margin	High margin

Source: Susan Greco, "Choose or Lose," *Inc.*, December 1998, p. 58.

He defined the categories as follows:

- *High volume/low margin.* Customers that provided revenues greater than $1 million per year, with gross margins of no more than 35 percent.

- *Low volume/low margin.* Customers that provided revenues of less than $1 million per year, with gross margins of no more than 35 percent.

- *Low volume/high margin.* Customers that provided revenues of less than $1 million per year, with gross margins in excess of 35 percent.

- *High volume/high margin.* Customers that provided revenues greater than $1 million per year, with gross margins in excess of 35 percent.

His immediate initial response was to simply drop only the customers in the low-volume/low-margin section. But on second thought, he decided to analyze the data even further to determine how profitable each customer was to the company by performing a contribution margin analysis on each customer

Equation 5-3 shows the contribution margin formula.

E Q U A T I O N   5-3

Contribution Margin

$$\text{Revenues} - \text{variable costs} = \text{contribution margin}$$
$$\rightarrow \text{Fixed costs and profits}$$

The contribution margin is the difference between revenues and all the variable costs (i.e., the costs that would not be incurred if this customer left) associated with a unit of product. Therefore, it is the profit available, after breakeven, to contribute to the company's fixed costs and profits.

The contribution margin analysis is presented in Table 5-8. Clearly, as you can see from the table, the least profitable business was not the low-margin/low-volume business but, in fact, the high-volume/low-margin business. Therefore, Morse attempted to raise its prices to customers who fell into these two categories. Several of them refused to accept the price increase, including Wal-Mart, so he dropped them. His growth strategy for returning the company to profitability included attempting to grow the volume of the remaining customers, who fell into the high-volume/high-margin and low-volume/high-margin categories, without decreasing prices. The second part of the strategy was the implementation of a policy that all new business had to have at least a 40 percent contribution margin. While his revenues in the immediate term went down, his net profits and cash flow increased dramatically. Ultimately, his revenues increased, as a result of his ability to maintain high quality standards and ship promptly. Most importantly, his profit dollars and percentages also increased.

T A B L E   5-8

Customer Analysis Calculation

	High Volume/ Low Margin/	Low Volume/ Low Margin	Low Volume/ High Margin	High Volume/ High Margin
Annual revenues	$12,000,000	$800,000	$900,000	$3,000,000
Variable costs	10,000,000	600,000	500,000	1,500,000
Contribution margin	$2,000,000	$200,000	$400,000	$1,500,000
Percentage	17%	25%	44%	50%

The lesson: Growth for the sake of growth, without regard to profitability, is both foolish and harmful and will inevitably lead to insolvency. This is what happened to the dot-com companies of the late 1990s. Many businesses engage in such growth in the name of gaining market share. But evidence repeatedly shows that the companies with the strongest market share, excluding perhaps Microsoft, are rarely the most profitable. Two recent examples illustrate the danger of focusing on sales. In 2006, Toyota sold approximately 9.02 million vehicles worldwide. During the same time period, GM sold 9.18 million vehicles. Despite this sales edge of 162,000 cars, Toyota earned $11.6 billion in profit, while GM lost $2 billion.[26] How did this happen? GM obviously wasn't focusing on profits. In the world of video games, the importance of profitability over market share is demonstrated in the battle among Nintendo, Sony, and Microsoft. Sony's Playstation and Microsoft's Xbox consoles have dominated the market for years. In early 2006, however, Nintendo had recorded close to a billion dollars in profit on its Wii console while Sony's game division was barely profitable and Microsoft lost money on Xbox.[27]

Additional support for the case for looking at the bottom line is evidence from a survey completed by J. Scott Armstrong and Kesten C. Green that showed that companies that adopt what they call "competitor-oriented objectives" actually end up hurting their own profitability. To restate their point, the more a firm tries to beat competitors, as opposed to maximize profits, the worse it will fare. A 2006 Harvard Business School study, "Manage for Profit, Not for Market Share," estimated that companies that let market share or sales volume guide their actions sacrifice 1 to 3 percent of their revenue. In hard numbers, a manager of a $5 billion business leaves between $50 and $150 million in his customers' and competitors' pockets every year by focusing on market share rather than the bottom line.

The drawbacks of high market share and lower profitability were further confirmed by a study of more than 3,000 public companies. The study's results showed that more than 70 percent of the time, firms with the greatest market share do not have the highest returns, as the examples in Figure 5-8 show. The study found that the key to success for smaller, more profitable competitors was their absolute vigilance in controlling costs and eliminating customers who returned low margins.

GROSS MARGINS

One of the initial financial ratios that business financiers examine when reviewing the income statement is the gross margin. What is a good gross margin? Well, a "good" gross margin, like all the other

F I G U R E   5-8

High Market Share versus High Returns

Category	High Market Share	Higher Returns
Discount stores	Wal-Mart	Family Dollar
Office furniture	Ricoh Company Ltd	Chyron Corp.
Pharmaceuticals	Johnson & Johnson	Alcon, Inc.

items we will be analyzing, is relative and depends on the industry in which a company operates. In general, gross margins of 35 percent and above are considered to be very good. Table 5-9 provides comparative gross margins for different companies.[28] See also Appendix A for common-sized income statement values for different industries.

T A B L E   5-9

Comparative Gross Margin Percentages

Company/Industry	Gross Margin, %
Amazon.com	22.6
Hewlett-Packard	47.1
Dell	16.6
Nike	43.8
Starbucks (2000)	56.0
Starbucks (2007)	23.3
Starbucks—espresso	90.0
Starbucks—coffee	70.0
Kroger	24.2
eBay	77.0
Yahoo!	59.3
Salesforce.com	76.1
Microsoft	79.1

Source: Company financial statements for FY'2007 as compiled by Reuters; USA Today, "Starbucks cultivates caffeine rush", April 30, 1996

Supermarkets generally have razor-thin gross margins, ranging between 10 and 15 percent. Computers, which have become almost a commodity product, have gross margins that are also very slim. That is why it is so difficult to compete in the computer hardware industry: because the average price at which a retailer sells a computer is only about 10 to 15 percent higher than what it costs to produce it. On the other hand, some computer manufacturers have been able to achieve gross margins that are higher than the industry average. One example was Compaq Computer, which was the number two computer manufacturer in the country before its merger with Hewlett-Packard in 2002. Compaq consistently had gross margins above 20 percent. The combined Hewlett-Packard had a corporate gross margin of 47.1 percent in 2007 largely due to its higher gross margin services and printer businesses. [28a]

There are several industries in which companies make very decent gross margins. For example, Nike's average gross margin is about 44 percent, whereas Starbucks, as indicated in Table 5-9, applies toward its gross profit 70 cents of every dollar it makes selling coffee. Or more profoundly, as Table 5-9 also shows, a cup of Starbucks espresso, with a 90 percent gross margin, costs only 10 percent of its selling price![29] Starbucks' overall corporate gross margin has fallen to roughly 23 percent in 2007, which is more than half of what its margins were just 7 years earlier. Much of this drop can be attributed to the increasing percentage of food and other lower margin products sold in its retail establishments Microsoft on the other hand still enjoys a gross margin of nearly 80 percent.

Gross margins are also very high in other businesses, some of them illegal. University of Chicago economist Steven Leavitt and Harvard sociologist Sudir Venkadisch undertook an analysis of the financial books of a drug gang—a very rare set of financial statements to analyze. Not surprisingly, they found that the gang was able to reap very high gross margins—approximately 80 percent—by selling crack cocaine.[30]

A venture capitalist once stated, "Gross margin is the entrepreneur's best friend. It can absorb all manner of adversity with two exceptions, philanthropy or pricing stupidity. Actually, in this case the two are synonymous."[31] Good gross margins provide a novice entrepreneur with breathing space, allowing him a chance to make costly mistakes and still be potentially profitable. On the other hand, in a low-gross-margin business—such as grocery stores, for example—management mistakes and waste, as well as theft and pilferage, must be minimized, because the margins are too thin to be able to absorb these costs. A low-gross-margin business must also have volume, whereas a high-gross-margin business may sacrifice unit volume sales because its ultimate profit comes from the high margins. The ideal business, like Microsoft, dominates its industry relative to units of volume, while at the same time maintaining high gross margins. This is a rarity. High-gross-margin industries inevitably attract competitors who compete on price, thereby reducing gross margins throughout the industry.

For example, independent retailers of books used to enjoy gross margins in excess of 35 percent. Those attractive gross margins were the primary reason that major chains such as Barnes & Noble and Amazon.com entered the market and now dominate it. Twenty years ago, independent retailers sold 60 percent of all book titles. Since 1991, the independents' share of the book market has declined from 32 percent to 10 percent. The big competitors increased because of the attractiveness of the gross margins.[32]

I always tell my Kellogg students, "If you leave here, start your own business, and are lucky enough to have good gross margins, for God's sake, don't brag about it." If someone asks you, "How's business?" your standard reply should be a simple shrug of the shoulders and a polite response of, "Not bad; could always be better." It is always tough to maintain high gross margins. One way companies are able to do so is to have a patent or copyright on the product, essentially giving them a legal monopoly for a period of time. That was the case with the product Nutrasweet, an artificial sugar sweetener whose patent expired in 1999.

Ironically, not every entrepreneur is interested in high-gross-margin businesses. One of the primary reasons, as stated earlier, is because heavy competition is inevitable. Therefore, those who are interested in low-margin businesses are those who view excellent operational execution as their competitive advantage or as a barrier to entry of competitors. For example, as noted earlier, the computer manufacturing industry is notorious for low gross margins. Despite this fact, Dell Computers is able to prosper as the number two manufacturer in the world because of its outstanding operations—it carries four days of inventory compared with ten days at Hewlett-Packard. This means that Dell can turn its inventory more than 83 times a year compared with the industry's average of 4.9. The attitude of an entrepreneur who knows his competitive advantage is best illustrated by Michael Dell, who stated that he was not happy with his company's inventory of four days—his ultimate goal is to measure Dell's inventory not in days, but in hours.[33]

Gross margins are a factor that the entrepreneur should focus on very heavily in the business plan as well as in operations. Good, healthy gross margins do not usually happen by chance. They may happen by chance for the "mom-and-pop" entrepreneur who runs a business haphazardly. Because the strategy is to sell whatever can be sold at whatever cost, the mom-and-pop enterprise expects to absorb the costs and take whatever falls to the bottom line.

A high-growth entrepreneur, in contrast, is one who manages with a plan in mind. This entrepreneur expects to grow the company at a certain rate and plans to have a certain level of gross margins. A high-growth entrepreneur is one who wants to have a company for the purpose of wealth creation and therefore is an absolute bulldog when it comes to managing gross margins. The question that logically follows is, how can gross margins be increased?

Cut Labor and/or Material Costs

The following are ways to reduce labor costs:

- Train the workforce so that productivity increases.
- Reduce the labor force and have fewer employees work more efficiently. GE, one of the most profitable companies in the world, did just this. Over an eight-year period, GE cut 208,000 jobs worldwide. In one division, it cut 1,800 jobs, and profits rose 21 percent.[34]
- Reduce employee absenteeism, which results in increased labor costs because of the need for overtime pay. Industry studies have shown that employee absenteeism is at its highest point since 1999 and can cost companies as much as 15 percent of their payroll.
- Make the workforce more productive by using technology. For example, technology has been used in McDonald's franchises to reduce labor costs. The production process has been automated to the point where one person can now do what it used to take four people to do in terms of cooking and food preparation.
- Increase volume. The cost per item produced or cost per service rendered should go down as the volume goes up.

Labor costs should go down as employees gain more experience. People learn more and therefore should become more efficient, even if this is not done through the introduction of new technology.

- Find a cheaper labor force. Companies can move their operations, for instance, to a different region of the country or abroad, where labor is cheaper. For example, Nike manufactures all its products outside the United States in low-labor-cost countries such as China and Thailand, where unskilled labor can cost as little as $0.67 per hour, or 3 percent of the average hourly compensation cost for production workers in the United States for the same year. Even skilled labor can be significantly cheaper outside the United States. Draft Dynamix, the leading fantasy sports draft software company, used software programmers in India to build its first product. The programmers cost approximately $20 per hour for work that costs as much as $60 per hour in the United States. Over the course of a year, outsourcing the work to India saved Draft Dynamix in excess of $90,000. The CEO of Draft Dynamix, Ted Kasten, provides perspective on overseas labor: "I would caution that it isn't a one-for-one savings. Working with overseas software consultants and programmers requires more time per task than a U.S. based programmer due to time differences and distance." "Still," he explains, "we wouldn't have made it without these programmers. The cash we saved from these labor costs enabled us to survive long enough to start generating revenue." Draft Dynamix recently licensed its product to CBS Sportline and ESPN.com, two of the leading fantasy sports Web sites on the Internet, and secured another round of angel financing. One cautionary note here: using labor outside the country sometimes has its own risks. After the September 11, 2001, terrorist attack in New York, Illinois-based Product Development Technologies Inc. (PDT) scratched plans to source a client's manufacturing job in Brazil. The company was worried about the reliability of air shipments from abroad. Making the parts at home squeezed profits on the $60,000 order because labor costs were 30 percent higher.

But as PDT's owner said, "We can't afford to be even a week late."[35]

- Provide employees with stock options, restricted stock units, or other incentive programs in lieu of higher salaries.
- Reduce employee benefit costs. Employer health insurance premiums have risen 81 percent since 2000. In fact, a survey of small businesses conducted by the National Federation of Independent Business and Wells Fargo showed that the cost of health insurance was the number one concern of small-business owners. The world of health insurance is ever changing, but options such as health savings accounts and health reimbursement arrangements offer mechanisms enabling employers to control costs.[36]
- Continually turn over the workforce, reducing the number of higher-paid unskilled workers. For example, fast-food restaurants expect and want a certain amount of annual turnover in their unskilled employees because newer workers cost less.
- Implement good management skills. One of the easiest ways to reduce labor costs is simply for entrepreneurs to manage their employees. They need to manage, referring to the good old way of managing people, which means stating expectations, giving employees the necessary tools, and holding them accountable for their performance.

The following are ways to reduce material costs:

- Obtain competitive bids from suppliers, which may allow for the purchase of materials at lower cost.
- Buy in higher volumes to get volume discounts. The problem here is the inventory carrying cost. Ideally, one does not want to increase inventory. Therefore, the entrepreneur should make commitments to its suppliers to buy a certain volume within a period of time. Such a commitment should result in price-volume discounts. The commitment versus buy strategy allows entrepreneurs to keep inventories low, costs down, and cash available for other investments or uses.

- Outsource part of the production. Someone else may be able to produce a piece of a product or render a specific part of a service at a lower cost.

- Use a substitute material that can be purchased at a lower cost in the production process. Ideally you want to keep the quality of the product the same, but there is a possibility that you can actually get a substitute material that may be less expensive.

- Manage waste, pilferage, and obsolescence. Materials that have been stolen, thrown away, or destroyed, or are just sitting around because of obsolescence, negatively affect material costs.

- Do quality control checks throughout the various stages of the manufacturing process before additional value is added. This is in contrast to the traditional way of checking quality only at the end of the process. Waste and rework costs are always greater using the process of checking quality at the end.

- Let the most experienced and trained person perform the most detail-oriented or labor-intensive work, for example, cutting all patterns, because they should be able to get more cuts per square yard than an inexperienced person. For example:

	Worker 1	Worker 2
Material cost per yard	$10	$10
Units cut per yard	4	2
Cost per unit	$2.50	$5

Thus, the cost per unit for Worker 1 is lower because there is less material wasted.

Raise the Price

Raising the price of the product or service will enable the entrepreneur to increase gross margins, assuming, of course, that costs do not increase proportionately. While much is made in the press of the various factors that can produce pricing power for a company, the best way to increase profitability through price increases is by differentiating and creating value for which the consumer will pay. Linear Technology, a $1.1 billion semiconductor company, is a prime example of creating pricing power through differentiation. In contrast to industry heavyweights like Intel, which focus on bigger clients with huge demand for commodity-like chips, Linear has chosen to operate on the periphery and sell to smaller clients with needs that Linear can service better than the competition. The result? Linear's chips are priced a third more than its rivals', and the company made a 39 percent net profit margin in 2006, besting the tech industry's best-known profit powerhouses, Microsoft Corp. and Google Inc., which earned 26 percent and 24 percent, respectively.[37]

Amazingly, there are companies that, for a short time, were successful in challenging the importance of business fundamentals with regard to gross margins. For the most part, this was true in the e-commerce industry, where most companies were primarily focused on growing revenues even when it was at the expense of gross margins. For example, buy.com formerly sold merchandise, including CDs, books, videos, software, and computer equipment, at cost and, shockingly, sometimes even below cost. The company guaranteed the lowest prices available on the Internet. The result was zero and sometimes negative gross margins! Despite these facts, buy.com, which was founded in 1996, had 1998 revenues of $111 million and a public market valuation in excess of $400 million.[38]

But reality set in, and by September 2001 the vultures were circling with stockholder class-action lawsuits. In just over a year, buy.com's stock price had dropped from its opening-day price of just over $30 a share to about $0.08 per share. Its stock was delisted from the Nasdaq on August 14, 2001. I hope your kid's college fund was not tied up in that one. All kidding aside, these kinds of infamous cases—where managers "fumble the fundamentals"—play out every day in far more subtle ways in every business sector. When entrepreneurs ignore the fundamentals of finance or simply trust someone else to stand guard, they invite trouble to the table.

Before we close this section on gross margin, let us analyze the Clark Company. What are the gross margins for the Clark Company? They are as follows:

- 2005: 70 percent
- 2006: 72 percent
- 2007: 64 percent

The company has excellent gross margins—in excess of 60 percent for all three years. However, one sees an 8 percentage point decline in gross margins in 2007, indicating that something has changed.

What are some of the possible reasons for a decline in gross margins?

- There may have been a change in the product mix being sold. A higher percentage of lower-margin items may have been sold.
- The cost of supplies may have gone up.
- The company may have changed its accounting system from a cash system to accrual. This change in accounting system results in no change in the timing of cash receipts; since this is a cash business and therefore the company does not have receivables, the change in the system will not affect the timing of when revenues are recognized. However, the accounting system change forces the company to recognize costs earlier. The result of this change is potentially lower gross margins because costs are being recognized earlier, and therefore lower net profit as well.
- The company may be buying from different suppliers at higher costs and/or selling to different customers.

An examination of the income statement shows that 2006 was the first year in which products were returned. Also, and more importantly, as the note at the bottom of the statement shows, there was a change in the accounting method, from cash to accrual. And as we just stated, the change does not affect revenues because this is a cash business, but it does have a negative effect on all three margins because more expenses are being recognized. Therefore, as a result of the change, we are not comparing "apples to apples" with the prior year.

NET MARGINS

What are acceptable net margins? We've determined that the Clark Company has outstanding gross margins. But how do its net margins compare? In general, net margins of 5 percent or better are considered very good. According to Hussman Funds, since 1955, the average profit margins of the 500 largest U.S. companies have ranged between 5.5 percent and 7.5 percent. In fact, 2006 was a banner year for large U.S. corporations, as the Fortune 500 largest U.S. companies generated a posttax profit margin of 7.9 percent, equivalent to $785 billion. This was a 29 percent increase over 2005 and obliterated the previous cyclical peak of $444 billion. The top three companies in terms of net income, throughout the world, were U.S.-based. The net margins of these companies are shown in Table 5-10.

T A B L E   5-10

Net Margin Top Ten

Company	Net Margin, %
Ambac Financial Group	45.3
Prologis	42.7
Public Storage	41.2
MGIC Investment	41.1
Linear Technology	40.3
Gilead Sciences	40.1
QUALCOMM	37.4
Yahoo!	36.1
Burlington Resources	35.7
Apache	35.2

Source: *BusinessWeek*, April 2006.

Privately owned companies want to minimize taxes, and therefore they reduce operating income, which in turn reduces their net income. The point being made is that the net income is usually a manipulated number that understates the company's true financial performance. A few exceptions might be companies that are preparing to go public or be sold. These companies may want to look as financially strong as possible.

In contrast, a publicly owned company aggressively seeks positive net margins, as high as possible, because the net margin affects the stock price. As one money manager remarked, "There is a greater tendency among companies to pull out the stops to generate the kind of positive earnings that Wall Street demands."[39] For example, a few years ago, America Online decided not to recognize some huge marketing expenses in its quest for positive annual earnings. The Securities and Exchange Commission unearthed this fact and forced AOL to take a charge of more than $385 million in 1996, wiping out all the profit the company had made up to that point.

The greatest example of this kind of chicanery was the case of Enron, the one-time darling of Wall Street. Through off-balance-sheet transactions, Enron masked hundreds of millions of dollars of losses in its effort to continually beat analysts' estimates. The house of cards eventually crumbled, and one year after ranking number seven on the Fortune 500, Enron filed for bankruptcy. The carnage was severe, with more than 5,600 employees losing their jobs and in many cases their life savings. Over 20,000 creditors were left holding $63 billion in debt, and tens of billions in shareholder value was lost.[40,41]

Government regulation has targeted this kind of fraudulent behavior, and it has had an impact. A 2002 survey indicated that 59 percent of CFOs disclosed more information in financial statements than they had previously done, and 57 percent said that they planned to disclose more information in the next 12 months.[42] Moreover, the Sarbanes-Oxley reform act has targeted this kind of abuse and changed the way in which corporate boardrooms and audit firms operate. However, this problem will never completely go away. Therefore, when analyzing the financial statements of a privately or publicly owned company, beware. Things—especially net income—may be significantly different from what the statements show.

The problem with looking at just net income for a public or private company is that income does not pay the bills. Cash flow pays the bills. Net income is typically an understatement of the company's cash flow because it includes noncash expenses such as depreciation and amortization. In addition, expenditures that have nothing to do with the operation of the company may also be included, thereby lowering the company's net income. It is common for owners of private companies to run certain personal expenditures through their income statement because they view it as one of the perks of ownership. Therefore, one must realize that net income can be, and usually is, a manipulated number. For example, the late Leona Helmsley, owner of several upscale hotels in New York while she was alive, made improvements to her personal home and charged them against her company, thereby reducing the taxes owed. She was convicted of tax evasion as a result and served time in prison. One of the smoking guns used to convict her was an employee who quoted her as saying, "Only poor people pay taxes."

The reality that net income can be a manipulated number is best illustrated by a controversy regarding the 1995 movie *Forrest Gump*. The movie has grossed over $600 million worldwide, making it one of the highest-grossing movies in history. A fellow who agreed to take a percentage of the movie's net income as his compensation wrote the story. Believe it or not, this movie never reported a positive net income, and thus the writer was due nothing. The issue was in dispute for a number of years and was recently resolved, finally opening the door for the long-awaited sequel to the original blockbuster. What's the entrepreneurial moral of the story? As an investor, never agree to take a percentage of the net income because you cannot control the expenses, be they real or make-believe.

Conversely, if you are the entrepreneur, always try to compensate investors based on net income, never on revenues. Basing compensation on revenues has gotten many entrepreneurs in financial trouble, because giving someone a percentage of revenues ("off the top") ignores whether a company has a positive cash flow.

The final problem that must be highlighted, with regard to putting too much importance on net earnings, is that the net earnings figure does not tell you where the earnings came from. Did they come from strong company operations or from financial instruments? A fundamentally sound company derives most of its earnings from operations, specifically from product sales or services rendered, not from interest earned on invested capital. The primary reliance upon interest earned would force the company to be in the money management business. Yahoo!, which had always been touted as one of the few profitable Internet companies, found itself being justifiably criticized in 1997 and 1998. The criticism came from the observation that "in 1997 and 1998, Yahoo's interest income accounted for nearly 40% of its net income. By comparison, Cisco's 1998 interest income was only 12.5% of its earnings and Microsoft's 15.5%."[43] As noted in Chapter 2, Yahoo! began an ugly downward spiral in 2001 and is struggling to recover.

Before we close this section, let us analyze the net income of the Clark Company. The net margins for the Clark Company are 25, 24, and 14 percent for 2005, 2006, and 2007, respectively. This would indicate that the company's net margins are outstanding. The trend, however, is downward, with the caveat that the final year was negatively affected by the change in accounting method previously discussed.

OTHER ISSUES TO CONSIDER

Is the Owner Managing the Business Full Time?

When evaluating the income statement of the Clark Company, one can find evidence that the owner may not be at the place of business on a full-time basis. First, there is an increase in wages, which may represent the hiring of a new employee to run the business, as the owner is taking more time off. An examination of a company's financial statements requires a thorough analysis of the wages section. It is important to ask: Who are the employees? Do these employees actually exist? In some cities like Chicago, dead men have been known to vote in elections, and they also appear on city payrolls. During the due diligence, if the name of an employee is provided, you should look to see if the last name of the employee matches the last name of the owner. It would also be wise to follow up with the question, "How many employees are relatives, and what are their specific tasks and responsibilities?" Wages may have increased because a relative of the owner has been added to the payroll and is being paid an exorbitant wage for doing nothing or for doing something as simple as opening and locking up the company every day.

Figure 5-9 presents financial projections for 2008 for the Clark Company, based on historical information.

F I G U R E 5-9

Clark Company Pro Forma Income Statement for 2008

	Best Case	Worst Case	Most Likely Case
Income			
Gross sales	111,187	95,303	103,245
Returns and allowances			
Cost of goods sold	31,132	35,262	33,555
Gross profits	80,055	60,041	69,690
Expenses			
Advertising	3,336	2,859	3,097
Bad debts	111	95	103
Automobile expense	1,112	953	1,032
Depreciation	835	835	835
Employee benefits programs			
Insurance	2,224	1,906	2,065
Interest			
Mortgage			
Other			
Professional services			
Office expense	9,200	9,200	9,200
Other business property	13,400	13,400	13,400
Repairs and maintenance			
Supplies	226	226	226
Taxes and licenses	1,112	953	1,032
Travel			
Meals and entertainment	173	173	173
Utilities	2,600	2,600	2,600
Wages	12,200	12,200	12,200
Other			
Freight	1,245	1,245	1,245
Sales tax	7,783	6,671	7,227
Total expenses	55,556	53,317	54,437
Net profit or loss	**24,499**	**6,724**	**15,253**

How can you be sure the numbers are correct? In all likelihood, they will not be. It is rare that the actual numbers meet the projections. Pro forma development is simply educated guessing.

Revenues

Historically, if we look at the Clark Company pro forma income statement shown in Figure 5-9, the best case is a decrease in revenue of 2 percent; the worst case is a decrease of 16 percent. And the most-likely-case scenario is taken as an average of these two extremes—a decrease of 9 percent. This is a reasonable, logical argument for preparing the projections for sales revenue.

Gross Margins

With regard to gross margins, there were no clear trends during the three years of data that were provided. Gross margins increased between 2005 and 2006 and then declined between 2006 and 2007. The best-case gross margin would be 72 percent, the worst-case gross margin would be 64 percent, and the most-likely-case scenario would be an average of the two—68 percent. Again, there is very logical reasoning behind the development of these projections, which is what financiers hope to find.

N O T E S

1. Jamie Pratt, *Financial Accounting*, 2nd ed. (Cincinnati, Ohio: South-Western Publishing Co., 1994), p. 709.
2. *Chicago Tribune*, July 25, 2000, p. 12.
3. Ibid.
4. Ibid.
5. Ibid.
6. *Crain's Chicago Business*, October 1, 2001.
7. Reuters.com office equipment industry company rankings, accessed in July 2007.
8. Reuters.com pharmaceutical industry company rankings, accessed in July 2007.
9. Amazon.com financials, as compiled by Reuters.com, July 2007.
10. Dell, 2006 Annual Report.
11. "The Wal-Mart of High Tech?" *Fast Company*, November 2004.
12. "What's Wrong with This Picture? Nothing!" *Inc.*, June 2007.

13. Lawrence H. Officer and Samuel H. Williamson, "Annual Inflation Rates in the United States, 1774–2006, and United Kingdom, 1265–2006," MeasuringWorth.com, 2007.

14. Team Marketing Report, www.teammarketing.com, 2007.

15. "NFL Ticket Prices Rise for Third Straight Year," *USA Today,* September 6, 2006.

16. 2007 *Fortune* ranking of fastest-growing industries in the Fortune 500.

17. Ibid.

18. "A Profit Gusher of Epic Proportions," *Fortune,* April 15, 2007.

19. Eric Nee, "Defending the Desktop," *Forbes,* December 28, 1998, pp. 53–54.

20. Richard Murphy, "Michael Dell," *Success.*

21. John Anderson, "The Company That Grew Too Fast," Inc.com from *Inc.* magazine, November 2005.

22. Howard Schultz, e-mail to senior Starbucks management, February 14, 2007.

23. CIT Commercial Services and *Home Furnishing News*, 2002 Customer Concentration Survey.

24. *Boston Business Journal,* June 18, 2004.

25. *Boston Herald,* June 12, 2007.

26. "Toyota Tops GM in World Auto Sales," MSNBC.com, April 24, 2007.

27. "In Praise of Third Place," *The New Yorker,* December 4, 2006.

28. *BusinessWeek,* September 7, 1998.

28a. 2007 corporate financial statements as compiled by Reuters

29. Bruce Horovitz, "Big Markups Drive Starbucks' Growth," *USA Today*, April 30, 1998, p. 1B.

30. Scott Woolley, "Greedy Bosses," *Forbes,* August 24, 1998, p. 53.

31. Mid-Atlantic Venture Partners, 1997.

32. Shawn Rea, "Buy the Book," *Black Enterprise,* February 1999, p. 176.

33. Dell financial data as compiled by Hoovers, July 2007.

34. Robert Sherrill, "Corporate Cannibalism at GE," *Chicago Sun-Times,* November 22, 1998, p. 20E.

35. James B. Arndorfer, "Attacks Show Risks of Exporting Jobs," *Crain's Chicago Business,* October 1, 2001.

36. Bruce Phillips, "Small Business Problems and Priorities," National Federation of Independent Business, June 2004.

37. "Pricing Power: In a Tech Backwater, a Profit Fortress Rises," *Wall Street Journal,* July 10, 2007.

38. Alex Gove, "Margin of Error," *Red Herring,* February 1999, p. 140.
39. Thor Valdmanis, "Cooking the Books, a Common Trick of the Trade," *USA Today,* August 11, 1998.
40. "The Fall of Enron," NPR.com.
41. "From Collapse to Convictions: A Timeline," CBS News Online, October 23, 2006.
42. "The Fear of All Sums," *CFO Magazine,* August 1, 2002.
43. *Forbes ASAP,* February 22, 1999, p. 24.

CHAPTER 6

Cash Flow Management

INTRODUCTION

Nothing is as important to a business as positive cash flow. As I often tell my students, "For any business, depending on the entrepreneur's gender, positive cash flow is King or Queen!" Without cash, an entrepreneur will not be able to buy inventory or equipment, make payroll, pay bills and utilities, or repay debt. Cash is necessary not only to keep a business going, but also to grow the business. Seth Godin is the founder of Yoyodyne, an online direct-marketing company that he later sold to Yahoo! for $30 million. As an entrepreneur who bootstrapped his business for the first few years, he notes that happiness for a business owner boils down to one simple thing: positive cash flow.[1] Companies that cannot achieve positive cash flow are essentially nonvoluntary not-for-profit organizations that eventually become insolvent. That is the reason why so many dot-com companies became dot-bombs.

TYPES OF CASH FLOW

A business's cash flow is commonly referred to as EBITDA, which is an acronym for earnings before interest, taxes, depreciation, and amortization. EBITDA is the cash available to service debt (i.e., make principal and interest payments), pay taxes, buy capital equipment, and return profits to shareholders after paying all of a company's operating expenses. A company's EBITDA is calculated as shown in Equation 6-1.

EQUATION 6-1

EBITDA

	Net Earnings
plus	Interest
plus	Taxes
plus	Depreciation
plus	Amortization
equals	**EBIDTA**

It should be noted that a company's true cash position includes the adding back of depreciation and amortization. While these two items can be expensed on an income statement, they are noncash expenditures, as was explained in Chapter 4. Their presence on an income statement helps the company's cash flow by reducing its taxable profits. This practice of adding back depreciation and amortization is the reason why a company with negative net earnings on its income statement can still have a positive cash flow.

While EBITDA and free cash flow, or FCF, are important for the entrepreneur to understand, she must also understand that these are simply cash flow descriptions used for cash flow statement purposes. They describe what the cash flow of the company should ideally be. Unfortunately for entrepreneurs, the ideal and actual are often miles apart. It is common to hear entrepreneurs say, "On paper my cash flow numbers show the company to be rich and making plenty of money, but in reality we are cash-poor and starving." The reason this comment is so often made is that money owed to the company has not been paid. For example, the company could have had an extraordinary month of growth in revenues such that all of the actual cash had to be used to finance that growth by paying overtime to employees and paying for the raw materials used to make the product. About 90 percent of the month's products were shipped on the last day of the month, and the terms are net 30. Such a scenario describes a situation in which, on the income statement for that month, the cash flow looks strong, but the reality is that the cash will not actually arrive until at least 30 days later. This "paper-rich, cash-poor" situation resulted from taking advantage of the opportunity to increase profitable revenues.

Paper-rich, cash-poor as it relates to poor cash flow management occurs when the money from the customer is past due. To succeed, the entrepreneur must be an absolutely vigilant bulldog about maximizing the actual day-to-day cash flow of the business.

Ensuring that a company has adequate cash on hand to fund its operations and pay off its obligations is essential. It is important to put a system in place that enables the entrepreneur to properly monitor and manage both expected cash receipts (i.e., cash inflows) and payables (i.e., cash outflows). The lack of an efficient cash flow management system can have severe negative consequences for a company's bottom line. For example, for service companies, whose expenses are heavily front-loaded into labor costs, profits diminish with every additional unnecessary week that it takes to get costs reimbursed. For manufacturers, this problem is even more severe, since they often have to spend large amounts of money up front on materials, production, and inventory, and they have long lag times between cash outflows and the receipt of money from customers. How does the delay in cash receipts diminish profits?

The importance of managing a company's cash needs accurately is highlighted by the following example. The Gartner Group is a high-tech consulting firm that generated $1.06 billion in revenues in 2006. When founder Michael Fernandez and his cofounders were raising capital for the company, they decided to limit the capital they raised to $30 million, even though they could have raised twice as much. They placed this limit because they wanted to restrict the amount of equity they would have to give up. However, they did not anticipate the problems they would face as they tried to develop a new product for their company, nor did they adequately assess their cash needs during this crucial period.

One problem that arose was that the manufacturer of the disk drives for the company's laptops went out of business. Given that there was only one company equipped to manufacture these drives, Gartner experienced production delays until a second manufacturer could be found. Once this manufacturer was identified, Gartner had to spend several months redesigning the disk drive so that the new manufacturer could produce it. In the meantime, the company ran out of money and was forced to file for Chapter 11. The lesson that Fernandez learned, the hard way, is that it is essential to focus on cash flow. As he notes, "We were obsessed with revenues and profits and trying to hold on to the equity," rather than on cash flow.[2] Today he insists that his executives and employees look at cash flow every single day. However, this is an area that few entrepreneurs focus on, particularly when they are starting their companies.

There are endless examples of entrepreneurs who neglect to pursue prudent cash flow management, particularly when their company is doing well. As Godin noted in 1998, "We think about this [cash flow] every day. But there are a lot of people who forget, when times are as good as they have been over the past few years, that the business world is cyclical and that you need money to make money."[3] The stronger the economy is and the faster a company is growing, the easier it can be to overlook cash flow controls, sometimes without suffering immediate negative consequences. But eventually, when there is a downturn in the economy, the entrepreneur may face a cash crunch. As a CPA once told me, "The best thing about volatile economic conditions is that they remind managers to refocus their attention on the basics." In fact, during a cash flow crisis, fast growth usually exacerbates the problems because companies spend cash on supplies and payroll—often at an accelerated rate because of fast growth—while waiting long periods to collect receivables.

A case in point is Douglas Roberson, president of Atlantic Network Systems, a data and voice systems integrator, whose company's revenues quadrupled from $100,000 in its first year to $460,000 in the next. During this growth period, the members of his staff did not concern themselves with cash flow because sales were growing at such a phenomenal rate. "I actually believed that the more money companies owed us, the better shape we were in," Roberson confessed.[4] It was not until his company went through an extended period in which it was unable to collect its receivables that he realized the importance of managing cash. His company had to use all its existing lines of credit to keep its operations going while waiting for bills to be paid. It was a real-life lesson. He, like most entrepreneurs, learned that managing cash flow was different from just accumulating sales. As he noted, "If you don't do serious projections about how much cash you'll need to handle sales—and how long it will take to collect on invoices—you can wind up out of business, no matter how fast you're growing."[5]

CASH FLOW FORECASTS

Preparing a cash flow forecast allows an entrepreneur to determine a business's financing needs. If an entrepreneur finds that the business has a forecasted cash shortage as a result of rapid growth, then it might be necessary to raise external money to meet the company's financial needs. A good cash flow forecast will allow the entrepreneur to determine the exact amount of cash needed and also when it is needed. In general, there are several reasons why businesses raise outside capital. First, seasonal needs, such as holiday sales, may require the purchase of additional materials and the payment of additional production expenses to meet this temporary increase in demand. Second, more capital may be needed to finance long-term sales growth. As a company's sales grow, more inventory must be purchased and additional workers will be needed. All these activities will require additional cash, which may not be on hand. A good cash flow forecast will allow an entrepreneur to forecast financing needs for these activities. Third, an entrepreneur may have to purchase expensive capital equipment or make expensive repairs to existing equipment.

Entrepreneurs must know that projected cash flow determines the amount of capital a company needs in the future. The following steps should be taken to make that determination:

- Prepare a 3- to 5-year (i.e., monthly annual projection) cash flow projection.
- To make the projection, use FCF *plus* debt obligations (i.e., interest and principal payments), which is called net cash flow.
- Choose the largest cumulative negative cash flow number—this is the capital needed.

To better illustrate these steps let's look at the 5-year net cash flow numbers for the Johnson Company, shown in Table 6-1.

With the information in Table 6-1, the Johnson Company can easily determine its capital needs by completing the chart in Table 6-2.

T A B L E   6-1

Projected Net Cash Flow Calculation

Year	Projected Net Cash Flow
1	−100
2	−90
3	−70
4	85
5	100

T A B L E   6-2

Cumulative Net Cash Flow Calculation

	Year 1	Year 2	Year 3	Year 4	Year 5
Projected NCF	−100	−90	−70	85	100
Cumulative projected NCF	−100	−190	−260	−175	−75

By plugging in the numbers from the cash flow projection, the Johnson Company would determine that $260 is needed because that is the largest cumulative number over the projected time frame.

The obvious question now is, when should you get the cash? There are two schools of thought in response to this question. The first is that you should get only what you need from year to year, or a "series of funding." The second is that you should get the maximum that you will need at once. Both have advantages and disadvantages, as shown here.

Obtain Series of Funding

Pros

- It keeps the entrepreneur disciplined and minimizes wasting money.
- The entrepreneur is paying only for current expenses.
- The new series of capital comes in at a higher valuation, thereby allowing less equity to be surrendered.

Cons

- There is no certainly that more capital will be available in the future.
- Resources must be allocated to securing additional funding.

Obtain All Funding at One Time

Pros

- There is no need to allocate resources to raise future funding.
- It avoids the risk of capital not being available in the future.

Cons

- Forecasts may be wrong as a result of incoming cash flows occurring earlier than Year 4, requiring less up-front capital. Additionally, in the case of an equity capital investment, too much equity is surrendered, or in the case of a debt capital investment, interest on unnecessary capital will be paid.
- Receiving too much capital at one time spoils the inexperienced entrepreneur and could lead to unnecessary waste of the capital.
- Invested capital comes in at a lower valuation.

CASH FLOW MANAGEMENT

Cash flow management can be as simple as preserving future cash by not spending as much today. For example, in order to deal with seasonal sales, a company may choose not to spend as much in October if December—when October's bills come due—is traditionally a poor sales month and won't generate enough receipts to cover those bills.[6] Cash flow management can also involve making somewhat complicated decisions about delaying payments to a supplier in order to use cash resources to temporarily increase production. Or it can involve making decisions about borrowing or using factoring companies to generate cash quickly to meet short-term cash shortages.

The relationship between the sources and uses of cash are shown in Equation 6-2.

EQUATION   6-2

Sources and Uses of Cash

Sources of cash − uses of cash = net cash flow
→ Fund operations and return to investors

Sources of Cash or Cash Inflows

- Accounts receivable
- Cash payments
- Other income (i.e., income from investments)
- Borrowing

Uses of Cash or Cash Outflows

- Payroll
- Utilities—heat, electricity, telephone, and so on
- Loan payments—interest plus principal
- Rent
- Insurance—health, property, and so on
- Taxes

Key Cash Flow Goals

The goal of good cash management is obvious: to have enough cash on hand when you need it. The major goal of prudent cash flow management is to ensure there is enough cash on hand to meet the demands for cash at any given time. This is done by getting cash not only from operations (i.e., managing cash inflows, including accounts receivable) and disciplined spending (i.e., managing accounts payable), but also through the use of external capital (i.e., borrowing). While this may appear to be a simple concept, in reality it is a process that even the most experienced financial officers and executives find difficult to carry out successfully.

The trick to handling cash flow is in the timing—as an entrepreneur, you want your customers to pay as soon as possible (if possible in advance), while you pay your suppliers and vendors as late as possible without jeopardizing your relationship with them or your credit standing. The idea is that money that is collected in receivables today, and that does not have to go out as payables, is, in fact, an important source of internally generated working capital.

While it may not be the most fun thing to do, it is important for an entrepreneur to spend time (at least an hour a day) working on cash flow. It is without a doubt one of the most crucial things an entrepreneur can do for a business. This exercise forces an entrepreneur to think about what he is doing in terms of cold, hard cash.

Cash Flow Ledgers and Projections

The cash flow ledger provides important information about the balance of the cash account, enabling the entrepreneur to assess the company's ability to fund its operations and also meet debt payments as they come due. It indicates, on a transaction basis, all cash received and disbursed during a month's period. Successful entrepreneurs are those who know their company's actual cash position on any given day. Therefore, it is recommended that the entrepreneur, especially the inexperienced and those in the early stages of their ventures, review their cash flow ledger at least weekly.

In addition to the ledger, a weekly cash flow projection summary, as discussed in Chapter 4, should be prepared when opening a business and every month thereafter. This projection indicates the anticipated cash inflow during the month along with the cash payments to be made. By doing this kind of projection each month, the entrepreneur can schedule payments to suppliers to match expected cash receipts. This planner allows the entrepreneur to be proactive with regard to the money owed to suppliers and enables the entrepreneur to let specific vendors know in advance that a payment will probably be late. The cash flow ledger and planner are simple and very useful tools that should be used to manage cash flow successfully. It is important to be consistent and work through each line item so that forecasts can be as accurate as possible.

To prepare cash flow forecasts, the entrepreneur should first look at historical cash flow, if this information is available. Construct monthly historical cash flows for at least the past year or, if possible, the past few years. It will be easier to forecast many items, such as utility bills, if what has been spent in the past is known.

Using these historical figures, prepare forecasts for the weekly cash flows for a month at a time. First, determine the cash inflows for each month—usually cash sales and accounts receivable. Then determine the cash outflows—utilities, payroll and other employee-related expenses, inventory, equipment purchases, and so on. Compare inflows with outflows to determine the company's net cash position.

The cash flow forecast allows an entrepreneur to track actual performance against forecasts and plans. Each month, an entrepreneur should compare the forecast with the actual results and calculate the variance between the actual amount incurred and the forecast line by line. Then calculate the percentage variance (i.e., the actual minus the forecast divided by the forecast). Focus on the areas where overspending occurred, looking at the dollar amount and percentage over the budget. Where the difference is significant, determine whether the expenditure was justified, and, if not, how to reduce it. By doing this every month, an entrepreneur will find that he can control expenses much more effectively.

ACCOUNTS RECEIVABLE

The major area of vulnerability for many entrepreneurs is accounts receivable. On any given day, it is estimated that 5 million businesses are behind on their bills.[7] As stated earlier, many entrepreneurs, particularly in the early or fast-growth stages of their business, focus more on generating sales than they do on collecting receivables. While this is never a good idea, it can turn into a disastrous situation if the economy slows down and more customers take longer to pay their bills—usually the result is a cash crunch for a company.

This problem is not unique to American entrepreneurs. In Australia, a survey conducted by Dun & Bradstreet and Roy Morgan Research showed that the majority of small and medium-sized enterprises no longer expect to be paid on time. As for the old standard 30-day payment period, only 30 percent of these firms expect to be paid within that time by their customers. In the U.K., 67 percent of small businesses indicated that late payment from other businesses was a cause of cash flow difficulties.[8] Every year, Dun & Bradstreet surveys small-business owners. The survey is designed to give an overview of current issues and problems facing these business owners, as well as a brief look at expectations for the coming year. In 2001, for the twentieth annual survey, small-business owners were asked about their priorities. For example, in the coming year, would they put more of an emphasis on increasing sales? What about collecting debt? The answers given are shown in Table 6-3, and they suggest that collecting customer debt is a secondary concern.

T A B L E   6-3

Dun & Bradstreet Small-Business Survey

	Sales	Control Costs	Financing	Uncollected Debt
Increase emphasis	67%	53%	16%	21%
Decrease emphasis	3%	4%	10%	7%
Same emphasis	28%	40%	59%	50%
Don't know/not applicable	2%	3%	16%	21%

Source: Dun & Bradstreet 20th Annual Small Business Survey.

In a similar study, the National Federation of Independent Business (NFIB) conducts a survey every 5 or 6 years to establish the priorities of small businesses. The results of this survey are enlightening: cash flow wasn't even a top ten concern. In fact, it is number 34![9]

Alan Burkhard, president of The Placers, Inc., a Wilmington, Delaware–based temporary placement and permanent job search firm, initially did not value the importance of having good financial controls for accounts receivable. He notes, "I always told myself that accounts receivable didn't create sales, so they weren't worth paying attention to."[10] This was his belief until a time when, although his company was generating record sales, he was having difficulty running his company because of cash problems. The root of the problem: an inefficient accounts receivable system.

"None of our customers paid us in any kind of timely fashion. And 60–70% of our delinquent accounts were actually owed by our regular customers. Every single week we had to pay salaries and payroll taxes for every temp we placed on a job. But it was taking us 60 or 90 days or longer to collect our bills from the companies that were hiring those temps."[11] By allowing its customers to take so long to pay, The Placers was actually giving them an interest-free loan to cover their own payroll costs.

Unfortunately, it is quite common for entrepreneurs to complain about their need for more working capital when in fact the company already has the money in accounts receivable. When you are an entrepreneur, you had better be an absolutely vigilant bulldog (as noted at the beginning of this chapter) when it comes to collecting your receivables. This is the lifeblood of the business—collecting your receivables as quickly as possible. Candidly, when I first owned my business, I was a bit of a wimp. I was scared that if I called the customers and said something, well, they would no longer do business with me. I learned very quickly that if you do not say something, you are not going to be sitting around for very long saying, "Where's my money?" Instead, you're going to be saying, "Where's my business?" The money simply needs to be collected by whatever means necessary. As one entrepreneur stated, "I get on the phone and beg."[12]

Accounts Receivable Systems

A good accounts receivable collection system is proactive. It also allows the entrepreneur to do business with customers that may not have a credit history, or even those who have a bad credit history. The major components of an effective system include these steps:

- Before you go into business, perform an analysis of the industry's payment practice. Is this an industry characterized by historically slow-paying customers, such as the government or health insurance companies? Figure 5-2 lists periodicals that can be used as part of an industry analysis. If an industry is characterized by slow-paying customers, this does not necessarily mean that you should not enter it; it simply means that you should be even more diligent about developing and maintaining a disciplined system.

- Have all new customers complete a credit report before you provide any services or products. The report should be simple but thorough and should contain the following information:
  - The age of the company
  - The owner(s) of the company
  - Whether the company has ever declared Chapter 7 or 11 bankruptcy and whether the owner has ever declared Chapter 13
  - The current name of the company and any previous names
  - The maximum credit level desired
  - The telephone numbers and fax numbers and/or addresses of three supplier references, along with the length and terms of the relationship with these suppliers
  - The name of the company's primary bank, its account number(s), and a contact number for the bank officer responsible for managing the company's accounts
  - Whether or not the company agrees to pay invoices according to your terms
- Consider the following options if a potential customer does not have a credit history or has a bad one:
  - At the time of order receipt, require an up-front payment equal to the cost of goods sold for the order, with the balance due at the time of shipment. This ensures that your costs are covered if the customer cancels the order after production has begun.
  - Obtain a 100 percent payment before work on the order can begin.
  - Require a 100 percent payment before or at the time of delivery (COD).
  - Request a 33 percent payment at order receipt and 33 percent at the time of shipment, with the balance due 30 days later.

- Contact all references immediately and inquire about their credit experience with the prospective customer. Questions should include:
  - How many years have they had this customer?
  - What is the maximum amount of credit they have provided this customer? Have there been any increases or decreases in the credit limit? If so, why?
  - What are their invoice terms?
  - Does the customer typically pay within 10, 30, 60, or 90 days?
  - Have they ever received any checks from this customer, and have any of them bounced?
  - Do they recommend this company as a good customer?
  - Have they had any problems doing business with this company?

If all references are satisfactory, inform your customers that their orders will be processed immediately. Also remind customers of the company's invoice terms and ask if they have any problems adhering to them. Specifically, ask customers how they normally pay their bills. The reason behind this question is that some companies have their own system for paying bills, regardless of the supplier's invoice terms.

Successful entrepreneurs know how their key customers pay their bills. For example:

- Some customers pay their bills once a month, typically on the thirtieth or thirty-first. To be paid on the thirtieth, the merchandise must be received by the tenth; otherwise, the payment will be made on the thirtieth of the next month.
- Some pay 30 days after receipt of the goods or services. Therefore, the supplier is penalized if the shipment is delayed by the carrier.
- Some pay 30 days after products that were damaged during delivery have been replaced.

It is also important to ask customers for the name of the accounts payable clerk who will be responsible for paying invoices. When I operated my business, you'd better believe that I knew every accounts payable clerk at every one of my customers. I knew their names, their kids' names, the flowers they liked. Heck, their employers must have wondered why we were so cozy. You know why? Any edge I could gain in getting my bills paid earlier was well worth a few timely cards, a few nice words, and flowers on a birthday.

Other important key steps toward the effective management of accounts receivable include the following:

- All invoices should be mailed on the same day that the product is shipped or services rendered. Do not hold invoices until the next day or the end of the week, and do not wait and send invoices once a month. Such a practice will certainly delay payment.

- Make sure that the invoice highlights the payment terms in bold capital letters or in a different color from the rest of the invoice. The terms should be printed at the top of the page of the invoice. The most common invoice terms are "2/10, net 30." This means that if the customer pays within 10 days of the invoice date, she is allowed a 2 percent discount. Otherwise, the entire invoice amount is due within 30 days of the invoice date.

- Manage the collection of accounts receivable. It is naïve to expect all customers to pay in a timely fashion. In the business of collecting receivables, the squeaky wheel does in fact get the oil.

- The entrepreneur should have a weekly receivables aging report showing the customer accounts that are outstanding for 30 days or more.

- For invoices that have not been paid seven days after the due date, automatic action of some kind should be taken.

- Excellent payment history is no longer than 10 days more than the invoice terms. If the terms are net 30 and payment occurs in 50 days, then no future orders should be sent before receipt of some kind of payment, as mentioned earlier.

Collecting accounts receivable can be an intimidating experience, especially for the inexperienced entrepreneur. In many instances, the new entrepreneur is afraid to implement a system similar to the one discussed here because of the fear of losing revenue if the customer gets offended. Such a concern is foolish and naïve. It is also a good idea to have someone other than you send the strong letters and make the tough phone calls. At my company, a woman named Angela—our CFO—was our resident pit bull. We had a system in place where our terms were net 30, and if we weren't paid by the thirty-fifth day, an automatic reminder went out to the customer—a neon green sheet of paper in a neon green envelope. It said, "Just a reminder if you've forgotten us." If we hadn't been paid five days after that, another notice—this one hot pink—went out. I had one customer call me to say, "Steve, every time I open one of these doggone notices, I get blinded by the sheets of paper. Why don't you stop sending them to me?" I replied, "Listen, I just own the company. Angela runs everything out there. Now the way that I can get Angela to stop is for you to simply pay on time. It's a simple solution."

But everyone has his own system, and occasionally the entrepreneur needs to show a little "tough love." I love the story that a business broker in Richmond, Virginia, Bette Wildermuth, tells about one of her clients. "This gentleman owns an excavation company. He always does excellent work, meets the developers' time schedule, and makes sure his crews clean up after themselves. Usually he gets paid within 10 days of completing the job. But every once in a while, a developer really drags things out. The excavator's solution: he puts on his muddiest contractor boots and goes to the developer's fancy office with the nice oriental rugs. When he arrives, he announces in a very loud voice that he has come to pick up the overdue check and plans to sit in the lobby until it's ready. Needless to say, this does tend to speed up the process."

For the entrepreneur who just doesn't have the stomach for collections, one option is to get "credit insurance," where the insurer pays the claim within 60 days and then assumes the responsibility for collection. Baltimore, Maryland–based American Credit Indemnity Company, the country's largest issuer of credit insurance, charges 1 percent of the sales insured and will insure only receivables from customers who historically have paid within 30 days.[13]

Remember, good customers typically expect to pay their bills within five to ten days after the due date unless they have a special payables system, as was mentioned earlier. Even those customers plan to pay, but according to their system. A bad customer is one who is very cavalier about paying bills. These types of customers will pay only when they are forced to do so, even when they have the money. Ultimately, the experienced entrepreneur sees that the latter are not profitable customers and does not mind losing them.

When such a decision has been made, extreme action should be taken, such as hiring a lawyer, at a cost of approximately $2,000, to get a "writ of attachment" within 60 days against the delinquent customer's corporate bank account. This action generally gets the customer's immediate attention for settling the delinquency.[14]

Before leaving the subject of an accounts receivable system, here are a few don'ts:

- Don't be rude to customers. Don't threaten them.
- Don't assume that a slow-paying customer is a thief or a bum. It may be that the customer has fallen on temporary tough economic times.
- Don't take legal action against a customer until the bill is at least 45 days past due and you have personally spoken to the customer and tried to get payment.
- Don't pay independent sales representatives until you receive payment from the customer. Some sales representatives do not care if a customer is a known delinquent payer. Taking an order from such a customer may not bother the salesperson, since she is not the one investing in raw materials. Therefore, discourage such action with a policy that specifies that sales representatives will not receive their full commission if payment is received more than a certain number of days late. For example, if the payment is 15 days late, the commission is reduced by 15 percent.

To check on the quality of accounts receivable, several ratios can be used. The first step in checking the quality is to determine what the company's collection ratio, or "days receivable" or "accounts receivable turnover," is. This ratio measures the quality of a company's accounts receivable. It shows the average number of days it takes to collect accounts receivable. To look at it another way, this ratio indicates the number of days, on average, that it takes a business to convert receivables to cash. Equation 6-3 shows the equation to calculate days receivable.

E Q U A T I O N   6-3

Days Receivable

Outstanding receivables/annual sales/365 days

The same formula can be restated as Equation 6-4.

E Q U A T I O N   6-4

Days Receivable

Outstanding receivables/average daily sales

In this case, average daily sales can be calculated using Equation 6-5.

E Q U A T I O N   6-5

Average Daily Sales

Average daily sales = annual sales/365 days

The goal is to get the customers to pay as soon as possible. Therefore, a low number is desirable. At a minimum, a company's days receivable should be equal to the industry's average. Also, it should not exceed the company's days payable ratio, because if it does, this indicates that bills are being paid faster than payments are being received.

For example, a company with $5 million in annual revenues and $800,000 in accounts receivable has an accounts receivable turnover ratio of 58.4 days, calculated as shown in Figure 6-1.

FIGURE 6-1

Receivables Turnover Ratio Calculation

$5 million in sales/365 days = $13,699 (average daily sales)
$800,000 in receivables/$13,699 = 58.4 days

This number would indicate that, on average, it takes the company approximately 58 days to convert receivables into cash. Is this good or bad? Well, most importantly, it depends on the invoice terms. If the terms are 30 days, this is bad even if the industry average is more. This says that customers are paying almost one month later than they should. That is money that could be reinvested and could generate returns if the company received it closer to the invoice terms.

Companies usually do not understand the importance of collecting their accounts receivable quickly and consistently. Entrepreneurs usually focus their resources on boosting sales, rather than on faster collection of receivables, because the benefits of higher sales are easier to quantify. Entrepreneurs sometimes ignore the costs of inefficient collection systems because they usually do not understand the effects of these inefficiencies on the company's bottom line. However, it is easy to quantify the benefits of faster collection of accounts receivable in terms of dollars saved. Faster collection means that the company will not have to use external financing for current payables. Equation 6-6 is the formula for calculating dollars saved as a result of faster collection of accounts receivable.

EQUATION 6-6

Dollars Saved

(Gross annual sales × annual interest rate) × days saved/365 days = dollars saved

In calculating dollars saved, use the most recent complete year's sales figures unless the company is growing rapidly and has a good projection for the current year. For the annual interest rate, include the cost of debt capital. To find the days saved, subtract the company's improved days sales outstanding (DSO) from its original DSO. The equation for DSO is shown in Equation 6-7.

EQUATION 6-7

Days Sales Outstanding[15]

$$\frac{\text{Average accounts receivable balance over past 3 months} \times 90 \text{ days}}{\text{Total sales over past 3 months}}$$

For example, suppose a \$4 million company, borrowing at the prime rate of 6.75 percent plus 2 points (i.e., 2 percent), improves its days sales outstanding by 5 days. The total amount of dollars the company saves by improving its collection of accounts receivable is shown in Figure 6-2.

FIGURE 6-2

Accounts Receivable Collection Savings

(\$4,000,000 × 8.75) × 5 days/365 days = \$4,795 in savings

ACCOUNTS PAYABLE

The ideal situation is to collect all your receivables quickly while paying your outstanding bills as late as possible without jeopardizing the service you get from your suppliers. However, delaying payables is not always necessarily a good thing. If you have cash on hand or can borrow at low rates, should you take discounts? Yes. As Jay Gohz, the author of *The Street Smart Entrepreneur*, explains:

> Suppose your supplier terms are 2, 10 net 30—2% discount if you pay in 10 days; the entire balance is due in 30 days. You don't take a discount and pay in 40 days instead of 30. Basically, you have borrowed from your vendor for 30 days, which is essentially one-twelfth of a year. The loan cost equals 2% (i.e., the 10-day discount) of the invoice annualized, which is 24%. If every month you lose a 2% discount, it is like paying 24% over the course of a year.

To determine whether or not the company's accounts payable are what they should be, analyze the accounts payable turnover ratio and compare it with the industry average. This ratio measures the average number of days it takes the company to pay its bills. The ratio can be calculated as shown in Figure 6-3.

F I G U R E   6-3

Accounts Payable Turnover Ratio Calculation

COGS/365 days = average daily costs

Accounts payable/average daily costs = number of days it takes to pay

Management of Accounts Payable

To improve the accounts payable days, the entrepreneur can take the following actions recommended by several professionals:

- Negotiate better payment terms, such as net 45 or net 60, instead of net 30.
- Time payments according to their due dates, such as 30 days following the receipt of material, rather than on some artificial schedule.
- Plan cash flow realities. For example, to avoid big cash outflows, some companies pay their employees' payroll biweekly and then pay their outstanding bills during the other two weeks of the month.
- Avoid interest penalty charges. If you have to stretch out your own payables because of temporary cash flow problems, make sure you are not late with those bills that incur additional interest charges.
- Communicate with your suppliers. If you establish a good working relationship with a supplier and make regular payments, you can usually avoid paying late charges by contacting the owner in advance if you expect to make a late payment or if you need to request a payment extension.
- Set scheduling goals. Try to establish a final date by which all payables are to be paid. While it is unrealistic to assume that you will always be on schedule, it is important to keep the accounts payable as close to the scheduled goal date as possible.

- Be organized. Keep a paper trail and keep close track of details, especially of the aging of bills. Invest in a good accounts payable system.
- Look for warning signs, including low cash levels, that could result in future problems paying vendors and suppliers. Reevaluate your collection controls to ensure that you are collecting cash as soon as possible.
- Prioritize. You can't devote the same amount of time to all payables. Prioritize payables based on some type of priority rating. For example, fixed expenses such as rent may be paid first, utilities second, and then other bills.
- Identify problems early. Look for accuracy of information on invoices from suppliers.
- Provide supervision from the top.
- Have specialists monitor the accounts payable daily.
- Try to stretch your accounts payable as much as possible without hurting your relationships with vendors and without damaging your credit status.

THE CASH GAP

You now own a business. Whether it's a manufacturing, retail, or service firm, you soon discover a simple truth: first *you* pay for the goods or services, and then eventually someone else—*your* customer—pays you. The period between payment of cash and receipt of cash is called the *cash gap* or *cash conversion cycle*. How long do your goods sit in inventory? How many days is it before you have to pay your supplier? Finally, how many days does it take your customers to pay you? The answers to those three questions are plugged into the cash gap formula, shown in Equation 6-8.

E Q U A T I O N   6-8

Cash Gap Calculation

	Inventory days
plus	Days receivable
minus	Days payable
equals	Cash gap

That interval between the payment of cash and the receipt of cash must be financed. The longer the time, the more interest a company must pay on capital borrowed from a lender, thereby using working capital. The wise way to reduce the need for working capital is to decrease the gap. The entrepreneur's goal must be to continually shorten the gap, because for each day that it is decreased, the daily interest cost saved goes entirely and directly to pretax profits.

Let's explore this concept in more detail, using an example and illustrations. We can make the following assumptions for the Varnadoe Company:

- Days inventory carried*: 40.5
- Days payable*: 40
- Days receivable*: 35
- Annual revenues: $50 million
- Gross profit*: 30 percent
- Cost of debt: 6 percent

Therefore, the cash gap can be calculated as shown in Figure 6-4.

F I G U R E   6-4

Cash Gap Calculation

	Inventory days	40.5
plus	Days receivable	35.0
minus	Days payable	40.0
equals	Cash gap	35.5 days

To determine the savings from reducing the cash gap by one day, the calculation shown in Figure 6-5 should be made.

As you can see from the figure, for every day that the cash gap is reduced, the savings of $5,753 will go directly to profits before taxes, thereby increasing the Varnadoe Company's cash flow. Using the Varnadoe Company's information, Figure 6-5 illustrates the cash gap concept.

---

* The formulas for these ratios can be found in Chapter 5.

F I G U R E   6-5

Cash Gap Reduction Calculation

Determine the company's daily revenues:
$50 million ÷ 365 = $136,986

Determine the cost of goods sold:
1.00 − 0.30 (gross profit) = 0.70

Determine the COGS for one day of revenue:
0.70 (COGS) × $136,986 (daily revenue) = $95,890

The cash gap:
35.5 days

Determine how much Varnadoe Company needs to borrow to cover 35.5 days of COGS:
35.5 × $95,890 (COGS for 1 day's revenue) = $3,404,109

Determine the interest expense to be paid on the borrowed money:
3,404,109 × 0.06 (cost of debt) = $204,246

Determine the savings from reducing the cash gap by 1 day:
$204,246 ÷ 35.5 (cash gap) = $5,753

There are only three ways in which a company can reduce its cash gap: (1) increase the number of days it takes to pay for inventory, (2) decrease the number of days it takes to collect receivables, or (3) increase the inventory turns. Let's analyze each.

Increase Days Payable

Most companies allow their customers up to two weeks past the due date before they consider the invoice seriously delinquent. Therefore, every entrepreneur should take advantage of these extra days by paying no earlier than two weeks after the due date. This shortens the cash gap because it extends payments that may have been due in 30 days to 44 days. Using the information from the Varnadoe Company, if days payable were increased 4 days to 44, the cash gap would be 31.5 instead of 35.5. Such a decrease would save the company $23,012 in interest payments (4 days × $5,753).

Decrease Days Receivable

This topic was discussed in great detail in Chapter 5. Some industries historically have lower days receivable than others. For example, manufacturing companies typically expect payment in 30 days, whereas retailers such as Amazon.com usually get paid immediately upon sale. They have no receivables because payment is required at the time of the order. In fact, in 2006 Amazon.com reported 13 days receivables, 80 days payables, and 39 days of inventory. The result was that Amazon.com's cash gap was a beautiful negative 28 days $(13+39-80=-28)$, which means that it raised interest-free money from its customers for almost a month. Specifically, with average cost of sales, which at the time was $22.6 million, the company raised $631 million ($22.6 million $\times$ 28 days), which it used to help pay overhead expenses.[16] Using the Varnadoe Company data again, if the days receivable were reduced from 35 to 29, the effect would be a 6-day reduction in the cash gap and therefore a $34,518 cash savings.

Increase inventory Turnover

The faster a company converts inventory into cash, the less cash it needs because it can reduce its days of inventory carried and decrease its inventory carrying costs, which was discussed in Chapter 5. A company that has successfully increased its inventory turns is Wal-Mart, known in some circles as the world champion of lean. Its inventory turnover was 4.1 in 1990 and 7.6 in 2005, an average increase of 3.1 percent per year. Another company that has been successful in improving its cash flow by turning inventory faster is Dell. It turns its inventory an amazing 83.7 times per year, compared with less than 5 times for traditional computer manufacturers.[17]

The hope is that, as a result of this rich discussion, it is now clear that every entrepreneur must know why cash gap analysis is important and how to use it as a proactive tool for operating the company. Every entrepreneur should do the complete analysis explained in this section at least annually and use the information for strategic planning for next year.

What is the ideal cash gap? It varies by industry. An industry comparison should be made annually using the Risk Management

T A B L E   6-4

Cash Gaps by Industry, 2006

	Receivables +	Inventory −	Payables =	Cash Gap
Manufacturing				
Bread and bakery	25	19	23	21
Bottled soft drinks	29	30	31	28
Women's dresses	41	54	26	10
Wholesale				
Office supplies	40	28	31	37
Auto	17	66	13	70
Toys, hobby goods	50	94	39	104
Retail				
Gasoline stations	5	9	13	0
Drugstores	20	50	32	38
Shoes	2	130	30	103
Service				
Equipment rental	7	N/A	N/A	7
Motels and hotels	8	N/A	N/A	8
Accounting firms	64	N/A	N/A	64

Source: Risk Management Association (formerly Robert Morris Associates), 2006.

Association (formerly Robert Morris Associates) guide. A few of the industries are highlighted in Table 6-4.

WORKING CAPITAL

The procurement, maintenance, and management of working capital seem to be some of the most common and challenging tasks facing entrepreneurs. Therefore, let's devote a little more time to the subject.

As was stated earlier in this chapter, the interval between a company's payment and receipt of cash must be financed. The money for this is called *working capital*, which consists of funds invested in all current assets, including inventory, accounts receivable, and cash. Gross working capital is used to finance only the company's current assets. Net working capital, which is a measurement of a company's solvency, is current assets minus current liabilities. The goal is to have positive net working capital. The greater the net working capital, the stronger the company's cash position relative to its ability to service its other expenses, including long-term debt.

Very few companies are able to finance their working capital needs internally. Therefore, external financing in the form of debt or equity is inevitable. How much working capital is ideal? One expert, Skip Grandt, a commercial lender with 20 years of experience, says that he likes to see a company have net working capital levels at 3 to 6 times its annual fixed costs.[18] A great resource for finding working capital levels for different industries is *CFO Magazine*'s annual working capital survey, which can be found on *CFO*'s Web site (www.cfo.com).

FINDING CASH

Entrepreneurs have frequently asked me to help them raise external financing from debt and/or equity investors. Most of the time, after reviewing the financial statements, I have told them that they do not need outside capital. They simply need to reduce their inventory and/or accounts receivable levels. That's right. Cash is often readily available to entrepreneurs who carry excessive amounts of these two assets.

What is the ideal level of inventory that an entrepreneur should carry? The formula to make this determination is shown in Equation 6-9.

E Q U A T I O N   6-9

Ideal Inventory Calculation

Ideal inventory = COGS/targeted inventory turns

Let's use the information from the Hoy Company to show how an entrepreneur can raise internal cash by applying this formula. The Hoy Company had the following numbers for 2008:

- Revenues: $30,848,000
- Cost of goods sold (COGS): $13,989,000

- Inventory: $9,762,000
- Inventory turns: 1.43 times
- Average industry inventory turns: 2 times
- Accounts receivable: $5,996,000
- Days receivable: 71
- Average days receivable for industry: 40

If in 2009, the revenues and COGS remained the same as in 2008, but the entrepreneur was able to turn inventory 2 times rather than 1.43 times, the cash savings would be dramatic. The ideal level of inventory is $6,994,500, determined by $13,989,000/2. The actual savings based on the 2008 inventory level would be $2,767,500 in cold, hard cash!

What is the ideal level of accounts receivable that an entrepreneur should carry? The formula to make this determination can be seen in Equation 6-10.

E Q U A T I O N   6 - 1 0

Ideal Level of Accounts Receivable

Ideal level of accounts receivable = average daily sales × targeted days receivable

Using the same information for the Hoy Company, if days receivable can be reduced from 71 to 40 days, the cash savings would be significant. To compute average daily sales, the annual revenue must be divided by 365. Therefore, $30,848,000/365 generates average daily sales of $84,515. This figure multiplied by 40 days receivable shows that the Hoy Company's ideal level of receivables should be $3,380,600. The actual savings based on the 2001 accounts receivable, or $5,996,000, would be $2,615,400 in cold, hard cash!

N O T E S

1. Jill Andresky Fraser, "Riding the Economic Rollercoaster," *Inc.*, December 1998, p. 126.
2. Michael Fernandez, "My Big Mistake," *Inc.*, December 1998, p. 123.
3. Fraser, "Riding the Economic Rollercoaster."

4. "Running on Empty," *Inc.*
5. Ibid.
6. Fraser, "Riding the Economic Rollercoaster."
7. Gini Graham Scott and John J. Harrison, *Collection Techniques for a Small Business* (Grants Pass, Oregon: Oasis Press, 1994).
8. U.K. Survey of Small Businesses, 2005.
9. Bruce D. Phillips, "Small Business Problems and Priorities," National Federation of Independent Business, June 2004.
10. Jill Andresky Fraser, "Getting Paid," *Inc.*, June 1990.
11. Ibid.
12. *Wall Street Journal*, October 25, 1999, p. 9.
13. *Chicago Sun-Times*, May 25, 1999, p. 48.
14. Ibid.
15. Source: Jill Andresky Fraser, "Collection: Days Saved, Thousands Earned," *Inc.*, November 1995.
16. *Journal of Accountancy*, October 1999, p. 29.
17. Dell company financials as compiled by Hoovers, July 2007.
18. Skip Grandt, interview with author.

CHAPTER 7

Valuation

INTRODUCTION

When I teach my MBA students about entrepreneurial finance, on Day 1 of the classes, I run through an exercise in which students attempt to value a company. You should know that many of these students have previously sat through high-level finance classes, know about discounted cash flows, and have their heads full of formulas. We look at the numbers. "Tell me what you would pay for the company," I demand. The valuations range from zero to $300,000. Actually, I tell them, when the company was sold, it went for $38,000. It sold for the price of its inventory. There is a story behind the valuation that is not quantitative. The owner had to sell the company, because his wife told him that if he didn't, she was going to leave him and retire down in Florida by herself. It had nothing to do with a multiple of cash flows, multiple of revenue, or anything other than that he simply had to get out of the business.

Here's the lesson: valuation is very tricky and can never be done in a vacuum. Entrepreneurs must learn the methods used to value companies and become comfortable with the "ambiguity of valuation" and the fact that the valuation process is not a hard-and-fast science. The story of Bain Consulting highlights this fact. In 1973, Bill Bain, a former vice president at Boston Consulting Group, and seven partners founded the consulting firm Bain Consulting. From the mid-1980s through 1993, it was estimated that Bain's revenues had increased from $100 million to $220 million.

During this time, the eight partners decided to sell 30 percent of the company to a Bain Employee Stock Option Plan (ESOP) for $200 million. This transaction gave the company an implied valuation of $666 million. A few years later, the vice presidents of the company took legal action against these partners, which ended in the partners returning $100 million to the company as well as the 70 percent of the company's equity that they held. This transaction, in which the eight partners essentially sold 100 percent of their equity back to the company, changed the valuation from $666 million to $200 million, a reduction of more than 70 percent! The point of this story is to show that even a world-class organization such as Bain, filled with brilliant MBA graduates from some of the finest business schools in the country, including Kellogg, Harvard, Stanford, and Wharton, could not initially come up with the "correct" valuation.

Let me repeat it again. The valuation of a company, particularly that of a start-up, is not an exact science. As Nick Smith, a venture capitalist in Minnesota, stated, "Valuation in a start-up is an illusion." Therefore, the true value of a company, be it a start-up or a mature business, is established in the marketplace. Very simply, a company's ultimate value is the price agreed to by the seller and the buyer. This fact can be traced back to the first century BC, when Publilius Syrus stated, "Everything is worth what its purchaser will pay for it."

One of the best examples of this fact is highlighted by the story of Apple Computer and Be, Inc. In October 1996, Apple Computer's CEO, Gil Amelio, began negotiations to buy Be, Inc., from its CEO, Jean-Louis Gassée. Be had developed a new operating system called BeOs that some people in the industry said "put Apple's Macintosh and Microsoft's Windows to shame."[1] Like most opportunistic entrepreneurs, Gassée was more than willing to sell his 6-year-old entrepreneurial venture, which he had financed with $20 million from venture capitalists and other private investors. In 1996, Be, Inc., had 40 employees and approximately $3 million in annual revenues. Amelio offered $100 million for the small company. Gassée thought the value of Be, Inc., was much greater and countered with a $285 million asking price, which amounted to approximately 10 percent of Apple's valuation.

Amelio refused to offer anything over the $100 million price. Instead, he bought the more established NeXt Software, Inc., which ironically had been founded by Steve Jobs, Apple Computer's founder and current CEO. Therefore, what was the value of Be, Inc., in 1996? It was an amount between $100 million and $285 million. And what happened to Be, Inc.? In September 2001, Nasdaq regulators told the company that they were delisting it for failing to maintain a minimum bid price of at least a dollar for 30 consecutive days. Be, Inc.'s shares were trading for about 14 cents. That same month, Be, Inc., announced that it would sell its remaining assets and technology to Palm Inc. for $11 million.

This overvaluation experience taught Gassée the valuable lesson that all entrepreneurs must learn: "pigs get fat and hogs get slaughtered." He could have been a nice fat happy pig by accepting the $100 million. Instead, he got greedy, a common trait of hogs, and got nothing.

Despite the fact that business valuation is not an exact science, entrepreneurs should determine a value for their company at least once a year. This process must not intimidate them. As has been repeatedly stated throughout this book, it is not brain surgery. In fact, it can be rather simple, and almost everyone can do it. What is the reason for performing an annual valuation of a company? There are many. If the entrepreneur does not determine the value of his company, then someone else will, and the entrepreneur will not be happy with the result. For example, if the entrepreneur is selling his business and relies entirely on a prospective buyer to determine its worth, the buyer will certainly look out for her own interests and price it low. The entrepreneur must, therefore, look out for his own best interests by establishing a price that he is comfortable with, using logical and acceptable valuation methods. Which methods are correct? As you will see later in this chapter, all of them.

Valuation involves estimating the worth or price of a company. Different industries use different methods to determine this value. Some industries use complicated quantitative models, while others use relatively simple approaches. Regardless of the methodology used, however, the valuation of a business incorporates not only a financial analysis of the company, but also a subjective assessment of other factors that may be difficult to quantify, including:

- Stage of the company
- Management team assessment

- Industry
- Reason the company is being sold
- Other general macroeconomic factors

Ultimately, the value of a company is driven by the present and projected cash flows, which are affected by all the factors just mentioned. As Bill Sutter, a former venture capitalist, said to a class of MBA students, "Where does value come from? Cash flow. It does not come from assets or revenues. It comes from cash flow."

VALUING THE CLARK COMPANY

At the beginning of this chapter, I shared the story about the owner whose selling price had more to do with his wife's threats than with any fancy formula. The company is called the Clark Company, and it is worth examining in a bit more detail. As we discussed in Chapter 5, the Clark Company had 2007 revenues of about $113,000. The cash flow that the business generated was an astonishing $45,000, or 39 percent of revenues. This was calculated after scrutinizing the income statement and asking questions of the seller. Remember, the starting point for calculating cash flow is net profit plus depreciation plus any other noncash item expenditures. In this case, we add the $16,000 in net profit and the $835 for depreciation. Cash flow calculations will often also include discretionary expenses that the new owners of the business would not incur if they were to acquire the company. For Clark Company, the additional add-backs include wages, which were in fact wages ($12,215) being paid to the owner's spouse.

The $8,965 allocated for office expenses were in reality personal expenditures that the owner was running through the company for a new car that his wife drove. In addition, as the owner of the business also owned the building that the business was renting, he was in effect renting the building to himself. The company was paying about $7,000 more than market value for the rent for this building.

Net income	$16,000
plus Depreciation	$835
plus Excess wages	$12,215

plus Personal expenses	$8,965
plus Excess rent	$7,000
equals	$45,015

This company is really "a little engine that could." To value this company or any other, many different valuation methods could be used. For example, using a conservative multiple of 3 in the multiple of cash flow valuation method, the company's valuation is approximately $135,000 (3 × $45,015). If another valuation method, such as multiple of revenues, was used, then a different value could be determined. For example, if a conservative 0.9 multiple of revenue was used, Clark Company's value would be $101,700. Clark actually sold for $38,000, which was the value of the inventory on hand. Why did it sell for the price of inventory? Again, the answer was that the owner had to sell it. His wife had told him that if he did not sell, she was going to leave him and retire in Florida by herself. The price was not determined by using a free cash flow, a multiple of cash flow, or a multiple of revenue method—or, for that matter, any other valuation method that is usually used in determining the value of a business.

Again, this case perfectly highlights two major points. One is that valuation is not a hard-and-fast science. The second is that the valuation of a business can never be done in a vacuum. A myriad of things affect valuation, quantitative as well as qualitative.

Before we proceed further, it is important that we clarify two terms that are commonly used when discussing valuation. Those terms are *premoney valuations* and *postmoney valuations*.

PREMONEY AND POSTMONEY VALUATIONS

Private equity investors routinely ask entrepreneurs, at the beginning of negotiations, for the value of their company. When an answer is given, the usual follow-up question is, is the valuation a premoney or postmoney valuation? Premoney means the company's value, using whatever method the entrepreneur chooses, before the investment. Postmoney is very simple. It means the premoney valuation plus the amount of the equity investment.

As we will see later in this chapter, there are several ways to determine the value of a company. These methods render a premoney valuation. Therefore, if the multiple of revenue method creates a $12 million valuation and the company is pursuing $3 million of private equity capital, the postmoney valuation will be $15 million if the equity capital is successfully raised.

The significance of the two valuation terms is to ensure that both parties, the entrepreneur and the investor, are viewing the valuation the same way. The other significance is that postmoney valuations determine how much equity the investor gets. This ownership amount is calculated by dividing the investment by the postmoney valuation. Using the previous example, if the premoney value is $12 million, then the person who invests $3 million will get 20 percent (i.e., $3 million invested divided by the sum of the $12 million premoney valuation plus the $3 million investment).

The problem arises when the investor thinks the value is postmoney and the entrepreneur considers it premoney. In that instance, if the $12 million valuation is thought to be postmoney, the premoney valuation would be $9 million. The investor thinks his that $3 million investment will get him 25 percent of the equity (i.e., $3 million divided by the sum of $9 million + $3 million), while the entrepreneur wants to give up only 20 percent.

This is the reason why it is imperative for both parties to quickly agree on what they mean. Therefore, when she is asked by investors whether the valuation is premoney or postmoney, the entrepreneur's answer should be a resounding, "Premoney with the equity amount for the investor determined by the postmoney valuation."

Another major point to be made is that the postmoney valuation of the last financing round is usually where the premoney valuation of the next round begins—unless there is an increase in the valuation using another agreed-upon method. In the earlier example, the first round, the "Series A," was financed at a $15 million postmoney valuation. Therefore, the premoney valuation for the next round of financing, the "Series B," will be $15 million, and if a new investor puts in $3 million, the new postmoney valuation will be $18 million. The Series B investor will receive 17 percent of the equity for his second round of financing. The Series A investor, who invested $3 million for 20 percent will now own 20 percent of 83 percent (the balance of the equity after Series B), or 16.6 percent of the company

Finally, the private equity industry has a rule of thumb that Series B financing should never be done at a valuation more than twice the Series A valuation.[2]

WHY VALUE YOUR COMPANY?

There are numerous reasons why an entrepreneur should know the value of her business. These include:

- To determine a sale price for the company
- To determine how much equity to give up for partnership agreements
- To determine how much equity to give up for investor capital

Let us discuss this final point in a little more detail.

How Much Equity to Give Up

It is quite common for entrepreneurs to establish the value of their companies unknowingly when they are raising capital. Many of them will determine the amount of capital they need and at the same time arbitrarily state the level of ownership they wish to retain. Such an act automatically places an implied value on the company. For example, if an entrepreneur is looking to raise $100,000 and says he wants to retain 90 percent of the company, the postmoney valuation is $1 million.

The most common minimum level of ownership that many start-up entrepreneurs seek is 51 percent. They believe this to be the minimal number they need to maintain their control of the company. Therefore, they are willing to give up 49 percent. The problem with arbitrarily giving up 49 percent for an investment is that it typically gives the company too low a valuation and little equity to sell to future investors.

Another very simple way to determine the level of equity to give up is by calculating the company's value using the methods that will be cited later in this chapter. This calculation should be done prior to taking any fund-raising action. After the valuation has been logically, rather than arbitrarily, calculated, the amount of equity capital needed, as explained in Chapter 10, should be determined. Once these two numbers have been identified, the entrepreneur is prepared to actively pursue investors because he can now inform investors what they will get for their capital. For example, if the company has a postmoney value of $2 million and the entrepreneur is raising $200,000, then the investor will get 10 percent of the company.

The entrepreneur should be aware of the fact that sophisticated and experienced investors will want to use a more complex formula to determine their future equity position. Investors may determine the equity stake that they want using calculations that factor in the company's present and future valuations along with time and their desired rate of return. In this instance, four, not two, variables are needed: the future expected value of the company, the amount of capital invested, the investors' desired annual return, and the number of years that the capital will be invested. This approach is shown in Equation 7-1.

E Q U A T I O N   7-1

Equity Stake

$$\text{Amount of investment} \times \frac{(1 + \text{Year 1 expected return}) \times (1 + \text{Year 2 expected return}) \times \cdots}{\text{future expected value of company}}$$

Using this formula, an entrepreneur who is seeking an equity investment of $400,000 for a company valued at $5 million can calculate the amount of equity she should expect to give up to an investor who wants to cash out in 4 years with an annual return of 30 percent. See for example, the calculation shown in Figure 7-1.

F I G U R E   7-1

Postequity Investment Ownership Calculation

$$\frac{\$400{,}000 \times (1 + 0.30) \times (1 + 0.30) \times (1 + 0.30) + (1 + 0.30)}{\$5{,}000{,}000}$$

or

$$\frac{\$400{,}000 \times 2.86}{\$5{,}000{,}000} = 0.23$$

This shows that the entrepreneur should expect to give up 23 percent of the company.

The final way to determine the amount of equity to give up requires knowing the equity investment amount, knowing the investor's desired return, and placing a value on the company before and after the investment. In the example in Figure 7-2, the entrepreneur established the company's value at the time of the investment at $10 million, and forecasted that the company's value would be $40 million in 5 years. The entrepreneur also found out, by asking the investor, that the investor expected an internal rate of return (IRR) of 38 percent, which is the same as 5 times the investment in 5 years. The $5 million investment would generate a $25 million return. Therefore, the $25 million return the investor would be entitled to equals 63 percent of the company's future projected value of $40 million.

FIGURE 7-2

Equity Amount Calculation

	Today	5 Years Later
Company value	$10 million	$40 million
Investors' equity	$5 million	$25 million
Investors' ownership	50%	63%

Regardless of the reason, however, every entrepreneur who owns a business, or who intends to own one, should have some idea of its worth. Thomas Stemberg, founder of Staples, Inc., gives excellent advice when he notes, "No one will ever value your business as highly as you do. No one really knows how a new business will fare. A company's valuation is very much a test of your own conviction."[3]

KEY FACTORS INFLUENCING VALUATION

As noted earlier, the value of a business is influenced by a multitude of factors, qualitative as well as quantitative. Before a final value for any company can be determined, the entrepreneur must identify and review these factors. This procedure is commonly referred to as completing a "contextual factor analysis." In other words, what is the general context in which the valuation is taking place? A proper valuation of a company does not occur in a vacuum. A solid valuation contextual factor analysis should include the following factors:

- The historical, present, and projected cash flow of the company.
- Who is valuing the company?
- Is it a private or a public company?
- The availability of capital.
- Is it a strategic or a financial buyer?
- The company's stage of entrepreneurship.
- Is the company being sold at an auction?
- The state of the economy.
- The reason the company is being valued.
- Tangible and intangible assets.
- The industry.
- The quality of the management team.
- Projected performance.

Let's discuss each factor in more detail.

Cash Flow Status

Historically, the value of a company has been largely driven by its present and projected cash flow. Contrary to this historical practice, however, over the last few years, technology companies, particularly Internet and e-commerce businesses, have created immense value without the existence or the projection of positive cash flow in the foreseeable future. Despite this fact, which we will analyze and discuss in more detail later in this chapter, the argument of this book is that all entrepreneurs should focus on creating and maximizing value by aggressively pursuing positive cash flow.

The idea that value comes from positive cash flow is rather simple and direct. The entrepreneurial pursuit of business opportunities usually comes with one basic goal in mind: to make more money than you spend—also known as positive cash flow. The other issues mentioned in Chapter 2 regarding why people choose to become entrepreneurs, including to create jobs, nurture an idea, and get rich, are simply by-products of the successful attainment of the goal of making more money than you spend.

Thus, the cash flow of the company is where its true value lies. This cash flow can be used to reward employees with special bonuses, reward owners and investors, or reinvest in the company to make it even stronger in the future. It should be noted that the timing of a company's cash flows can also affect its value, depending on who is valuing the company. For example, the entrepreneur who is buying a company should give the greatest importance to the targeted company's present, not future, cash flows. The reason is that future cash flows are uncertain. They are merely projections, with no assurance of achievement. Experienced entrepreneurs like Wayne Huizenga correctly refuse to pay for the unknown. When asked about valuation, Huizenga said, "We pay for what we know, today's cash flow, not tomorrow's."[4]

The other reason that buyers should base their valuation on today's cash flow is that future cash flow comes from the work put in by the new buyer. Paying the seller for the company's future performance would be rewarding the seller for the work the buyer will do. By doing so, the buyer would essentially be giving away the value that he will create. The craziness of the practice of valuing a company and paying the seller based on a company's future cash flow is something akin to the following. A prospective home buyer sees a house for sale in Beverly Hills that has been appraised at $10 million in its present condition and needs a lot of repairs. The buyer does due diligence and finds that once the repairs have been completed, the value of the house will be $30 million. With this information, the buyer makes an offer of $30 million, paying the seller for the work he is about to do!

Obviously, such a scenario is utterly ridiculous, and the same should hold true with a business. The value of a business to a buyer should be based on the company's most recent cash flow, not the future. The difference between the present and future cash flows belongs to the buyer. On the other hand, if the person valuing the company is the seller, she will want the valuation to be based on future cash flow because the future is always projected to be rosier than the present, which would lead to a higher valuation. In the case of a start-up, a valuation based on cash flow projected for the future is acceptable to investors and the entrepreneur because there is no historical or present cash flow.

Finally, the cash flow of a company directly affects its value based on the amount of debt it can service. This can be determined by working backward. The idea is that, for the buyer, the value of a company is primarily based on the amount of debt that can be serviced by the company's cash flow in 5 to 7 years (the typical amortization period for a commercial loan) under the worst-case scenario (the worst-case scenario should be the actual for the most recent year). Most highly leveraged acquisitions have capital structures consisting of 80 percent debt and 20 percent equity. Therefore, if an entrepreneur were able to get a 7-year commercial loan for 80 percent of the value of a company that had a worst-case projected cash flow of $100,000 for the first year, the company's value would be $875,000.

This valuation is based on the fact that 80 percent of the company's value equals $700,000 cumulative cash flow projected over 7 years. Thus, each percentage of ownership of the company is valued at $8,750, or 100 percent equals $875,000. This relationship between value, debt serviceability, and present cash flow is supported by a comment made by Sam Zell after he purchased the *Chicago Tribune* newspaper in 2007 with $8.2 billion in debt. Regarding the 2006 cash flow of $1.3 billion Sam said, "I don't think you need it to go up, you need for it not to go down."[5]

Who Is Valuing the Company?

Are you the entrepreneur who is selling the business or raising capital? Are you the buyer of the entire company or an equity investor? As Stemberg aptly points out:

> The central tension in a venture capital deal is how much the new company is worth. The company's valuation governs how much of it the entrepreneur will own. Venture capitalists yearn to keep the valuation low and take control. Entrepreneurs want to push the number up to raise the maximum amount of cash and keep control themselves.[6]

Stemberg's experience with venture capitalists highlights the tension that often exists between financiers (both venture capitalists and others) and the entrepreneur. He notes:

> I thought Staples was worth $8 million post-money when I went out to raise capital. I wanted to raise $4 million for 50% of the company. Relative to the company's value, are you the insurance company who has to pay a claim, or are you the claimant? The former wants a lower company valuation than the latter. Are you the party in a marriage divorce trying to minimize payments to your spouse as assets are being divided or are you the spouse? The venture capitalists wanted to value the company at $6 million. On January 23, 1986, I struck a deal: The venture capitalists would pay $4.5 million for 56% of the company. Staples was worth $8 million.[7]

The value placed on a business will depend on which side of the table you sit on: If you are the entrepreneur, you will want as high a valuation as possible so that you give up as little equity as possible. If you are the investor (e.g., the venture capitalist), you will want a low valuation because you will want to get as much equity as possible for your investment. As Scott Meadow, a 20-year veteran of the venture capital industry, said, "I'm going to pay you as little as possible for as much of your company as I can get."[8] This point is best illustrated by the experience by Stemberg that was just cited. The venture capitalists initially wanted 66.6 percent of Staples for their investment, compared with the 56 percent they received. Not all investors are as aggressive as Scott Meadow, mentioned earlier. Another venture capitalist is quoted as saying, "The key to valuing a company is to do it in a way that enables the investor to get his desired return, while keeping the entrepreneur happy and motivated." Obviously, this venture capitalist seeks a valuation that creates a "win-win" situation for the investor and the entrepreneur.

Public versus Private Company

Two companies of similar age, operating in the same industry, producing exactly the same products or services, and achieving the same level of revenues, profits, and growth rates, will have significantly different values if one is publicly traded (i.e., listed on the NYSE or Nasdaq stock exchange) and the other is privately owned. A publicly owned company will always have a greater value than a private one. Specifically, private companies have historically been valued at 15 to 25 percent less than similar companies that are traded publicly.[9] This difference in valuation is explainable by the following factors:

- According to Securities and Exchange Commission (SEC) rules, all public companies are required to disclose all details regarding the company's financial condition, past and present. These disclosures allow investors in public companies to make their investment decisions with more information. As private companies do not have to adhere to SEC disclosure rules and regulations, investors in private companies do not have access to this type of information.

- Investors in publicly owned companies have a ready market to buy and sell shares of stock. As you will see in more detail in Chapter 8, "Raising Capital," anyone can buy and sell the stock of public companies. That is not the case with the stock of private companies. Legally, private companies are supposed to sell stock only to "sophisticated" investors whom they know directly or indirectly. *Sophisticated* is loosely defined to include individuals with a certain minimum net worth who understand the risks associated with equity investing. Investors known "directly" means those who are associates, family members, or personal friends. Investors who are known "indirectly" are people known through others, for example, through a banker, lawyer, or accountant.

Therefore, publicly owned companies have greater value because they provide greater and more reliable information regularly to investors than do private companies. This fact supports the axiom "information is valuable." Publicly owned companies also have greater value because of the liquidity opportunities available to investors.

Availability of Capital

As seen in Table 7.1, purchase price multiples of EBITDA on transactions under $250 million in value reached an all-time high of 7.6 in 2006. The availability of capital is one of the main reasons for this increase. Between 2002, when multiples reached a 7-year low, and 2006, a number of factors converged to make this a golden era for sellers. First and foremost, the amount of credit available to investors reached historic levels. Low interest rates and the explosion of securitization of loans opened the spigot, enabling financial buyers to use leverage to target acquisitions. The proliferation of private equity firms, flush with new capital, has been another factor driving valuations higher. Armed with overflowing coffers and easily accessible credit, buyout firms spurred a record $2.7 trillion in M&A activity in the first half of 2007. Corporate buyers, traditionally the most lucrative exit option for sellers, have contributed their share to the multiple increase.

T A B L E   7-1

Purchase Price Multiples

Year	Price/Adjusted EBITDA
1995	5.5
1996	6.1
1997	7.0
1998	7.0
1999	6.3
2000	6.2
2001	5.9
2002	5.8
2003	6.4
2004	6.8
2005	7.5
2006 (June)	7.6

Source: Carter Morse & Mathias, "Strategic Buyers in Perspective," November 2, 2006.

As noted in Chapter 5 and shown in Table 7.2, corporate profitability was at an all-time high in the mid-2000s, riding a strong economy and years of cost cutting. This had firms flush with cash and looking for ways to spend it. In 2006, cash and cash equivalents for S&P 500 firms were more than 6 times as high as in 1995 and even twice as high as in the dot-com era. Additionally, other factors such as the entrance of hedge funds and second-tier lenders into the market and the increasing presence of foreign buyers as a result of a weaker dollar also supported these higher multiples.

T A B L E   7-2

U.S. Corporate Profits, 1995–2006

Year	U.S. Corporate Profits (Billions of Dollars)
1995	697
1996	786
1997	869
1998	802
1999	851
2000	818
2001	767
2002	886
2003	993
2004	1,183
2005	1,331
2006	1,616

Source: U.S. Department of Commerce.

In 2008, the situation has changed drastically, as the international credit markets have tightened significantly as a result of the increasing fallout from the U.S. home mortgage crisis. While the situation is still unfolding, the reduction in liquidity resulting from the softer credit markets is likely to lead to a decline in purchase price multiples. As Scott Sperling, co-president of buyout firm Thomas H. Lee Partners, said in an interview, "Prices have gotten much higher than historical trading levels for many of these companies. That's probably not sustainable if debt markets adjust to more normalized levels."[10] The results of a survey of investment bankers lends support to a more difficult environment for financing in 2008 and beyond: 68 percent of the bankers in the survey said that the availability of financing is getting worse, and only

11 percent said that it is getting better.[11] Moreover, corporate profits and the economy are slowing, and both factors should work to bring down acquisition prices.

Venture capital fund-raising levels tend to track the economy and the stock market. Typical of this historical pattern, venture capital funds were awash with investable capital in the years leading up to 2007 and early 2008. While fund-raising at this point in time was still far below the $83 billion raised in 2000, venture capital fund-raising became more plentiful again. This has moved median premoney valuations from a low of $10.7 million in 2002 to $18.5 million in 2006.[12] VentureOne Corp., a Dow Jones company, tracks venture capital investments. As indicated in Tables 7-3 and 7-4, the availability of capital can vary dramatically by the sector or industry that the firm competes in, and also by the round class. All of this impacts premoney valuations. Firms in hotter industries get a higher premoney valuation, as do firms that are further along in their evolution.

T A B L E 7-3

Median Premoney Valuation by Industry Group, Millions of Dollars

Industry Group	2001	2002	2003	2004	2005	2006	2007, Q2
Health care	16.00	14.70	14.70	15.89	18.32	19.75	17.85
Information technology	16.70	10.00	9.55	12.50	15.00	19.48	15.70
Products and services	15.00	8.00	8.70	8.90	10.15	13.00	5.40

Source: Dow Jones VentureOne

T A B L E 7-4

Median Premoney Valuation by Round Class, Millions of Dollars

Round Class	2001	2002	2003	2004	2005	2006	2007, Q2
Seed Round	3.18	2.68	2.00	1.70	1.80	2.50	2.40
First Round	8.00	6.00	4.90	6.00	5.94	6.00	7.30
Second Round	18.00	13.00	13.00	12.25	15.00	17.80	16.00
Later Round	40.00	24.10	21.00	29.30	32.80	36.00	35.25
Restart	17.50	8.00	8.90	11.19	21.50	24.70	23.85

Source: Dow Jones VentureOne

Strategic or Financial Buyer

The value of a company is also affected by who the buyer is. Corporations, such as those in the Fortune 500, have historically valued companies at higher prices than do financial buyers, entrepreneurs with financial backing from leveraged-buyout funds (i.e., leveraged buyouts, or LBOs), and other private equity sources. As stated previously, a significant reduction in the amount of available credit typically reduces the buying power of private equity firms and returns the spread between financial and strategic buyers closer to historical norms. In situations where financial buyers have an abundance of available funds, they often pay higher prices for attractive companies; in these instances, financial buyers will often pay higher prices than strategic buyers. Table 7-5 shows the average EBITDA multiples by sectors, and Table 7-6 shows the multiples by year.

TABLE 7-5

Average EBITDA Multiples by Sector

	Financial Buyers	Strategic Buyers
Manufacturing	6.8	7.0
Services	7.3	7.1
Retail	8.2	8.4
Health care	5.2	6.1
Communications	10.9	11.0
Overall	7.4	7.5

Source: Thomas Financial, 2000.

TABLE 7-6

Average EBITDA Multiples by Year

	Financial Buyers	Strategic Buyers
2001	5.8	8.8
2002	5.8	6.0
2003	6.3	6.4
2004	6.6	7.8
2005	7.5	7.6
2006	7.2	7.2
2007	8.3	7.0

Source: S&P Leveraged Commentary and Data, 2008

Speculation

There are some companies that gain all of their value based on future projected performance. This was the case with the vast majority of Internet and e-commerce companies, which we will examine in more detail later in this chapter, which typically had modest revenues and no history of profits.

In response to the question, "Are Internet stocks overvalued?" one business writer responded, "Let's put it this way: They sell more on hype and hope than on real numbers."[13] That is the reason why Amazon.com, at the end of March 1999, had a 27 percent greater market value than Sears, a company with revenues more than 15 times greater—and, more importantly, with actual profits compared with losses for Amazon.com, as Figure 7-3 shows. After the market crash in 2001, both companies took a huge hit from investors, but Amazon.com was slapped silly. Later that year, Sears's market capitalization was listed at $11.2 billion, while Amazon was valued at just over $2 billion—a 91 percent drop from its value in 1999. In mid-2007, the picture shown in Figure 7-4 suggests that maybe the speculators in Amazon were on to something, as Amazon.com has become one of the world's most successful online retailers.

F I G U R E   7-3

Valuation Comparison (1999)

	Sears	Amazon.com
Value	$18.6 billion	$23.6 billion
Revenues	$9.0 billion	$293 million
Net profit (loss)	$144 million	($62 million)

F I G U R E   7-4

Valuation Comparison (2007)

	Sears	Amazon.com
Value	$22.6 billion	$28.4 billion
Revenues	$52.7 billion	$11.4 billion
Net profit (loss)	$1.5 billion	$0.25 billion

Stage of Company Development

The earlier the stage of the company, the lower its value. A company in the early seed stage will have a lower value than a company in the more mature growth stage. The reason is that there is less risk associated with the later-stage company. It has a history. Therefore, entrepreneurs are generally advised to develop their products and companies as much as possible before they seek outside private equity financing. Unfortunately, many entrepreneurs learn this lesson too late. They procure equity financing in the earliest stages of the company, when the valuation is extremely low and the leverage is on the side of the investors.

This problem is further exacerbated by the fact that early-seed-stage entrepreneurs typically need relatively little money to start their company and/or develop prototypes. It is not uncommon for these entrepreneurs to need as little as $25,000 or as much as $200,000. When equity investors come in at this stage, they want to own at least 50 percent of the company in return for their investment. Their investment of $25,000 to $200,000 for half the company results in a postmoney company valuation of only $50,000 to $400,000. This creates major problems for the entrepreneur later because he is left with little stock to sell to future investors.

Another common problem that arises is the "seller's remorse" that entrepreneurs feel once they realize that they gave up so much of their company for so few dollars. This was the feeling that Joseph Freedman had with the company he founded in 1991, Amicus Legal Staffing, Inc. (ALS). He raised $150,000 for 65 percent of the company, thereby giving the company a value of only $230,769. In 1997, Freedman sold ALS to AccuStaff, and his investors received $13 million, or 65 percent of the price, for their initial $150,000 investment.[14] Table 7-7 provides average venture capital investment amounts by round.

TABLE 7-7

Median Amount Invested by Round

Round	Amount (Millions of Dollars)
Seed round	1.0
First round	4.9
Second round	9.5
Later round	12.1

Source: Dow Jones Venture One/Ernst & Young, first quarter of 2007.

Auction

When a company is being sold via an auction process, it theoretically will ultimately be valued based on what the market will bear. This process typically has multiple potential buyers bidding against each other. The result is usually a nice high price for the seller. For example, in 2007, Microsoft outbid Google and Yahoo! for the right to buy a portion of Facebook. Microsoft's $240 million investment for 1.6 percent of Facebook gave the company a value of $15 billion! At the time, Facebook's revenues were less than $50 million.

State of the Economy

The condition of the country's and possibly even the world's economy can dramatically affect the valuation of a company. As stated earlier in this chapter, the value of companies being started up or purchased increased annually for 5 years until 2000. It is not merely a coincidence that this occurred at the same time that the U.S. economy experienced the longest period of continuous economic growth without a recession, as stated in Chapter 2.

A strong economy translates into an increased availability of investor capital, which in turn, as we mentioned earlier in this chapter, translates into leverage for the entrepreneur. Obviously, the converse is true. The value of companies typically declines as the economy worsens because investors have less money to invest. Therefore, the economy affects the availability of capital, which in turn affects the value of companies.

This is not just economic theory, but a fact, evidenced by, for example, what occurred during the last recession. In 2001, the United States went into a recession. Capital raised (i.e., available for investing) by all private equity firms (i.e., venture capital, LBO, and mezzanine funds) was $89.2 billion. The next year, 2002, was the first full year of the recession. Capital raised for the year plummeted to $33.6 billion, a 62 percent decrease from a year earlier. Every year since 2002, the economy has improved, and the private equity available to entrepreneurs has correspondingly increased, as the data in Table 7-8 show.

Reason for Selling

The value of a company that is being sold is directly related to the reason behind the sale. A company has its greatest value if the

T A B L E   7-8

Commitments to Private Equity Partnerships

Year	Total Funds (Number)	Amount Raised (Millions of Dollars)	Average per Fund (Millions of Dollars)
1990	151	11,160.6	73.9
1991	69	7,889.4	114.3
1992	139	16,341.6	117.6
1993	169	20,199.0	119.5
1994	239	29,387.3	123.0
1995	276	36,337.9	131.7
1996	260	41,040.3	157.8
1997	375	61,074.7	162.9
1998	451	91,538.7	203.0
1999	601	109,650.6	182.4
2000	807	181,116.3	224.4
2001	439	89,223.2	203.2
2002	296	33,588.3	113.5
2003	263	42,519.1	161.7
2004	356	70,782.3	198.8
2005	412	124,861.4	303.1
2006	408	178,686.9	438.0
2007	432	207,305.1	479.9

Source: National Venture Capital Association, 2008.

entrepreneur is not selling as a result of personal or business pressures. For example, the value of a company that is being sold because of the threat of insolvency brought on by cash shortages will be much less than the value of the exact same kind of company that does not have financial problems.

The same holds true for personal reasons. The value of a company that is being sold, for example, to settle the estate of divorcing owners will be lower than it would be if that circumstance were not driving the sale. Other personal reasons that may negatively affect the value of a company include, but are not limited to, illness or death of the owner(s) or members of the owner's family and internal conflict (i.e., business or personally related) among the owners.

Because these personal and business problems can negatively affect the value of a company that is being sold, it is common for owners to disclose as little as possible about the real reasons for the sale. That is why it is essential for any entrepreneur who is buying a company to do thorough due diligence to determine the reason the company is being sold *before* valuing the company and making an offer. The major lesson to be learned from this section is that information is valuable. The same lesson was the highlight of an earlier section in this chapter, which discussed the reason why public companies have greater value than private companies.

Tangible and Intangible Assets

The tangible and intangible assets of a company will also affect the company's value. Most of the value of manufacturing companies typically lies in tangible assets. The age and condition of these assets—such as machinery, equipment, and inventory—will have a direct impact on the company's value. For example, if the equipment is old and in poor condition as a result of overuse or lack of maintenance, the company will have a lower value than a similar company with newer and better-maintained equipment.

The same holds true for intangible assets, including a company's customer list, patents, and name. For example, if a company's name is damaged, the company will have less value than another company in the same industry with a strong, reputable name. That is the reason why AirTran Airways changed its name from Value Jet Airlines. The latter's name had been severely damaged as a result of a disastrous plane crash in 1996.

Type of Industry

The industry that a company competes in is also very important to its valuation. It is not uncommon for two separate companies in different industries, but with similar revenues, profits, and growth, to have significantly different valuations. As we will see later in this chapter, that was most certainly the case a few years ago when comparing Internet and e-commerce companies with companies in almost any other industry. Based on the price/earnings ratio (P/E ratio) valuation method, which we will also discuss in more detail later in this chapter, the industries with the highest and lowest valuations were the ones shown in Figure 7-5.

F I G U R E   7-5

Highest and Lowest Industry P/E Ratios

Highest P/E Ratios		Lowest P/E Ratios	
Industry	Ratio (Trailing 12 Months)	Industry	Ratio (Trailing 12 Months)
Wireless networking	353.4	Homebuilding	6.1
Power	222.8	Retail building supply	9.4
Utility (foreign)	106.6	Building materials	11.0
Insurance (property and casualty)	105.6	Steel (general)	11.7
E-commerce	96.1	Trucking	11.7
Internet	62.5	Financial services	11.9

Source: Aswath Damodaran, Stern School of Business, January 2008.

The reasons why some industries had greater value than others were the sexiness of the industry and its growth potential. Those companies that were viewed as being sexier, with high and rapid growth potential, typically were valued greater than those companies in staid, conservative, and moderate-growth industries, despite the fact that—as we saw earlier in this chapter when comparing Sears and Amazon.com—the conservative industries were immensely more profitable.

Quality of Management Team

The quality of the management team, which is primarily measured by the number of years of experience each member of the team has and the individual members' success and failure rates, will affect the value of a company that is being sold or is raising capital from external investors. In the situation where a company is being sold and the existing managers require the new owners to retain them, the value of the company will be negatively affected by the evaluation of the management team. If the new owner views the old management team as poor, then she will be less willing to pay a high price for the company because she will have to pay to further train or replace team members. The chance that the management team may need to be replaced adds risk to the future of the company, which in turn decreases the value of the company.

Private equity investors will give greater value to a company that has experienced management. The reason is exactly the same as that just mentioned: risk. The greater the risk, the lower the valuation. For example, two start-up companies looking for the same amount of investor capital will have significantly different valuations if one company's management is composed of people with start-up experience and the other's has none.

VALUATION METHODS

There are numerous ways to value a company, and seemingly, almost no two people do it the same way. Methods may differ from industry to industry, as we will see later in this chapter, as well as from appraiser to appraiser. It is important to know that there is no single valuation methodology that is superior to all the others; each has its own benefits and limitations. But ultimately, most business appraisers prefer and use one method over another. Typically, the commitment to one method comes after experimenting with several methods and determining which consistently provides the valuation that the person is most comfortable with.

Candidly, valuation is part gut and part science, and simply saying that you believe in one valuation method is all well and good. The rubber hits the road when you actually risk your own capital using one or more of these methods to value a business. The point is that an entrepreneur's valuation method is determined by experience; without that valuable experience, it is strongly recommended that the entrepreneur use at least two different valuation methods to determine a company's range of valuations.

Valuation methods basically fall into three categories: (1) asset-based, (2) cash flow capitalization, and (3) multiples. In the world of entrepreneurship, if there is a most popular and commonly used valuation category, it is multiples, and within this category, the most popular method is the multiple of cash flow.

MULTIPLES

Multiple of Cash Flow

The cash flow of a company represents the funds available to meet both its debt obligations and its equity payments. These funds can be used to make interest and/or principal payments on debt, and also to provide dividend payments, share repurchases, and reinvestments in the company. One way of valuing a company is by determining the level of cash available to undertake these activities. This level of cash is determined by calculating earnings before interest, taxes, depreciation, and amortization—EBITDA.

In this valuation methodology, EBITDA is multiplied by a specified figure (i.e., the multiplier) to determine the value of the company. In general, as shown here, a multiplier of between 3 and 10 is used. However, buyers' market or sellers' market, sales growth, industry growth potential, variability in a company's earnings, and exit options available to investors are all factors that affect the level of the multiplier used in valuation. The multiple is not static, but evergreen. It can change for a myriad of reasons.

As venture capitalist Bill Sutter, a graduate of Princeton University and Stanford Business School, stated:

> Virtually every conversation about a company's valuation in the private equity industry starts with a 5 times cash flow multiple discussion. The multiple will go up for qualitative reasons like super management and higher growth and will go down for other types of industries that are recessionary, where risk and volatility is perceived to be higher.[15]

Another means of reducing or improving valuations based on cash flow multiples is to adjust EBITDA. The adjusted EBITDA should be calculated after the entrepreneur's salary has been deducted. The reason is that the entrepreneur is entitled to receive a market-rate salary. This salary should be treated as a legitimate expense on the income statement. If the owner's salary is not recognized, then the company's EBITDA will be artificially inflated, resulting in an overvaluation of the company. This result would not be in the best interest of a buyer, who would pay more for a company, nor would it be in the best interest of an investor, who would get less equity for her investment. In the case of a buyer, the proper way to determine EBITDA is to replace the seller's salary with the new salary anticipated by the buyer, as long as it is at a justifiable market-rate level. The calculation is shown in Equation 7-2.

E Q U A T I O N   7-2

EBITDA Salary Adjustment

Adjusted EBITDA = EBITDA + seller's salary − buyer's salary

For example, if a company in an industry that commonly uses a multiple of 7 had an EBITDA of $500,000, one would assume a valuation of $3.5 million. But suppose further analysis of the seller's financial statements shows that he took a salary of only $50,000 when similar-size companies in the same industry paid their owners $125,000. If the buyer intends to pay himself the market rate of $125,000, then the company's value, using the EBITDA multiple of 7, should be $2,975,000 [i.e., ($500,000 + $50,000 − $125,000) × 7]. This $525,000 difference is an 18 percent overvaluation!

Please note that the change in the owner's salary would also affect the amount of taxes paid by the company. Since the new salary would decrease the operating profit, the taxes would also decrease.

As stated earlier, multiples of EBITDA up to 10 are not uncommon. For example, in 2008, Mars, the candy manufacturer, agreed to buy Wrigley, the gum company, for $23 billion, or 19 times EBITDA, whereas the packaged food industry generally averages a 12 multiple.[16] But this author discourages acceptance of such multiples unless you are the seller of the entire company or a portion of it. For a buyer, it is suggested that multiples no greater than 5 should be accepted. The reason is that valuation should be such that cash flow, under the worst-case scenario, will be able to completely service the debt obligation in the typical 5- to 7-year amortization period.

At a 5 multiple, if the capital structure is 60 to 80 percent debt, as is common, then it can be serviced within 7 years. For example, if the Grant Company's EBITDA is $1 million, a buyer should pay no more than $5 million. With an 80 percent, or $4 million, loan at 7 percent, if the cash flow over the next 7 years remained the same and no major capital improvements were needed, the total $7 million could comfortably service the debt obligation.

Multiple of Free Cash Flow

Finally, for companies requiring major investments in new equipment in order to sustain growth, it is common to use a multiple of the company's free cash flow (FCF) instead of just EBITDA. This is a more conservative cash description that yields a lower valuation. For multiple purposes, FCF is calculated as shown in Equation 7-3.

EQUATION 7-3

Free Cash Flow

$$FCF = EBITDA - \text{capital expenditures}$$

Manufacturing companies are usually valued based on a multiple of FCF. On the other hand, media companies such as television stations are usually valued based on a multiple of EBITDA. For example, in 1995, Westinghouse and Disney purchased CBS and ABC, respectively. Westinghouse paid 10 times EBITDA, and Disney paid 12. In fact, a quick review of the television broadcasting industry (see Table 7-9) will highlight the earlier point regarding the "evergreen" aspect of multiples.

TABLE 7-9

Television Broadcasting Industry Multiples

Years	Selling Multiple
1980s	10–12
Early 1990s	7–8
1996	16
2007	15

It should be noted that the EBITDA and FCF multiple methods correctly value a company as if it is completely unleveraged and has no debt in the capital structure. The adding back of interest, taxes, and depreciation to the net earnings eliminates the relevance of whatever debt the company presently carries. This is the proper way to value a company, especially if you are a buyer, because the seller's chosen capital structure has nothing to do with the buyer and the capital structure she ultimately chooses. The company's present capital structure could be loaded with debt because the owner wants his balance sheet to look dreadful as he begins asset settlement negotiations as part of his upcoming divorce. Therefore, the company should be valued without regard to its existing debt. Once the buyer determines the value she wants to pay, she can agree to inherit the debt as part of her payment. For example, if the company's value is $5 million, the buyer can agree to pay it by assuming the $1 million of long-term debt that the seller owes and paying the $4 million balance in cash.

Multiple of Sales

This multiple is one of the more widely used valuation methods. Sales growth prospects and investor optimism play a major role in determining the level of the multiple to be used, and different industries use different multiples. In the food industry, businesses generally sell for 1 to 2 times revenue, but sales growth prospects can have an impact on raising or lowering the multiplier. For example, Quaker Oats, a strategic buyer, paid $1.7 billion, or 3.5 times revenue, for Snapple in 1995 at a time when similar companies were being sold for a sales multiple of 2 or less. Quaker's rationale: it expected rapid growth from Snapple.

However, that rapid growth did not happen. Two years later, Quaker sold Snapple to Triarc Cos. for $300 million, equivalent to a little more than 50 percent of its annual revenues of $550 million. Quaker's obvious overvaluation of Snapple was instrumental in the CEO's departure from the company. On the other hand, Triarc's owners were given the greatest compliment after buying Snapple when someone said, "They stole the company!"[17] In 2001, PepsiCo acquired Quaker for $13.4 billion.

Other industries that are commonly valued on a multiple of revenues include the radio station industry. Typical valuations are 2.0 to 2.5 times revenues for small-market stations, 3 to 3.5 times for middle-market stations, and 4 times for large-market stations. Another such industry is professional services firms, which are typically valued at 1 to 3 times revenues. But the most prominent industry that used the multiple of sales model is technology, especially the Internet industry, which will be discussed in more detail later in this chapter.

The shortcoming of this method is that it ignores whether the company is making cash. The focus is entirely on the top line. Therefore, this valuation method is best suited for those entrepreneurs who are focusing on growing market share by acquiring competitors. The idea is to buy new customers and rely on your own operational skills and experience to make each new customer a cash flow contributor. This method is best carried out by entre-preneurs who are well experienced in operating a profitable ven-ture in the same industry as that of the company being acquired.

Multiple of Unique Monthly Visitors

This valuation method has surfaced primarily in the Internet space. In 2005, News Corporation purchased MySpace for $580 million, or $2.93 per unique monthly visitor. The next year, Google purchased YouTube for $1.65 billion, or $4 per unique monthly visitor. Additionally, in 2008, NBC Universal agreed to buy the Weather Channel for $3.5 billion. At the time of purchase, the Weather Channel's Web site had 37 million unique monthly visitors, making it a top 15 Web site. This purchase price translates into a price of $9.40 per unique monthly visitor.[18]

P/E Ratio Method

Another common valuation method that falls in the multiples cat-egory is the price/earnings ratio. The P/E ratio model is com-monly used when valuing publicly owned companies. The P/E ratio is the multiplier used with the company's after-tax earnings to determine its value. It is calculated by dividing the company's stock price per share by the earnings per share (EPS) for the trail-ing 12 months. For example, a company with a stock price of $25 per share, 400,000 shares outstanding, and trailing 12 months' earnings of $1 million will have a P/E ratio of 10, calculated as shown in Figure 7-6. In the figure, the P/E of 10 means that it costs $10 to buy $1 in profit, or conversely, that an investor's return is 10 percent. This return compares very favorably with the 5.8 percent historical average returns of long-term bonds.[19]

F I G U R E   7-6

Price/Earnings Calculation

Price per share/EPS
EPS = earnings/number of shares outstanding
$25/($1,000,000/400,000)
$25/$2.5 = 10

The average historical P/E multiple for the Dow Jones Industrial Average and Standard & Poor's 500 is 16. In 1998, during the heart of the stock market rise, the S&P multiple was 28 and the Dow 22.[20] In late 2001, in the heart of the market crash, the S&P multiple was 23.5 and the Dow multiple was 57.3. If you exclude Honeywell (P/E of 731, due in large part to GE's attempted acquisition), the Dow multiple was 32.9. That multiple is higher than the historical averages for some good reasons. The Dow consists of larger blue-chip companies that tend to have less volatility, and during the economic downturn, investors were migrating to these safer companies. Consequently, the P/E multiples of these companies tended to be higher than normal.

P/E multiples are published daily in the business sections of newspapers, showing the ratios for publicly traded companies in comparable businesses. Companies in the same industry may have different P/E multiples despite the fact that they have similar annual earnings and a similar number of outstanding shares. The difference may be related to the price of the stock. Investors may be willing to pay a higher stock price for one company because of its higher forecasted growth rate, the presence of more experienced management, the settlement of a recent lawsuit, or the approval of a new patent. In this example, the company with the higher stock price would have a higher P/E multiple and therefore a higher valuation. Thus, it can be concluded that when a company has a P/E multiple that is higher than the industry average, it's primarily because investors have a positive view of the company's growth opportunities and expect relatively reliable earnings. Conversely, lower P/E multiples are associated with low growth, erratic earnings, and perceived future financial risk.

Be mindful of the fact that the use of P/E multiples is ideally for publicly owned companies. But P/E multiples are sometimes used to value private companies.

The ideal way to value a private company using a P/E multiple is to find the public company that is the most comparable. The most important criterion to look for is a company with exactly the same, or as close as possible, products or services. The objective is to select a company in the same business. The other important criteria are as follows:

- Revenue size
- Profitability

- Growth history and potential
- Company age

After the best comparable is determined, the P/E multiple should be discounted. The reason? As stated earlier in this chapter, the value of a publicly owned company will always be higher than that of a private company with exactly the same revenues, profits, cash flow, growth potential, and age, as a result of liquidity and access to information. The result is that private companies are typically valued 15 to 25 percent lower than public companies. Therefore, the P/E multiple of a public company that is selected as the best comparable should be discounted by 15 to 25 percent.

MULTIPLE OF GROSS MARGIN

As a rule of thumb, the multiple of gross margins should be no higher than 2. Therefore, a company with revenues of $50 million and gross margin of 30 percent has a value of $30 million (i.e., $50 million $\times$ 0.30 = $15 million; $15 million $\times$ 2 = $30 million).

DIFFERENT INDUSTRIES USE DIFFERENT MULTIPLE BENCHMARKS

Before we close out the discussion of multiples, it is important to highlight the fact that different industries use not only different multiple numbers but also different benchmarks. They include the following:

- Distribution companies in the soft drink and alcoholic beverages industry are valued at a multiple of the number of cases sold.
- The pawnshop industry, which provides loans averaging $70 to $100 at annual interest rates ranging from 12 to 240 percent, typically uses one of two valuation methods: the multiple of earnings model or the multiple of loan balance model. There are over 15,000 pawnshops in the United States, and approximately 6 percent are publicly owned. These public pawnshops are valued at a multiple of 18.5 times earnings, which is significantly higher than the figures for private shops, which are valued at between 4 and 7 times earnings.

While this multiple of earnings valuation model is not unique to pawnshops, the model of a multiple of loan balance is. A pawnshop's loan balance provides evidence of the number of its customer relationships, which is its greatest asset. Thus, the multiple range commonly used to value a pawnshop is 2 to 4 times its outstanding loan balance.

Rules of thumb are often used to make quick estimates of business values. The 2008 *Business Reference Guide*, published by the Business Brokerage Press, is a great resource for anyone involved in valuing, buying, or selling a privately held business. Table 7-10 is a sample of some businesses and the "rule-of-thumb" multiples outlined in the guide.

TABLE 7-10

Rule-of-Thumb Valuations

Type of Business	Rule-of-Thumb Valuation
Accounting firms	100–125% of annual revenues
Auto dealers	2–3 years net income + tangible assets
Bookstores	15% of annual sales + inventory
Coffee shops	40–45% of annual sales + inventory
Courier services	70% of annual sales
Day-care centers	2–3 times annual cash flow
Dental practices	60–70% of annual revenues
Dry cleaners	70–100% of annual sales
Employment and personnel agencies	50–100% of annual revenues
Engineering practices	40% of annual revenues
Florists	34% of annual sales + inventory
Food and gourmet shops	20% of annual sales + inventory
Furniture and appliance stores	15–25% of annual sales + inventory
Gas stations	15–25% of annual sales
Gift and card shops	32–40% of annual sales + inventory
Grocery stores	11–18% of annual sales + inventory
Insurance agencies	100–125% of annual commissions
Janitorial and landscape contractors	40–50% of annual sales
Law practices	40–100% of annual fees
Liquor stores	25% of annual sales + inventory
Property management companies	50–100% of annual revenues
Restaurants (nonfranchised)	30–45% of annual sales
Sporting goods stores	30% of annual sales + inventory
Taverns	55% of annual sales
Travel agencies	40–60% of annual commissions
Veterinary practices	60–125% of annual revenues

Source: Business Brokerage Press via bizstats.com.

As one further point of reference, the *Newsletter of Corporate Renewal* suggests that the value of any company should be no more than 2 times its gross margin dollars.[21] In conclusion, when valuing a company using any one of the aforementioned multiple models (i.e., revenues, cash flow, earnings, and gross margins), it should be noted that the multiples are not static. They are constantly changing and should be adjusted up or down, depending on several factors.

If an industry is experiencing a downturn, thereby making it a buyer's market, then the multiples will typically decline. The television industry is a perfect example. During the 1980s, television stations were selling for 10 to 12 times EBITDA. By the turn of the decade, however, the multiples had gone down to 7 to 8. The reason? The country was in the early stages of a recession. Fewer advertising dollars were going to television stations because of more competition from the new cable industry. Also, the major networks decreased the amount of payments they were making to their affiliate stations. The combination of these factors created a buyer's market for network-affiliated television stations. By 1995, the multiples had changed again. The reason for the increase was aptly described in a *Chicago Tribune* article:

> Television stations normally sell for 8 to 10 times cash flow. But some of the recent sales sold at multiples of 15 to 20. A strong economy and an even more robust advertising market helped make TV stations virtual cash cows, producing profit margins ranging from 30 to 70 percent. The approach of a presidential election year in 1996 and the Olympic Games in Atlanta should provide further stimulus to the ad market.[22]

Another interesting example is the newspaper industry in 2007. Since 1940, the number of U.S. daily newspapers has steadily declined. In addition, more recently, advertising revenue for newspapers has come under siege from other media, including the Internet. As Warren Buffett said at his annual investors' meeting in May 2006, newspapers appear to have entered a period of "protracted decline." Consequently, share prices of newspapers have been in free fall, down 20 percent in 2005 and 14 percent in 2006.[23] To illustrate, Google's market capitalization in mid-2007 was approximately 4 times that of the five largest newspapers, yet Google's EBITDA of $5.8 billion was equivalent to the $5.5 billion generated by these newspapers. Table 7-11 demonstrates this point.

T A B L E   7-11

Valuation Comparison

	Top Five Newspapers	Google
Total EBITDA	$5.5 billion	$5.8 billion
Market cap	$37.5 billion	$158.5 billion
Multiple of EBITDA	6.87	27.42

Source: Company financials via Yahoo! Finance.:

There are many factors that may justify an increase or decrease in a company's multiple relative to the industry's typical multiple. An example of multiples increasing occurred in the funeral home industry. Historically, this industry was characterized by primarily small "mom-and-pop" family owner/operators. These small businesses were selling for 2 to 3 times EBITDA. But in the early 1990s, the value of companies in this fragmented industry of over 25,000 funeral homes began to change dramatically. Four companies, which are now publicly owned, began a fierce battle, competing with one another to grow their companies rapidly by consolidating the industry. The four companies, Service Corporation International, Stewart Enterprises Inc., Loewen Group Inc., and Carriage Services, Inc., in many instances sought the same funeral homes, so that by the end of 1998, funeral homes were selling for 8 to 10 times EBITDA.

In 1997, the industry saw the beginning of a decline in these multiples because the growth began to slow. As one business analyst said, this industry is suffering from overvaluation of companies financed by too much debt that cannot be repaid because of an "outbreak of wellness"—fewer people are dying.[24] About 2.3 million people die each year in the United States, with a typical average annual increase of 1 percent. But in 1997, for the first time in a decade, that number decreased. There were 445 fewer deaths in 1997 than in 1996. One interesting reason for this decline was the weather. Most people die in the harsh winter. The past few winters in the United States have been relatively mild. The industry's growth was also hurt by the increasing popularity of cremations, which cost half the price of traditional burials.[25]

The final example of an ever-changing multiple was that applied to high-growth Microsoft. From 1994 to 1996, Microsoft's multiple of revenues more than doubled, from 6 to 14.[26]

ASSET VALUATION

In the past, the value of a company's assets had a great significance in determining the company's overall valuation. Today, most American companies do not have many tangible assets because each year fewer things are produced in the United States. Most are produced overseas in low-wage-paying countries like China, India, and Taiwan.

The result is that over time, the value of a company is dependent less on its assets than on its cash flow. Asset value tends to be most meaningful in cases in which financially troubled companies are being sold. In that case, the negotiation for the value of the company typically begins at the depreciated value of its assets.

CAPITALIZATION OF CASH FLOWS

Free Cash Flow Method

The most complicated and involved valuation model is the free cash flow model, also known as the discounted cash flow or capitalization of cash flow model. It is a model that relies on projections filled with assumptions, because there are so many unknown variables. Therefore, it is the model most commonly used to value high-risk start-ups.

Simply stated, free cash flow is the portion of a company's operating cash flow that is available for distribution to the providers of debt (i.e., interest and principal payments) and equity (i.e., dividend payments and repurchase of stock) capital. This is the cash that is available after the operating taxes, working capital needs, and capital expenditures have been deducted.

Using this valuation method, one approach is to forecast the FCF as the Japanese do: for 25 years without regard to what happens later, because its discounted value will be insignificant. Another similar, and more commonly used, approach is to separate the value of the business into two time periods: during and after an explicitly forecasted period. The "during" period is referred to as the *planning period*. The "after" period is referred to as the *residual*.

The FCF valuation formula—Equation 7–4—is the sum of the present value (PV) of the free cash flow for the planning period and the present value of the residual value.

E Q U A T I O N   7-4

Free Cash Flow Valuation

	PV for the FCF planning period
+	PV residual value
	FCF value

To calculate the PV of the FCF for the planning period, the following steps must be followed:

1. Determine the planning period. It is customarily 5 years.
2. Project the company's earnings before interest and taxes (EBIT) for five years. The use of EBIT assumes that the company is completely unleveraged; it has no debt in its capital structure.
3. Determine the company's EBIT tax rate. This will be used to calculate the exact amount of adjusted taxes to be deducted. These are "adjusted" taxes because they ignore the tax benefits of debt financing and interest payments, since this model, as stated previously, assumes a capital structure that does not include debt.
4. Determine the amount of depreciation expense for each of the 5 years. This expense can be calculated in several ways:
    a. Assume no depreciation expense because the capital expenditures for new assets and the corresponding depreciation will cancel each other out. If that assumption is made, then there should also be a zero for capital expenditures for new assets.
    b. Using historical comparables, make the future depreciation expense a similar constant percentage of fixed assets, sales, or incremental sales.
    c. Using the company's actual depreciation method, forecast the company's value of new assets from capital expenditures and compute the actual depreciation expense for each of the forecasted years.

5. Determine the needed increase in operating working capital for each year. The working capital required is the same as the net investment needed to grow the company at the desired rate. The working capital can be calculated as shown in Figure 7-7. The increase in working capital would simply be the change from year to year.

F I G U R E   7-7

Working Capital Calculation

	Current operating assets excluding cash
minus	Current operating assets excluding cash
equals	**Working capital**

6. Determine the investment amounts for capital expenditures. Capital expenditures are made for two purposes. The first is to repair the existing equipment in order to maintain the company's present growth. The other is for new equipment needed to improve the company's growth. As was stated in 4a, the new asset cost can be zeroed out by the depreciation expense. Therefore, only the capital expenditures needed for maintenance would be highlighted. As stated earlier, that amount can be determined by using historical comparables.

7. Determine the company's expected growth rate (GR).

8. Determine the discount rate (DR). This rate should reflect the company's cost of capital from all capital providers. Each provider's cost of capital should be weighted by its prorated contribution to the company's total capital. This is called the *weighted average cost of capital (WACC)*. For example, if a company is financed with $2 million of debt at 10 percent and $3 million of equity at 30 percent, its WACC, or discount rate, can be determined as follows:

   a. Total financing: $5 million

   b. Percent of debt financing: 40 percent ($2 million/ $5 million)

   c. Percent of equity financing: 60 percent ($3 million/ $5 million) *d.* (Debt amount × debt cost) + (equity amount × equity cost)

    e. $(0.40 \times 0.10) + (0.60 \times 0.30) = 0.22$

A final point: please note that the tax-shield benefit of the debt financing is incorporated in the WACC.

9. Input all the information in the FCF planning period formula, Equation 7-5.

EQUATION 7-5

Free Cash Flow for the Planning Period

	EBIT
−	Tax rate
+	Depreciation
−	Increase in operating working capital
−	Capital expenditure
	FCF for the planning period

10. Once the FCF for each year has been determined, a present value of the sum of the periods must be calculated. The discount rate is required to complete the calculation shown in Equation 7-6.

EQUATION 7-6

Present Value of Free Cash Flow for the Planning Period

PV of FCF planning period:

$$\frac{\text{Year 1 FCF}}{(1 + DR)} + \frac{\text{Year 2 FCF}}{(1 + DR)^2} + \frac{\text{Year 3 FCF}}{(1 + DR)^3} + \frac{\text{Year 4 FCF}}{(1 + DR)^4} + \cdots$$

Next, the present value of the residual must be determined. To do so, the first year's residual value must be calculated by simply forecasting the FCF for Year 6, the first year after the planning period. Then all the information should be put into the PV residuals formula, Equation 7-7.

E Q U A T I O N   7-7

Present Value Residuals

PV residuals:

$$\frac{\text{First year residual value/(discount rate } - \text{ growth rate)}}{(1 + \text{discount rate}) \times \text{number of years to discount back}}$$

The final number from this calculation should then be added to the PV of the FCF number to determine the company's value.

Let's determine the value of Bruce.com using the FCF model. The company is forecasting a conservative 10 percent growth rate. Its WACC is 13 percent, and its tax rate is 52 percent. The forecasted annual FCF is presented in Figure 7-8.

F I G U R E   7-8

Forecasted Annual Free Cash Flow Calculation, in Thousands of Dollars

	2000	2001	2002	2003	2004
EBIT	$1,398	$1,604	$1,789	$1,993	$2,217
− Tax (52%)	727	834	930	1,036	1,152
+ Depreciation	—	—	—	—	—
− Increase in working capital	56	144	158	175	191
− Capital expenditure	16	18	20	21	24
Forecasted annual FCF	**599**	**606**	**681**	**761**	**850**

The PV of the FCF planning period is determined as shown in Figure 7-9. With an estimated Year 6 FCF valuation of $960,300, the PV residual can be calculated using the equation in Figure 7-10. Now we can determine the value of Bruce.com. As you can see in Figure 7-11, Bruce.com's value is $19,798,746.

It should be noted that 88 percent of the company's value comes from the residual value. Also, this FCF valuation formula is very sensitive to slight changes in the growth and discount rates. For example, if the discount rate were 0.17 instead of 0.13, an 18 percent difference, the value of Bruce.com would decrease by 57 percent, to $8,430,776. The PV residual would be $6,264,187, and the PV of the FCF would be $2,166,589.

F I G U R E   7-9

Present Value of Free Cash Flow for the Planning
Period Calculation

PV of FCF for the planning period:

$$\frac{599}{(1 + 0.13)^1} + \frac{606}{(1 + 0.13)^2} + \frac{681}{(1 + 0.13)^3} + \frac{761}{(1 + 0.13)^4} + \frac{85}{(1 + 0.13)^5} =$$

$530,088 + $473,437 + $469,655 + $466,871 + $461,956 = $2,402,007

F I G U R E   7-10

Present Value of the Residual Calculation

PV residual:

$$\frac{\$960,300/(0.13 - 0.10)}{(1 + 0.13)^5} = \frac{\$960,300/0.03}{1.84} = \$17,396,739$$

F I G U R E   7-11

Valuation Calculation

$17,396,739	PV of the residual
+ 2,402,007	PV of the FCF
$19,798,746	Bruce.com valuation

The criticisms of this model are that it is too theoretical and complex and that it is filled with uncertainties. The three major uncertainties are the FCF projections, the discount rate, and the growth rate. Nobody truly knows. It is all educated speculation. As Bill Sutter, the venture capitalist at Mesirow Partners and a Stanford Business School graduate with a major in finance who was mentioned earlier in this chapter, noted in a lecture to graduate business school students:

> Valuation is remarkably unscientific. You can take out your FCF models, Alcar models, talk about your capital asset pricing model and betas until you are blue in the face. I have not used any of those since I got out of business school. Frankly, that is not the way we operate. You can use it for your finance class but you are not going to use it out in the real world.

VALUING TECHNOLOGY AND INTERNET COMPANIES

In most instances, the valuation methods discussed in this chapter were not applicable when valuing start-up Internet and related technology companies during the 1990s. The P/E ratio method could not be used because the companies had no "E." Until 2000, Internet companies that had negligible or no present cash flow streams, and in most instances did not expect to get positive cash flow streams for years to come, had been valued at extremely high prices at the time they went public. Examples of this include Netscape, Yahoo!, and Amazon.com, to name just a few of the better-known brand names.

When Netscape, the Internet browser company, went public in 1996, the value of its stock went from $28 to $171 per share over a three-month period, despite the fact that the company had never made a profit. AOL eventually acquired Netscape.

In 1995, two Stanford Ph.D. students founded Yahoo!, the Internet search engine company. In 1996, with annual revenues of $1.4 million and profits of only $81,000, the company went public at a valuation of $850 million. In 1999, Yahoo!'s $19 billion market value was equivalent to that of CBS, which had 37 times Yahoo!'s revenues.

Finally, the most famous e-commerce company, Amazon.com, which went public in May 1997 at a value of $500 million despite the absence of any historical, present, or near-term projected profits, once had a value greater than profitable Fortune 500 companies such as Sears, as noted earlier in this chapter. Another example: the Internet firm Epigraph had expected revenues of $250,000 in 1999 and $1.4 million in 2000. When asked when his company might become profitable, the founder responded, "Oh, come on. We're an Internet company!"[27]

In the late 1990s, the prices of Internet and technology companies soared enormously: Dell Computer rose 249 percent in 1998, Amazon.com went up 966 percent during the same year, and Yahoo! went up 584 percent, while eBay rose 1240 percent from its initial offering price. These valuations called into question whether conventional valuation methods were applicable in estimating the worth of Internet stocks. As one stockbroker noted, "I don't know how you value these things. It's a new set of rules. The Internet stocks are bizarre and outrageous."[28] And as we all discovered, many of those high-flying Internet stocks could be hazardous to one's health.

A prominent investor, Warren Buffett, the CEO of Berkshire Hathaway, who has forgone any significant investment in technology-related stocks, was also baffled by these stocks' valuations. At a 1999 news conference, he cheerfully closed a discussion of how he thought business schools should teach the principles of valuing companies by saying, "I would say for a final exam, here's the stock of any Internet company, what is it worth? And anybody who gave an answer, flunks."

Warren Buffett and others who believed that Internet stocks were valued more on hope and on hype than on real numbers were justifiably concerned that most Internet companies had high debt levels, few assets, and, most importantly, a limited, if any, history of profits. Despite this, investors were more than willing to pay premium prices for their stocks, with the expectation that these companies would eventually produce significant earnings.

Therefore, given all this controversy, what was (were) the best method(s) to use for valuing technology and Internet companies? Quite frankly, all of them had major drawbacks. The least practical method seemed to be a multiple of earnings or cash flow. As stated earlier, most of these companies had not only negative earnings but also negative cash flow. For example, in 1998, *Forbes* magazine identified what it called "the Internet landscape," which included 46 companies that covered the breadth of the Internet market, from semiconductor chips to sports commentary. Only 14 (or 35 percent) of the companies had had at least a breakeven net income for the previous 12 months. Despite this fact, the value of the lowest company was $182 million.[29]

Using the comparable valuation method also created problems. The process of borrowing a valuation from a similar company that had been priced by an acquisition or some other event did not work very convincingly either, says columnist Jim Jubak, especially given the fact that all Internet companies might be overpriced.[30] For example, two Internet service providers, Mindspring Enterprises Inc. and EarthLink Network Inc., were sold in 1998. Their selling prices translated into a value of $1,500 per subscriber. In mid-1998, America Online (AOL), the largest and most prominent Internet service

provider—now operated by Time Warner—had 14 million sub-
scribers. If AOL were valued based on comparable subscriber rates,
the company's value at the time would have been $21 billion, not the
actual $14 billion. Thus, using the comparable method would have
foolishly suggested that AOL was 33 percent undervalued.

Even the most popular and seemingly acceptable valuation
method for the Internet industry, the multiple of revenues, had many
justifiable critics. The rule of thumb was to use a multiple of between
5 and 7 times a company's projected, not current, revenues to determine valuation. The multiple would go up or down depending on
the company's revenue growth rates and gross margins.

Criticisms of this model included the fact that a 5 to 7 multiple for companies that had low or no profits seemed excessively
high when a company like Sears was valued at a revenue multiple
of 1 and a profitable media company such as Gannett was valued
at a multiple of 5. The other problem was that the value was based
on projected revenues, not present. If Amazon.com as of the third
quarter of 1999 had been valued based on present revenues, the
multiplier would have been an astonishing 20 times. Even more
astounding is that, because of the use of projected revenues, a company like Yahoo! had a $19 billion market value, similar to that
of CBS television, despite the fact CBS had revenues 37 times those
of Yahoo!.

Another example of the craziness of the revenue valuation
model previously used to value Internet companies was a company called Rhythms NetConnections, a high-speed Internet access
firm. Rhythms NetConnections, with revenues of $5.8 million, was
valued at $3.1 billion, or 539 times revenues. In defense of this
multiple, the founder said it was justified because Rhythms
NetConnections was growing exponentially, doubling its size
every quarter.[31] On August 1, 2001, Rhythms NetConnections and
all of its wholly owned U.S. subsidiaries voluntarily filed for reor-
ganization under Chapter 11.

To get a sense of perspective, let us look at the Standard &
Poor's Industrial 400. If the companies on this list were valued
based on multiples of revenues, their historical median from 1956 to
1997 is 0.9 times. The highest the multiple ever got during the 1990s
in a frothy public market was a whopping 2.2 multiple of sales. The
previous record multiple was 1.25 times, in the mid-1960s.

The final criticism of the revenue method was based on the discovery that many Internet companies were reporting "virtual revenue." The revenue was not real. For example, the companies recognized as revenues the value of the ad space that they exchanged with each other for space on their sites. While the recognition of revenue in such a situation had to be offset by an expense on the income statement, the expense became irrelevant because valuation was based only on revenues. Since the expense was irrelevant, this practice encouraged companies to inflate the price of their bartered ad space. Another challenge to this practice was the fact that there was no guarantee that if the ad space had not been bartered, it would have been sold. Thus, bartering was very important to a company's reported revenue. Internet.com did not include bartered ads in its revenues. Its CEO, Alan Meckler, says that this hurt the value of his company's stock, because competitors that included barter appeared to be doing better.[32] Figure 7-12 lists several public companies that, according to their company reports, included bartered ads in their revenue in 1998.

FIGURE 7-12

Bartered Advertisements

Company	Percent of Revenue from Barter
CNet	6
Yahoo!	<10
EarthWeb	11
SportsLine USA	20

Not surprisingly, private companies that were planning to go public realized the value of recognizing barter. Deja.com, an online chat site that went public in 1999, reported 1998 revenues of $5 million. Over 25 percent of that reported revenue came from barter. After 6 years of no profits, Deja.com went out of business in 2001 and sold its assets to the search engine Google.

Given the fact that most Internet and e-commerce companies did not have earnings or positive cash flows, the commonly used and accepted valuation model was a multiple of revenues. Therefore, the companies were in constant aggressive pursuit of increased revenues to bolster their valuations. As stated earlier, this practice of rewarding revenues without regard to profit seemingly encouraged more companies to recognize "virtual revenue." The standard accounting rules, which have now been revised, vaguely stated that retailers that do not assume the risk of holding inventory are "business agents" and should book as revenue only the difference between what the retail customer pays and the wholesale price. Therefore, if a retailer charges a customer $200 for a bike that will be shipped to the customer directly from the manufacturer (i.e., drop-shipped) and the manufacturer charges the retailer $100, the amount of revenue recognized by the retailer should be the $100 difference, not $200.

The vagueness of the accounting rules resulted in Internet companies recognizing revenues differently. This inconsistency made some companies seem significantly larger than others. For example, Preview Travel's CFO, Bruce Carmedelle, said that rival Priceline.com appeared to be 10 times larger even though it "sells only a few more tickets than we do." At one time, Priceline.com counted as revenue what customers paid for airline tickets, while Preview counted only the commissions it got from carriers.

This virtual revenue phenomenon also occurred when a company generated sales both by shipping inventory from its warehouse and by having the products shipped directly from its supplier's warehouse to the end customer. Ideally, the revenue amounts should have been recognized differently. In the former case, the amount of revenue that should have been recognized was the total price that the customer paid. In the latter case, where the product was being drop-shipped, the revenue recognized should have been only the difference between the retail and wholesale prices. Xoom.com, now part of NBCi, was one of the companies that adhered to this practice. But many other companies, such as Theglobe.com, booked revenue the same way in all cases, although some items came from company warehouses and others from suppliers.[33]

Theglobe.com would soon see its world come crashing down. From its opening-day high of $97 in 1998, the stock was delisted and trading for just 7 cents a share in late 2001. The technology industry, which came under justifiable criticism for overvaluation of companies without profits, began using the multiple of gross margin method. This method became more popular after it was realized that the multiple of revenues method had encouraged these companies to generate revenue without regard to gross, operating, or net profits. The result of the revenue method was the creation of companies such as Buy.com that sold products at prices below cost. This was sheer madness.

Beginning in April 2000, the valuation of technology companies began declining rapidly. For example, IWon purchased Web portal Excite.com in 2001 for $10 million. In 1997, Excite.com was worth $6.1 billion. As a comparison to their lofty status in 2000, Table 7-12 list the current P/E ratio (where it exists) for the five firms with the highest P/E ratios in the 2000 *USA Today* Internet 100 (now the Internet 50). As you can see, only two of the firms are still publicly traded today—at P/E ratios significantly lower than in 2000; one firm, Exodus Communications, went bankrupt; and two firms were acquired at fractions of their market values just 8 years earlier.

T A B L E   7-12

Current Status of Firms with Highest P/E Multiples in the 2000 USA Today Internet 100

Firm	2000 P/E	2008 P/E
Infospace.com	599.3	22.8
Exodus Communications	634	N/A (bankrupt)
Vertical Net	854	N/A (acquired for $15 million in 2007)
Covad Communications	922	N/A (acquired for $1.02 per share)
CMGI	1,228	18.77

Another thing that positively affected the value of publicly traded Internet companies was the fact that they had "thin floats." This means that most of the company's stock was controlled by insiders, such as the management team and other employees. Therefore, public investors held very little stock. The result was that it did not take a lot of buying by the public to increase the share price. Examples of companies that had thin floats are listed in Table 7-13. In contrast, companies with typical levels of stock held by the public include those listed in Table 7-14.

T A B L E   7-13

Companies with Thin Floats, 1999

Company	Held by Insiders	Public Float
eHome	69%	31%
Amazon.com	65%	35%
Broadcast.com	65%	35%
eBay	91%	9%
Yahoo!	49%	51%

T A B L E   7-14

Publicly Held Stock Levels

Company	Held by Insiders	Public Float
Microsoft	94%	6%
AOL	92%	8%
Adobe Systems	92%	8%
Dell Computer	92%	8%
Intuit	92%	8%

Source: *Barron's*, December 21, 1998.

While we correctly criticized the looniness of valuations during the Internet craze, it is important that the lesson learned be greater than a few jokes. The primary lesson learned is that whether one operates in a new economy, an old economy, or a future economy, financial fundamentals, relative to profitability and valuation, will always be important because they have passed the test of time.

N O T E S

1. Julie Schmidt, "Apple: To Be or Not to Be Operating System Is the Question," *USA Today*, September 24, 1996.
2. Thomas G. Stemberg, *Staples for Success: From Business Plan to Billion-Dollar Business in Just a Decade Knowledge Exchange*, 1996.
3. Ibid.

4. Ibid.
5. *Chicago Tribune,* April 7, 2007.
6. Stemberg, "Staples for Success."
7. Ibid.
8. Ibid.
9. Udayan Gupta, "Companies Enjoy Privacy as Need for Public Deals Ebbs," *Wall Street Journal,* December 17, 1995.
10. "Sperling Says Debt Crunch Could Tighten PE Purse Strings," Deal Journal, *Wall Street Journal,* July 25, 2007.
11. Bill Haynes, "Industry Risk—Merger Professionals Bullish about Continued Availability of Debt," Global Association of Risk Professionals, July 19, 2007.
12. "Venture Capital Industry Overview," Dow Jones VentureSource.
13. *Forbes,* July 27, 1998, p. 112.
14. Stephanie Gruner, "The Trouble with Angels," *Inc.,* p. 47.
15. Bill Sutter, classroom presentation at Kellogg School of Management, March 10, 1999.
16. *Crain's Chicago Business,* May 5, 2008, p. 2.
17. Jeanne Dugan, "Will Triarc Make Snapple Crackle?" *BusinessWeek,* April 28, 1997.
18. *Chicago Sun-Times,* July 7, 2008.
19. *Wall Street Journal,* March 30, 1998.
20. *Forbes,* June 15, 1998.
21. *Newsletter of Corporate Renewal,* February 14, 2000.
22. Tim Jones, "Rich Harvests in Television's Killing Fields," *Chicago Tribune,* October 22, 1995.
23. Project for Excellence in Journalism, "The State of the News Media 2007."
24. Brian Edwards and Mary Ann Sabo, "A Grim Tale," *Chicago Tribune,* October 29, 1999, Section 6N.
25. Ibid.
26. *Barron's,* September 15, 1997.
27. *Crain's Chicago Business,* September 27, 1999, p. 57.
28. *Forbes,* July 27, 1998, p. 112.
29. "Jubak's Journal: Putting a Price on the Future," *Forbes.*
30. Ibid.
31. Robert McGough, "No Earnings? No Problem! Price-Sales Ratio Use Rises," *Wall Street Journal,* November 26, 1999, pp. C1–2.

32. Matt Krantz, "Web Site Revenue May Not Be Cash," *USA Today*, September 9, 1999, p. 1B.

33. Matt Krantz, "Vague Rules Let Net Firms Inflate Revenue," *USA Today*, November 22, 1999, p. 1B.

CHAPTER 8

Raising Capital

Money is always dull, except when you haven't got any, and then it's terrifying.

Sheila Bishop, *The House with Two Faces* (1960)

INTRODUCTION

As Gene Wang, a successful business owner, noted, for the entrepreneur who is in the capital-raising stage, there are four important things to do:

1. Never run out of money.
2. Really understand your business or product.
3. Have a good product.
4. Never run out of money.[1]

These are great words of advice, but for many entrepreneurs, accomplishing points 1 and 4 is easier said than done.

One of the most common complaints about entrepreneurship concerns money. Entrepreneurs repeatedly lament the fact that raising capital is their greatest challenge because there seemingly is never enough and the fund-raising process takes too long. These are not groundless complaints. Thomas Balderston, a venture capitalist, said, "Too few entrepreneurs recognize that raising capital is a continuing process."[2] Also, it is extremely tough, as it should be, to raise capital, be it debt or equity, for start-ups, expansions, or acquisitions. The process typically takes several years and multiple rounds.

The founding and funding of Google is a classic example of this process. Initially, college friends Sergey Brin and Larry Page maxed out their credit cards to buy the terabytes of storage that they needed to start Google. Next, they raised $100,000 from Andy Bechtolsheim, one of the founders of Sun Microsystems, and another $900,000 from their network of family, friends, and acquaintances. Subsequently, Google raised $24 million from two venture capital firms and $1.67 billion from its IPO. The company was $3\frac{1}{2}$ years old when it raised venture capital, and $8\frac{1}{2}$ when it had its initial public offering (IPO).[3]

Why is it so difficult to raise capital? The most logical reason is that capital providers are taking major risks in financing entrepreneurial ventures. Remember the statistic cited in Chapter 2? Roughly 60 percent of businesses fail within the first 4 years, and almost nine out of ten fail within 10 years. Over a long time window, the success rate is only 10 percent. Given this fact, capital providers are justified in performing lengthy due diligence to determine the creditworthiness of entrepreneurs. It may seem sacrilegious for this author to say, but it must be said: those who become entrepreneurs are not entitled to financing simply because they joined the club.

As stated in Chapter 1, one of my objectives for this book is to supply you with information, insights, and advice that will, I hope, increase your chances of procuring capital. Here are some words on the advice front: since it is so tough to raise capital, the entrepreneur must be *steadfast and undeviating* in this pursuit. Recall from Chapter 2 that this is one of the traits of successful high-growth entrepreneurs. They are not quitters. They are thick-skinned enough that hearing the word *no* does not completely deter or terminate their efforts. A great example of an entrepreneur with such perseverance is Howard Schultz, the CEO of Starbucks. When he was in search of financing for the acquisition of Starbucks, he approached 242 people and was rejected 217 times. He finally procured the financing, acquired the company, and today boasts a public company that has 12,400 locations and more than 145,000 employees.[4]

VALUE-ADDED INVESTORS

Howard Schultz and all other successful high-growth entrepreneurs know not only that it is important to raise the proper amount of capital at the best terms, but that it is even more important to raise it from the right investors. There is an old saying in entrepreneurial finance: whom you raise money from is more important than the amount or the cost. The ideal is to raise capital from "value-added" investors. These are people who provide you with value in addition to their financial investment. For example, value-added investors may give the company legitimacy and credibility because of their upstanding reputation.

Value-added investors also include those who help entrepreneurs acquire new customers, employees, or additional capital. A great example of an entrepreneur who understands the importance of value-added investors is the founder of eBay, who accepted capital from the famous venture capital firm Benchmark. Ironically, eBay did not really need the money. It has always been profitable. It took $5 million from Benchmark for two reasons. The first was that it felt that Benchmark's great reputation would give eBay credibility. The second was that it wanted Benchmark, which had extensive experience in the public markets, to help eBay make an IPO.

Another great example of an entrepreneur who understood the importance of a value-added investor is Jeff Bezos of Amazon.com. When pursuing venture capital financing, Bezos rejected money from two funds that offered a higher valuation and better terms than Kleiner Perkins Caufield & Byers (KPCB), which he accepted. When asked why he took KPCB's lower bid, he responded, "If we'd thought all this was purely about money, we'd have gone with another firm. But KPCB is the gravitational center of a huge piece of the Internet world. Being with them is like being on prime real estate."[5]

In addition to investing $8 million, KPCB also helped persuade Scott Cook, the chairman of Intuit, to join Amazon.com's board. KPCB also immediately helped Bezos recruit two vice presidents and, in May 1997, helped him take Amazon.com public.

While these two examples highlight only venture capitalists, it must be made perfectly clear that there are several other sources of value-added capital.

SOURCES OF CAPITAL

The source of capital that gets the most media attention is venture capital funds. But in reality, as Figure 8-1 shows, these funds have been a small contributor to the total annual capital provided to entrepreneurs. According to the 2006 Global Entrepreneurship Monitor (GEM) report on financing, eliminating venture capital would not make a perceptible difference in entrepreneurial activity overall because fewer than 1 in 10,000 new ventures has venture capital in hand at the outset, and fewer than 1 in 1,000 businesses ever has venture capital at any time during its existence. According to the GEM, across the world, 62 percent of start-up funds comes from the entrepreneurs themselves, with the remaining 38 percent coming from external sources.[6]

FIGURE   8-1

Sources of Small-Businesses Financing

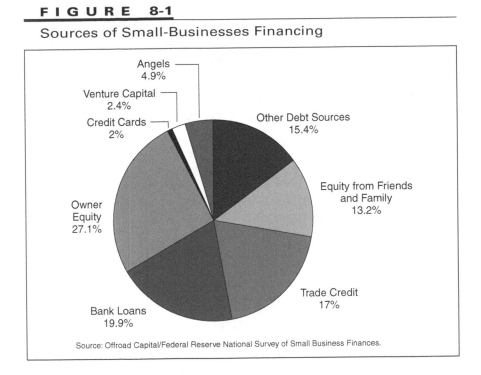

Source: Offroad Capital/Federal Reserve National Survey of Small Business Finances.

Money from friends, family, and the owners themselves is a bit more difficult to track. Table 8-1 shows data from a study conducted a few years back that examines the more formal sources of financing for entrepreneurs, and it shows that banks, with $179 billion in annual loans to small businesses at that time, were the most active backers of entrepreneurs. The number two providers, with $9.6 billion, were nonbank financial institutions such as GE Capital and Prudential Insurance. Venture capital was less than one-tenth of the amount of capital provided by banks. These relative levels have not changed drastically today.

TABLE 8-1

Sources of Capital for Entrepreneurs

Banks	$179 billion
Nonbanks	96 billion
Angels	30 billion
Venture capitalists	10 billion
Other	20 billion
Total capital	$335 billion

The fact that banks are more important to entrepreneurship than venture capitalists can be further highlighted by the fact that even the most active venture capitalist will finance only 15 to 25 deals a year after receiving as many as 7,000 business plans. The result is that in fiscal year 2000, after receiving approximately 8 million business plans, the entire venture capital industry invested in a record 5,380 companies. This is akin to a pebble in the ocean compared with banks. Arthur Andersen reported that each year, approximately 37 percent of the more than 20 million small-business owners apply for a commercial loan, and bankers reject only 25 percent.

THE INVESTMENT IS IN THE ENTREPRENEUR

While there are many sources of capital, there are basically two ways to finance a business: the capital can be invested in the form of debt or in the form of equity. Be it debt or equity, the most important determinant of whether the capital will be provided is the entrepreneur and his management team. As venture capitalist

Richard Kracum of Wind Point Partners said, "During the course of 70 investments we have made in many different kinds of situations over a 16 year period, we have observed that the quality of the CEO is the top factor in the success of the investment. We believe that the CEO represents approximately 80% of the variance of outcome of the transaction."[7]

The importance of the entrepreneur can be further supported by a statement from Leslie Davis, former vice president at South Shore Bank in Chicago, who said, "The most important thing we consider when reviewing a loan application is the entrepreneur. Can we trust him to do what he said he would do in his business plan?" Banks, just like venture capitalists, bet on the jockey. Now, the horse (the business) can't be some run-down creature knocking on the door to the glue factory, but ultimately, financial backers have to trust the management team. What are investors primarily looking for in entrepreneurs? Ideally, investors prefer people who have both entrepreneurial and specific industry experience.

As Table 8-2 shows, investors grade entrepreneurs as either "A," "B," or "C." They believe the best entrepreneurs to invest in are the "A" entrepreneurs, people who have experience as an owner or even an employee in an entrepreneurial firm, and also experience in the industry that the company will compete in.

T A B L E   8-2

Investor Ratings of Entrepreneurs

Rating	Experience
A	Entrepreneurship and industry
B	Entrepreneurship or industry
C	No entrepreneurship or industry

The second most desirable investment candidates are the "B" entrepreneurs, who have experience either in entrepreneurship or in the industry, but not both.

The last category of people is the least attractive to investors. People who fall into this category should try to eliminate at least one of the shortcomings prior to seeking capital. As one investor said, "There is nothing worse than a young person with no experiences. The combination is absolutely deadly." There is nothing a young person can do about her age except wait for time to pass. But experience can be gained by working for an entrepreneur and/or in the desired industry.

The financing spectrum in Figure 8-1 best depicts the financing sources typically used by start-up entrepreneurs. In Chapter 9, "Debt Financing," we will discuss each of these sources in greater detail. And at the end of Chapter 9, we will show how one entrepreneur became successful by using almost all the sources. Using all the sources is quite common among successful high-growth entrepreneurs.

FIGURE 8-2

Financing Spectrum

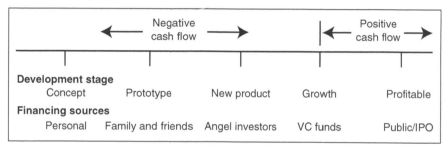

NOTES

1. *Chicago Sun-Times*, April 4, 1996, p. 44.
2. *Business Philadelphia Magazine*, November 1996.
3. Global Entrepreneurship Monitor, "2006 Financing Report," p. 14.
4. Starbucks, 2006 Annual Report, Starbucks home page, www.starbucks.com.
5. *The New Yorker*, August 11, 1997.
6. Global Entrepreneurship Monitor, "2006 Financing Report," p. 12.
7. *Buyouts*, February 19, 2001, p. 56.

CHAPTER 9

Debt Financing

INTRODUCTION

Bill Gates has a rule that Microsoft, rather than incurring debt, must always have enough money in the bank to run for a year even with no revenues.[1] In 2007, Microsoft had $23.4 billion in cash on its balance sheet.[2] Unfortunately, 99.9 percent of entrepreneurs will never be able to emulate this financing plan. Therefore, they must be willing to pursue and accept debt financing.

Debt is money provided in exchange for the owner's word (sometimes backed up by tangible assets as collateral as well as the personal guarantees of the owner) that the original investment plus a predetermined fixed or variable interest rate will be repaid in its entirety over a set period of time.

As we saw in Chapter 8, banks have been by far the biggest source of capital for entrepreneurs on an annual basis. In June 2004, commercial banks had a total of $1.4 trillion in business loans outstanding (in other words, total loans, not just the notes written that year). Of that, 38 percent, or $522 billion, was in small-business loans (loans of less than $1 million).[3]

In today's environment, lenders want to see a company's capital structure with debt equivalent to no more than 4.3 times EBITDA.[4]

TYPES OF DEBT

There are basically four types of debt: senior, subordinated (some-times called sub debt), short-term, and long-term. The first two refer to the order of entitlement or preference that the lender has against the debt recipient. Senior debt holders have top priority over all other debt and equity providers. The senior holders are the "secured creditors," who have an agreement that they are to be paid before any other creditors. If the company is dissolved, the senior holders are entitled to be paid first and "made whole" as much as possible by selling the company's assets. After the senior debt holders have been completely repaid, the remaining assets, if there are any, can go to the providers of subordinated debt.

A lender does not automatically get the senior position simply because he made the first loan. The lender must request this posi-tion, and all other present and future lenders must approve it. This can sometimes be a problem because some lenders may refuse to subordinate their loan to any others. If the other lenders will not acquiesce, then the loan is generally not made.

Sub debt, also referred to as mezzanine debt, is subordinated to senior debt but ranks higher than equity financing. The term *mezzanine* comes from the theater, where there are often three levels, with the middle level being called the mezzanine. Both types of debt are used for financing working capital, capital expenditures, and acquisitions. Mezzanine financing usually occurs after senior lenders exhaust their lending capabilities. Finally, because it is in a subordinate position, mezzanine debt is typically more expensive than senior debt.

Mezzanine and senior debt, in addition to equity, constitute a company's capital structure, which describes how the company finances itself. Therefore, when a company's capital structure is said to be highly leveraged, this means that it has a large amount of long-term debt.

Debt that is amortized over a period longer than 12 months is considered long-term debt (LTD). It can be senior or mezzanine. It is found in the balance sheet in the long-term liabilities section. Loans for real estate and equipment are usually multiyear, long-term debt obligations.

In contrast, short-term debt (STD) is that which is due within the next 12 months. STD comes in two forms: revolver debt, which is used for working capital, and current maturity of long-term debt. It is found in the balance sheet in the current liabilities section. This debt typically has a higher cost than does long-term debt. Short-term debt is usually used to buy inventory and to fund day-to-day operating needs.

Let's look at the strengths and weaknesses of debt financing.

Pros

- The entrepreneur retains complete ownership.
- The cost of capital is low.
- Loan payments are predictable.
- There is a 5- to 7-year payback period.
- It can involve value-added lenders.
- It provides tax benefits.

Cons

- Personal guarantees are required.
- The lender can force the business into bankruptcy.
- Amounts may be limited to value of the company's assets.
- Payments are due regardless of the company's profits.

SOURCES OF DEBT FINANCING

The major sources of debt financing are personal savings, family and friends, angels, foundations, government, banks, factors, customer financing, supplier financing, purchase order financing, and credit cards. Let's review these sources in more detail.

Personal Savings

An entrepreneur often uses her own money to finance the company. This is especially true in the early stages of a start-up. The Global Entrepreneurship Monitor's "2006 Financing Report" showed that 62 percent of the funds available to start-ups across the globe came from the entrepreneurs themselves.[5] The primary reason for this is that banks and other institutional debt providers do not supply start-up capital because it is too risky. Start-ups have no history of cash flow that can be used to repay the debt obligation.

Using the entrepreneur's own capital is commonly referred to as "bootstrapping." This is how, for example, Ernest and Julio Gallo started their wine business in a rented warehouse in Modesto, California, in 1933, at the heart of the Depression. After researching the industry at the local library, they decided to start their business using what little capital they had, and they convinced local farmers to provide them with grapes and defer payment until the wine was sold. They also bought crushing and fermenting equipment on 90-day terms. Today, the company started by these two bootstrappers enjoys annual worldwide sales of more than $900 million. Other examples of bootstrapping include Domino's Pizza, Hallmark Cards, Black & Decker, and Ross Perot's EDS.[6]

Often the start-up investments are made in the form of equity instead of debt. But there are no rules that require such an equity investment. An entrepreneur's ownership stake does not have to come from his capital investment. In fact, it should come from his hard work, called "sweat equity." My advice is that all investments that the entrepreneur makes in his company should be in the form of debt at a reasonable interest rate. The repayment of this debt allows the entrepreneur to receive capital from the company without the money being taxed because it was simply the return of the original investment. The interest payment would be deductible by the company, reducing its tax liability. The entrepreneur would be required to pay personal taxes on the interest earned.

All of this is more favorable to the entrepreneur than if the capital were invested as equity. In that case, if it were repaid by the company, it would be taxed at the investor's personal tax level, and any dividends would also be taxed. Unlike interest payments, dividends paid are not tax-deductible. Therefore, the company would receive no tax reduction benefits.

Family and Friends

As stated earlier, it is virtually impossible to procure debt financing for start-ups. Therefore, an obvious viable alternative is family and friends. The benefit of raising debt capital from this source is multifold. Raising money may be easier and faster because the lenders are providing the capital for emotional rather than business reasons. They want to support the family member or friend. That was the case with Jeff Bezos's first outside lenders, who were his parents. Another benefit, especially with debt, is that if repayments cannot be made, these lenders may be more conciliatory than institutional lenders. Unlike the latter, they are not likely to force the entrepreneur into bankruptcy if he defaults on the loan.

The negative aspects of procuring money from family and friends exceed the positives, however. First, these are typically not value-added investors. Second, they may not be "sophisticated investors," which we will discuss in more detail later in this chapter. They may not understand either the risk of the investment or its form. Regarding the first point, they may not really comprehend the fact that such an investment might be completely lost, yielding no capital return at all. They expect to be repaid no matter what happens. They also may not realize that as debt investors, they are not entitled to any ownership stake, only a predetermined interest payment and the return of their original investment. This usually becomes an issue when the entrepreneur is extremely successful in increasing the company's value. In such a case, many family members and friends may not be content with simply having their principal returned and earning interest on that money. They expect to share in the firm's value appreciation. In essence, they expect their debt to be treated as equity. If it is not, they feel that they have been cheated by their own child, grandchild, niece or nephew, or childhood friend.

This final point leads to the greatest problem with raising debt capital from family and friends: there is a risk of irreparably damaging or losing important personal relationships. As one professor said, "Remember these are people whom you eat Thanksgiving with, and it may not be safe to sit next to your uncle if you have lost all his money and he has sharp utensils in his hands."

In closing, my advice is to refrain from raising debt capital from family and friends. If this cannot be avoided, adhere to the following recommendations:

- Raise money only from those who can afford to lose the entire amount. Do not get money from a grandparent who has no savings and lives on a fixed government income.

Make it clear to the family members that they are putting
their entire investment at risk; therefore, there is a chance
that it may not be repaid.

- Write a detailed loan agreement clearly highlighting the
  interest, the payment amounts, and the expected payment
  dates.
- The agreement should give the investor the right to
  convert any or all of the investment into company stock,
  thereby giving the investor an ownership stake if
  desirable.

  Alternatively, the agreement should be that the
  investment is mezzanine financing, which is debt with
  equity. The investor receives all of the investment back,
  interest, and an equity stake in the company.
- Personally guarantee at least the amount of the investment
  and at most the investment plus the amount of interest
  that the investment could have gained had it been put in a
  safe certificate of deposit. Today that would yield
  approximately 4 percent.

Angel Investors

Angel investors are typically wealthy individuals who invest in
companies. (The term was originally coined to describe individuals who were patrons of the arts.) They are different from family
and friends in that they usually do not know or have a relationship
with the entrepreneur prior to the investment. In addition, they are
sophisticated investors who thoroughly understand the risk of the
investment and are comfortably able to absorb a complete loss of
their investment. Angel investors are typically former entrepreneurs who focus on industries in which they have experience.
Prominent examples of companies that received angel investing
are the Ford Motor Company, The Body Shop, and Amazon.

With venture capital increasingly looking toward later-stage
investments, money from angels has provided the bulk of seed and
start-up capital in the United States, with some estimates placing
that percentage at as much 90 percent of all early-stage capital
provided in the country.[7] A University of New Hampshire study

estimated that in 2006, there were 234,000 active angel investors in the United States who annually provided $50,000 to $500,000 per deal in debt and equity to entrepreneurs. In 2006, angels funded 51,000 businesses at a cost of $25.6 billion. These numbers grew 10.8 percent and 3.0 percent, respectively, from 2005.[8] While increases in available capital from angels obviously delight entrepreneurs, they generate the opposite response from many in the institutional venture capital community, since they create more competition for deals and increase valuations. Some venture capitalists call money from angels "dumb money," alleging that it is far less than value-added money. In my opinion, such insulting comments are simply sour grapes.

For many years, angel investing has been an important part of the financial support and mentoring available to entrepreneurs that assists them in bridging the financing gap between the individual investments of friends and family members and the institutional venture capital provided by traditional VC firms. Increasingly, though, angel investors are formalizing into angel investor groups in order to attract better deals; provide infrastructure and support for the tax, legal, and other issues that arise from angel investing; and provide more formal support systems that allow them to increase their real and perceived "value added."[9] In 2006, there were nearly 250 formal angel investor groups in the United States, up from just below 100 groups in 1999.[10]

While most angels demand equity for their investments, there are some who have invested debt in companies that had "shaky credit" and had been dumped by their banks. In those instances, the angels restructured the loans at significantly higher interest rates.

The positive aspect of getting debt financing from angels is that they can be more flexible in their terms than an institution like a bank. For example, the angel can make a 10-year loan, whereas the maximum term of a bank's commercial loan is typically 5 to 7 years. Also, angel investors, unlike banks, make their own rules for lending. A bank may have a rule that a loan will not be provided to any applicant who has declared personal bankruptcy. The angel, on the other hand, uses her own discretion in determining whether she wants to make a loan to such a person.

On the negative side, the cost of debt capital from angels is usually higher than that of institutional financing. It is not unusual for these investors to charge entrepreneurs 2 percent per month, which equals an astounding annual rate of 24 percent. Not only is such a rate higher than the 2 to 3 percent over prime that banks usually charge their best customers, but it is also greater than the 18 percent that some credit cards charge their customers. The other negative is that, unlike banks, which cannot legally interfere with their customers' day-to-day business operations or strategy, the angel typically expects to be involved. For some entrepreneurs, this may ultimately cause problems.

When most people think about formal organizations that provide debt capital, banks are the first ones that come to mind. But as stated earlier, there are other types of debt providers. Let's review and discuss a few of these nonbank sources of capital.

Foundations

Another interesting source of capital for entrepreneurs is philanthropic organizations, including the Ford Foundation, the MacArthur Foundation, the Wieboldt Foundation, and the Retirement Research Foundation. Historically, these organizations have provided grants and loans only to not-for-profit entities. But since the beginning of the 1990s, they have broadened their loan activity to include for-profit companies that provide a social good. Eligible companies are those that explicitly state their intention to improve society by doing such things as employing former convicts, building homes in economically deprived areas, providing child-care services to single mothers, or offering computer training to low-income families. Specific examples include the MacArthur Foundation's loan to a Washington, D.C., publisher that tracks the economic policies of states. The loan was used by the company to purchase additional computers. Another example is the inventory loan that the Wieboldt Foundation made to a Chicago company called Commons Manufacturing that makes window blinds that go into public housing.[11]

Foundations also provide grants to community development corporations (CDCs), which, in turn, use the money to provide business loans. The objectives of the CDCs are the same as foundations', which is to lend capital to businesses that provide a benefit to society. An example of such a CDC is Coastal Enterprises, an organization in Maine that provides capital to companies that employ low-income people in Maine.

These loans from foundations and CDCs are called *program-related investments (PRIs)*. More than 550 organizations throughout the world provide PRIs, including those listed in Figure 9-1.

FIGURE 9-1

Program-Related Investment Organizations

Bhartiya Samruddhi Investments and Consulting Services
Hyderabad, India

BRIDGE Housing Corporation
San Francisco, California

Cooperative Housing Foundation
Silver Spring, Maryland

Corporation for Supportive Housing
New York, New York

Enterprise Corporation of the Delta
Jackson, Mississippi

MBA Properties
St. Louis, Missouri

MacArthur Foundation
Chicago, Illinois

Peer Partnerships
Cambridge, Massachusetts

Shorebank
Chicago, Illinois

Wieboldt Foundation
Chicago, Illinois

One of the attractive aspects of PRI loans to entrepreneurs is that interest rates can be as low as 1 percent with a 10-year amortization period. Another positive element is that the foundations can be considered to be value-added investors.

The David and Lucile Packard Foundation was the nation's largest PRI program in 2005, providing over $26 million in PRI investments.[12] If more information about PRIs is desired, two sources are a book entitled *Program Related Investments: A Guide to Funders and Trends* and *The PRI Directory: Charitable Loans and Other Program-Related Investments by Foundations*.

Government

Local, state, and federal government agencies have programs for providing loans to entrepreneurs. These programs are typically part of a municipality's economic development or commerce department. Some government loans are attractive because they offer below-market rates. SBA and CAP (capital access program) loans are usually market-priced, which we will discuss later. They are provided to companies that are geographically located in the municipal area, that can prove their ability to repay, and, just as importantly, that will use the money to retain existing jobs or create new jobs. Regarding the retention of jobs, entrepreneurs in Chicago have accessed capital from the city for the acquisition of a company based on the fact that if they did not buy the company, someone else might do so and move it, along with the jobs, to another city. Other entrepreneurs have procured expansion debt capital with the agreement that for every $20,000 that the city provides, one new job will be created in 18 to 24 months. Practically every town, city, and state provides such job-related debt financing.

The negative aspect of these loans on the local and state levels is that they often take a long time to procure. The applicant has to complete a lot of paperwork, and the process can take as long as 12 months.

A great periodical for identifying federal, state, and local government economic programs is *The Small Business Financial Resource Guide*, which can be received free by writing to the U.S. Chamber of Commerce Small Business Center at 1615 H Street, NW, Washington, D.C. 10062. It can also be ordered online through MasterCard's Web site at www.mastercard.com.[13]

Another drawback for some entrepreneurs is that the applicant must personally guarantee the loans. Personal guarantees will be discussed in more detail at the end of the discussion of debt.

Capital Access Programs

One local government program that does not take as long is your state or municipality's capital access program (CAP). There are presently 25 states and several cities that operate CAPs, which were first introduced in Michigan in 1986.[14] By 1998, CAPs had provided more than 25,000 loans totaling nearly $1.5 billion. While this is a pittance compared with the $19.1 billion guaranteed by the SBA, CAPs are rapidly becoming popular, as they compete with SBA loans.

The CAP loan product is a "credit enhancement" that induces banks to consider loan requests that they might otherwise have rejected because of deficiencies in collateral or cash flow. The mechanism for a CAP loan typically involves the bank and the borrower paying a fee ranging from 3 to 7 percent of the loan amount to a loan-loss reserve account held at the bank. This loan reserve contribution is then matched by state or local money, with the total reserve ranging from 6 to 14 percent of the loan. This amount is used to cover any loan losses.[15]

Banks seemingly like this state or local government–sponsored loan program because the banks, not the government agency, set the terms, rates, fees, and collateral. They do not have to get approval from any other organization or agency. Entrepreneurs like it for the same reason. The bank has the flexibility to approve a loan that may not qualify for SBA financing for one reason or another. Another attraction is that entrepreneurs have stated that CAP financing is faster than SBA loans. CAPs differ in the size of the eligible loans, the nature of eligible borrowers, and the size of the loan-loss reserve. Check with your state or municipality's economic development agency to determine if a CAP exists.

Small Business Administration Loan Program

Federal business loan programs fall under the authority of the U.S. Small Business Administration, which is the largest source of long-term small-business lending in the nation. Each year, the SBA guarantees loans totaling more than $19 billion. And since its inception in 1953, the agency has helped fund approximately 20 million businesses. There are two primary reasons for the popularity of SBA loans. First, the length of an SBA loan can be longer than that of a regular commercial loan. For example, an SBA-guaranteed loan can be for as long as 10 years for a working capital loan, compared with 1 to 5 years normally. Second, the SBA guarantees loans to borrowers who cannot get financing elsewhere.

It should be made perfectly clear that the SBA does not provide loans directly to entrepreneurs. It uses other financial institutions, banks and nonbanks, to do the actual lending. The SBA gives these approved institutions the authority to represent it as a lender and will guarantee up to 85 percent of the loan. For example, a lender, with the SBA's approval, may provide a $100,000 loan to the entrepreneur. If the recipient defaults on the loan, the lender has only 15 percent at risk because the SBA guarantees the balance of the loan.

Most of these loans go to established businesses. About one-third, or just over $6 billion, of SBA loans are lent to new businesses each year. A few start-ups that received SBA loans are Ben & Jerry's, Nike, Federal Express, Apple Computer, and Intel.

Some people foolishly believe that they can default on the loan because there will be minimal consequences. Nothing could be further from the truth. Remember, all SBA loans are personally guaranteed. Also, the lender, despite the SBA guarantee, will doggedly pursue the payment of as much of the loan as possible before requesting SBA reimbursement. The lender's reputation is on the line, and if the lender's loan default rate becomes too high, the SBA will discontinue that bank's participation in the program.

SBA lenders fall into three categories: general, certified, and preferred lenders. General lenders are those that have a small volume of deals or very little experience in providing SBA loans. Therefore, they must submit all of an applicant's loan information to the national SBA office to obtain its approval before they can approve a loan. The process can take several weeks and even months. In contrast, the other types of SBA lenders can act faster.

The most active and expert lenders qualify for the SBA's streamlined lending programs. Under these programs, lenders are given partial or full authority to approve loans, which results in faster service from the SBA. Certified lenders are those that have been heavily involved in regular SBA loan-guarantee processing and have met certain other criteria. They receive a partial delegation of authority and are given a 3-day turnaround on their applications by the SBA (they may also use regular SBA loan processing). Certified lenders account for 4 percent of all SBA business loan guarantees. Preferred lenders are chosen from among the SBA's best lenders and enjoy full delegation of lending authority in exchange for a lower rate of guarantee. This lending authority must be renewed at least every 2 years, and the SBA examines the lender's portfolio periodically. Preferred loans account for more than 21 percent of SBA loans.[16]

To find a list of the SBA lenders in any state, go to www.sba.gov or contact the SBA hotline at 800–827–5722. There is a publication available for each state that is updated at least every 2 years. It lists all the lenders and shows whether they are general, preferred, or certified. The SBA also posts a state-by-state listing of SBA preferred or certified lenders online

The SBA's most popular lending programs are the 7(a) Loan Guaranty, Micro Loan, and 504 (CDC) Loan programs. Before we look at each of these programs, let's discuss a few of the general highlights of SBA financing terms.

Depending on the program, loans can be amortized for as many as 25 years. Interest rates vary. The SBA charges the lender a fee between 3 and 3.5 percent of the loan, which is usually passed on to the loan recipient. And all investors with a stake of 20 percent or more in the company must personally guarantee the loan. Finally, if the loan is to be used to purchase another company, the seller must subordinate his financing of the company to the SBA. In fact, the SBA might require the seller to agree to "absolute subordination." In this case, no payments can be made to the seller as long as SBA money is outstanding.

To be eligible for an SBA loan, the business must qualify as a small business, be for-profit, not already have the internal resources to provide the financing, and be able to demonstrate repayment ability. The SBA uses varying requirements to determine whether a business is small; these requirements depend on various factors, including the industry in which the company operates. For example, because the SBA targets smaller companies, the applicant can't have a workforce the size of GE. If the company is in manufacturing, it cannot employ more than 1,500 people, and the maximum number of employees for a wholesale business is 100. The SBA's requirements and guidelines can be found at www.sba.gov.

A few types of businesses that are ineligible for SBA financing are not-for-profit organizations and institutions, lending companies, investment firms, gambling companies, life insurance companies, religion-affiliated companies, and companies that are owned by non-U.S. citizens.

7(a) Loan Guaranty program. The majority of SBA loans are made under this program. In 2006, $19.1 billion was guaranteed through 100,197 loans, with an average loan of $190,000.[17] (Figure 9-2 shows the top five 7(a) loan markets by state.) Essentially, the 7(a) program is a conventional bank loan of up to $2 million that receives an SBA guarantee. The SBA guarantees 85 percent of these loans up to $150,000 and 75 percent above $150,000. The proceeds can be used to purchase commercial real estate, business equipment, and machinery. They can also be used to refinance existing debt, for construction financing, and for working capital.

F I G U R E   9-2

Top Five SBA 7(a) Loan Markets by State, 2001

Top States	Total Loans, in Millions
California	$1,994
Texas	$918
New Jersey	$851
Minnesota	$567
Virginia	$415

Source: Small Business Administration.

There are personal net worth eligibility criteria for 7(a) loans. For example, for a $250,000 loan, the owner's net worth must be less than $100,000.

SBA Express Loan program. Express loans allow lenders to offer revolving credit lines that are renewable annually for up to 7 years and are administered within 36 hours. They are meant to overcome the difficulties that lenders face in making smaller loans that are too expensive to underwrite as part of the traditional 7(a) program. Under this program, loans under $25,000 do not require collateral. Lenders use their own application forms. The maximum loan amount is $350,000, with a 50 percent SBA guaranty. In some areas, there are special versions of this program for veterans (Patriot Express) and those doing business in low- and moderate-income areas (Community Express).

Loan prequalification. Business applicants with needs of less than $250,000 can be reviewed and potentially authorized by the SBA before the loans are taken to lenders for consideration. The program employs intermediary organizations to assist borrowers in developing a viable loan application. Small Business Development Centers (discussed later in this chapter) provide this service for free. For-profit organizations will charge a fee. The application is expedited by the SBA after submission. Interest rates, maturities, and guarantee percentages follow the 7(a) guidelines.[18]

Micro Loan program. Nonprofit groups such as community development corporations are the primary issuers of micro loans. These are the smallest loans guaranteed by the SBA, at levels as small as $450. The maximum is $35,000, with the average loan being $13,000. Since 1992, the SBA has provided loans totaling more than $321 million to over 28,000 borrowers. Interest rates on these loans are generally between 8 and 13 percent. In 2006, the Micro Loan program provided more than $33 million in loans to more than 2,500 borrowers. There are 170 intermediaries that disburse these loans.[19]

504 (CDC) Loan program. This loan program is a long-term financing tool for economic development within a community that is offered through certified development companies (CDCs) in an area. The program provides growing businesses with long-term, fixed-rate financing for major fixed assets, such as land and buildings. The funds cannot be used for working capital or inventory, consolidating or repaying debt, or refinancing. CDCs are nonprofit corporations set up to contribute to the economic development of their community and retain jobs. CDCs work with the SBA and private-sector lenders to provide financing to small businesses.

There are 270 CDCs nationwide, each covering a specific area. Loan amounts vary, but can be as large as $4 million. In 2006, the SBA approved 9,720 loans totaling $5.61 billion under this program.[20]

Nonbank SBA Lenders

As stated earlier, the SBA guarantees loans made by both banks and other financial institutions. These other lenders compete with banks by offering lower rates and faster loan approval. The SBA refers to these firms as small business lending companies (SBLCs).

One of the largest non-bank lenders is CIT Small Business Lending, a division of CIT Group Inc., which is a publicly traded global commercial finance company. CIT has been named the top SBA 7(a) lender for nine consecutive years and is one of the top lenders to minorities, women, and veterans in the country. The following are examples of some of CIT's primary lending criteria:

- Adequate historic cash flow to cover the debt
- Business debt to net worth ratio must meet industry average
- Borrowers must be actively involved in the day-to-day operation of the business
- Satisfactory personal credit histories are required for all principals and guarantors
- No past bankruptcies or felony arrests

Other prominent large non-bank SBA lenders include the Small Business Loan Source and Loan Source Financial. Unfortunately, as of this writing, the number of nonbank lenders is decreasing. Banks have lowered their rates to a point at which the nonbanks can no longer compete. One reason that banks have been able to do this is that their cost of capital is lower than that of nonbanks. Banks use the deposits they have, whereas nonbanks must get their money from the public capital markets. Another reason is that banks are using their commercial loans as "loss leaders." They will sacrifice returns on business loans to increase the number of customers who use many of their other services, such as online banking, personal savings, loan accounts, and cash management programs. Nonbanks that have departed from or significantly decreased their loan business include Heller Financial, Transamerica Finance, and The Money Store.[21]

Banks with SBA Loan Programs

Approximately 6,000 of the 8,799 banks in the country (down from 14,000 in 1997) use the SBA's guaranteed loan program. Certified lender status is held by 850 banks and preferred lender status by 450 banks. The Small Business Administration produces an annual report on the small-business lending activities of the nation's leading commercial banks. The SBA analyzes lending patterns and ranks "small-business-friendly" banks in every state and on a national level. The SBA says that its goal is to give small businesses an easy-to-use tool for locating likely loan sources in their communities. It also aims to nudge banks to compete more aggressively for small-firm customers. The report is a great resource for entrepreneurs trying to determine which banks will be more likely to lend a sympathetic ear and, more importantly, some cash for their business. The most recent report is titled "Small Business and Micro Business Lending, 2006–2007" and can be found at http://www.sba.gov/advo/research. This report covers micro lending (under $100,000) and small-business lending (between $100,000 and $1 million).

Advice for Getting an SBA Loan

It has been estimated that the SBA will approve less than 50 percent of requested loans. Some advice for improving your chance of obtaining an SBA-guaranteed loan is provided here:

- *Clean up your personal financial problems.* Most of the rejected loans are rejected because of the applicants' poor personal credit history. Before applying, the entrepreneur should reduce his credit card debt, and also the number of credit cards he has. Financiers are aware of these numbers and view holding too many credit cards negatively. It is especially important for loan applicants to know their three-digit credit or FICO score, which ranks their creditworthiness on a scale from 501 to 990. Finally, before applying, the entrepreneur should check with the major credit bureaus and make sure there are no errors on his credit reports. The bureaus are Equifax (www.equifax.com), TransUnion (www.transunion.com), and Experian (www.experian.com). Americans are entitled to one free credit report per year.

- *Define your goals realistically.* Apply for a specific dollar amount, and identify in detail how the funds will be used. Develop realistic, logical financial pro formas that show that even under the worst-case scenario, the debt can be repaid. At a minimum, most lenders want to see that a company's annual cash flow is 1.25 times its total annual loan obligations (principal and interest). Do not plug in numbers. Do not ask for money that you cannot forecast being paid back.
- *Begin early.* Apply for financing at least 6 months before the money is needed.
- *Work with experienced lenders.* Apply to institutions that have certified or preferred lender status.
- *Submit an excellent business plan.* Follow the guidelines and advice presented in Chapter 3 regarding the development of a business plan. Make sure the entire plan, especially the executive summary, is well written, clear, and thorough. Just as important, check and recheck all numbers, making sure that they are correct and that the math is perfect. All numbers must add up.
- *Collect preapplication information.* Loans for existing and start-up businesses require much of the same information, including:
  - The personal tax returns of all investors with at least 20 percent ownership for the past 3 years
  - The personal financial statements for all investors with at least 20 percent ownership
  - The ownership documents, including franchise agreements and incorporation papers

  A few pieces of information are needed for an existing business that are not needed for a start-up and vice versa:

  For an existing company:
  - Tax returns for the past 3 years
  - Interim financial statements
  - Business debt schedule

For a start-up company:
- Business plan
- Potential sources of capital
- Available collateral

- *Do not lie.* Never lie. An entrepreneur's greatest asset is his reputation.

Other SBA Programs

Small Business Development Centers (SBDCs). There are more than 1,000 SBDCs, most of which are located in universities throughout the country. This program is a collaborative effort between the SBA, the academic community, the private sector, and state and local governments. The centers provide management and technical assistance as well as assistance in the preparation of loan applications. The services are tailored to the local economies they serve.

SCORE. This advisory group has 389 chapters and 10,500 retired and active senior executives and small-business owner volunteers. They provide marketing advice, business plan preparation, and business planning, and they handle approximately 10,000 cases per month. Information can be found at www.score.org.

Small Business Training Network. This network is an online training resource for small-business owners. The resource offers online courses, workshops, publications, information resources, learning tools, direct access to electronic counseling, and other forms of technical assistance. It can be found at www.sba.gov/training.

Banks without SBA Loan Programs

Historically, banks without SBA programs (those that use personal guarantees as their primary collateral), including some community development banks, have not been viewed as great friends to entrepreneurs. The reason is that most were asset-backed lenders that determined the loan amount using a strict formula, such as 80 percent of the value of accounts receivable plus 20 percent of inventory and

50 percent of fixed assets. Given this formula, start-ups could never get loans, and companies with tangible assets were limited to the amount mandated by the formula regardless of the true amount needed.

With the "entrepreneur generation" of the mid-1990s came the advent of an increasing number of banks that were cash flow lenders, like the SBA for small businesses. Recent research from the SBA suggests that, much like other dot-com phenomena, this type of lending has waned. A study of banking and small and medium enterprise financing by the SBA showed that 90 percent of loans under $1 million by small domestic banks required collateral.[22] The focus on small business has remained, however, and credit is generally more available to small firms than was the case many years ago. Large banks like Bank of America, Chase, Citigroup, and Wells Fargo have taken aim at the small-business market. While it is true that much of this focus is on credit lines/credit cards of under $100,000, these banks are increasingly focusing on small business.

Overall, the traditional rules of bank financing still apply. Entrepreneurs will need to pass a full credit analysis, including a detailed review of financial statements and personal finances, to assess their ability to repay. Banks will require collateral and will want to understand what kind of assets you can liquidate to pay them. They will also want to get comfortable with your business plan and how it fits within larger macroeconomic conditions. In general, the bigger your business, the easier it will be to secure financing. The Federal Reserve Bank of New York refers to this as the "Five Cs."[23] These are Capacity to repay, the Capital you have committed, your personal Commitment to the business, the Collateral you have to secure the loan, the conditions of the loan, such as economic climate and the purpose of the loan, and Character in the general impression you make.[24] As stated earlier, the SBA report on small business and micro business lending in the United States provides statistics on the top lenders to small businesses in each state and nationally.

Community Banks

Unlike the large banks, community banks have usually been seen as a friend to the entrepreneur. As Larry Bennett, director of the Center for Entrepreneurship at Johnson & Wales University, notes,

"There is a huge difference in banks' receptivity to lending to entrepreneurs." The biggest difference is that local and regional banks will more readily agree to customize loans to fit entrepreneurs' needs.[25] These are typically small independent banks that specialize in certain types of targeted lending. After years of consolidation, community banks are making a comeback. There are more than 9,000 such banks in the country, some of which are listed in Figure 9-3. To find out who and where they are, contact the Independent Community Bankers of America at 1–800–422–8439 or visit www.icba.org.

FIGURE 9-3

Various Community Banks

Community Bank	Investment Focus
Mechanics and Farmers Bank Durham, North Carolina	African Americans
Michigan Heritage Bank Novi, Michigan	Equipment leasing
United Commercial Bank San Francisco, California	Asian small-business community
Legacy Bank Milwaukee, Wisconsin	Urban families and entrepreneurs
First Truck Bank Charlotte, North Carolina	Small and women-owned businesses

Entrepreneurs should choose the bank that best fits their needs. Bill Dunkelberg, chief economist at the National Federation of Independent Business and chairman of a small bank in Cherry Hill, New Jersey, explains how entrepreneurs should think about choosing a bank. He says that small businesses should "figure out if they fit better with the point scoring model [or] if playing golf with the loan officer would help." In short, Dunkelberg is saying that larger banks will look more at the numbers behind your business, whereas small community banks will get to know the entrepreneur and may be more willing to work a bit more with her.[26]

Community Development Financial Institutions (CDFIs)

CDFIs primarily provide loan financing to businesses that are generally unbankable by traditional industry standards. They are typically community development loan funds, banks, credit unions, and community development venture funds. The pricing on these loans is a bit higher to reflect the additional risk, from 0.5 to 3.0 percent above normal loan rates. There are about 1,000 CDFIs nationwide. In 2005, CDFIs funded more than 2,000 small and medium-size businesses and held $739 million in outstanding loans and investments. Another 5,800 companies received loans of $35,000 or less. CDFIs can make riskier loans because they are not restricted by regulation. CDFIs can also be value-added investors. There is no listing of every CDFI, but the Treasury Department has a partial list at www.cdfifund.gov, and more resources can be found at www.cdfi.org.

CDFIs can be useful for starting up or growing a business when bank financing is not an option and your returns are not high enough to attract the interest of angel investors or venture capital firms. CDFIs also can be useful for owners with less than perfect credit. CDFIs typically fund businesses in economically depressed or rural areas.

Personal Guarantees

One of the greatest drawbacks to debt financing from banks for many entrepreneurs is the personal guarantee, which is collateralized by all one's assets, including one's home. While such a guarantee is not required for loans from all capital sources, it is for any SBA financing. Leslie Davis, a former commercial lender, said that it is not unusual for entrepreneurs to say, "I cannot agree to personally guarantee the loan because my spouse will not let me." In those cases, she immediately rejects the loan, because, as she explains, "If the spouse does not completely believe in the entrepreneur, why should we?"

One of the greatest fears that entrepreneurs have is losing their homes. Bankers estimate that at least 90 percent of first-time business owners use their homes as collateral. These are the entrepreneurs *and* spouses who are completely committed. Should they worry? Yes and no. If the borrower defaults and a personal guarantee is backed partially or completely by his home, the lender has the legal right to sell the home in order to recoup its investment. But private banks and the SBA typically attempt to work with the entrepreneur to develop a long-term repayment plan that does not include selling the house. This point was supported by an SBA director who said, "Our position as far as personal residences is to try to work with the individual borrower as much as possible. We look at the home as collateral of the last resort. We certainly don't want to retain assets, especially not residential real estate."[27]

Therefore, it is good advice to communicate regularly with the lender after providing a personal guarantee, so that if the loan becomes a problem, it can be restructured prior to default. Loan officers have been trained to receive bad news. They do not necessarily like it, but they like surprises even less. Keep the loan officer informed. The loan officer wants you to repay the loan and succeed, and will help if you pursue the problem early. Even when default is inevitable or occurs, the loan officer will still help you as long as you communicate, are open with information, are willing to negotiate, and agree to a payment plan that could take 10 to 15 years. Most importantly, demonstrate a "good-faith effort" to work things out.

The worst thing you can do when you are facing default is to become difficult, noncommunicative, or threatening. Do not attempt to negotiate by threatening that you will declare bankruptcy if the lender does not give you what you want. Such threats usually upset the lender, and if you carry out the threat, it will be more harmful to your future than to the lender's. In such combative cases, the lender will not only pursue the home that was used as collateral, but also seek to garnish any future earnings that the entrepreneur may have to fulfill the entire debt obligation.

Try to work things out. As stated in Chapter 1, most successful high-growth entrepreneurs fail at least 2 times. Give yourself another chance by making the bad experience a win-win situation for both you and the financier. The financier wins by receiving payment, and you win by keeping a strong reputation and putting yourself in a position to receive financing from the same lender for future deals. As one bank executive explained, "If you've had some financial trouble in the past, it doesn't mean that I'll turn you down. I'll be curious about how you responded to the trouble."[28]

Nonbank Financial Institutions without SBA Loan Programs

Many nonbank financial institutions without SBA programs also provide long-term debt financing to entrepreneurs. Included in this group are national insurance companies, such as Northwestern Mutual and Prudential. Their loans can be used for working capital, business acquisitions, and equipment and machinery. These institutions tend to have higher minimum loan levels than banks that service entrepreneurs. For example, Prudential's loan level ranges between $10 and $15 million. Another difference from traditional bank lending is that if the insurance company were a subordinated lender, the loan would be for only 1 to 1.5 times EBITDA. As the senior lender, nonbank financial institutions will be similar to banks, lending as much as 3 times EBITDA. Another attraction is that these institutions are not asset lenders; they are cash flow lenders. As one supplier said, "We don't look at collateral upfront. We look at management's work history, and then the cash flow of the business. Banks don't usually do that."[29] The final significant difference is one of their main attractions: be it senior or subordinated debt, they can amortize the loan over 15 years. This compares very favorably with the maximum 7 years that banks traditionally offer.

Person-to-Person (P2P) Lending

For prospective entrepreneurs who have had difficulty qualifying for traditional commercial or SBA loan products because of poor credit ratings and/or an unproven track record, an increasingly popular alternative for start-up capital is person-to-person (P2P) lending. At Web sites like Prosper.com, Zopa (www.zopa.com), Lending Club (www.lendingclub.com), and GlobeFunder (www.globefunder.com), entrepreneurs are able to connect with people across the globe who desire to lend small sums of money to strangers for the promise of higher returns than they might see with their traditional personal banking products. P2P lending allows individuals to lend to each other at a set rate for a fixed period of time, offer built-in solutions for loan repayment and tracking, and employ social networking capabilities that allow borrowers to tell the stories associated with their need for capital.[30]

The maximum loan amount at a P2P site is typically $25,000 (although maximum loan amounts are expected to increase to as much as $100,000 in the future), with loans often syndicated among several lenders.[31] Each of the major sites employs a slightly different model, but all typically require that borrowers register on their site, submit to a basic credit check (with required minimum credit scores of approximately 640), and have a debt/equity ratio of around 30 percent. Currently, roughly 20 percent of the loans on the four major P2P sites (Prosper, Zopa, LendingClub, and GlobeFunder) are for business purposes.[32]

While rates on P2P sites can be more attractive than using credit card debt to finance a business, there are downsides to consider. These loans typically require both principal and interest to be paid down every month (whereas several types of bank loans allow only interest payments at first). Additionally, the fixed payment periods associated with these loans can often be difficult to manage for seasonal businesses. Finally, it is almost impossible to renegotiate these loans once their terms are set.[33]

P2P lending will not replace traditional commercial lending anytime soon, but it is a growing niche. Entrepreneurs are especially cautioned to carefully consider their overall debt levels and ability to repay before obtaining a P2P loan, since these products do not come with the built-in sanity checks that a commercial banker brings to the traditional bank loan process.

CREATIVE WAYS TO STRUCTURE LONG-TERM DEBT

Debt is usually structured so that it is amortized over 5 to 7 years, with interest and principal payments due each month. For the first-time or inexperienced entrepreneur, it is recommended that you ask for more lenient terms. The purpose is to give you a little breathing room immediately after you procure the loan, so that your entire focus can be on operating the company and not becoming a slave to servicing debt. The options for repaying the debt could include:

- Making payments quarterly or semiannually.
- Making only interest payments each quarter, with a principal balloon payment at the end of Year 5 or Year 7.
- Making no payments at all until three to 6 months following the loan closing; then paying interest only for the balance of the fiscal year, followed by quarterly payments of interest and principal for four to 6 years.
- With SBA loans, structuring fixed principal and interest monthly payments even with a variable rate. If interest rates go down, you pay down the principal faster. If interest rates rise, you'll have a balloon payment at maturity.

These are only a few suggestions that every entrepreneur should consider pursuing. As is obvious, these structures free up a lot of cash in the early stages—cash that the entrepreneur can use to solidify the financial foundation of the company. These options, or any variation of them, are not typically offered automatically by the lender. The entrepreneur must ask for them during negotiations.

LONG-TERM DEBT RULES TO LIVE BY

In summary, here are a few final pieces of advice relative to debt financing:

- Always take the maximum number of years allowable for repayments. Try to include a no-prepayment-penalty clause in the agreement.
- Get a fixed rather than a floating rate of interest. Know what your future payments will always be.
- Expect loan application rejection. Do not be thin-skinned.
- After getting the loan, keep your investors informed. Send them monthly or quarterly financial statements and, if possible, send out a quarterly status report. Invite lenders to visit your business at least once a year. A few of these suggestions may actually be required as stipulated in your loan documents.
- When things go wrong, renegotiate.

- Keep excellent and timely financial statements. Historical statements should be readily available at any time. They should be neatly stored in an organized filing system.
- Once the loan application has been submitted, expect to hear from a loan officer by telephone before or after normal working hours. This is one of the ways bankers evaluate the working habits of the entrepreneur. Does she come in early and stay late? Or is she an 8:00 a.m. to 5:00 p.m. person? (To prove you are not the latter, call the loan officer at 6:00 a.m. or 9:00 p.m. and leave a message on his voice mail that you are in your office and working and thought he might be doing the same, because you had a question for him.)

DEBT FINANCING FOR WORKING CAPITAL

Up to this point, the sources of capital discussed could have been used for business acquisitions, start-ups, or working capital. As stated before, most entrepreneurs find access to working capital their greatest problem. Therefore, in addition to the aforementioned sources, here are other sources of debt financing specifically for working capital.

Factors

Factoring firms, or factors, are asset-based lenders. The asset that they use for collateral is a company's accounts receivable (AR). By way of example, a company sells its AR, at a discount, to a factor. This allows the company to get immediate cash for the products shipped or services rendered. Factoring is one of the oldest financial tools available, as it dates back to the Mesopotamians. It was also a tool of the American colonists, who would ship furs, lumber, and tobacco to England. Eventually, the U.S. garment industry became a user. Today, factoring has over $120 billion in annual volume in the United States. Worldwide, factoring volume is over $1.5 trillion annually.

The usual agreement is that when the product is shipped, copies of the shipping document, called the bill of lading, and the invoice are faxed to the factor. Typically, within 48 hours, the factor deposits 70 to 90 percent of the invoice amount into the client's account. When the customer pays the bill, which is usually remitted to the factor in accordance with instructions on the invoice, the factor takes the 70 to 90 percent that it had advanced to the client plus 2 to 4 percent for the use of its capital. The balance is sent to the client.

There are two types of factors, recourse and nonrecourse. The former buys accounts receivable with an agreement that it will be reimbursed by the client for receivables that cannot be collected. The latter type takes all of the risk of collecting the receivables. If a receivable is not paid, the client has no obligations to the factor. Obviously, the fees charged by nonrecourse factors are greater than those charged by recourse factors.

Regardless of the type of factor, before reaching an agreement with a client, the factor investigates the creditworthiness of the client's customers. In most instances, the factor will "cherry-pick," or select, certain customers and reject the accounts of others. The rejected customers are those that have a history of slow payment.

The factoring industry has continued to grow for a number of reasons. First, factors provide immediate access to cash. This can be particularly helpful for fast-growing companies or companies that are in immediate need of liquidity. Alton Johnson of Bossa Nova Beverage Group used factoring to avoid giving up equity during the early stages of the firm's growth. This got the firm to profitability without giving up precious equity. In some industries, factoring is actually the most profitable way to go. For example, Roger Shorey, president of Accurate Metal Fabricators, a Florida-based kitchen-cabinet company, receives discounts for immediate payment that exceed the costs of factoring. Another force driving the growth in the factoring industry has been globalization. Factoring is an excellent way for small companies to manage the uncertainty of a new export market.[34]

On the flip side, there are some clear negatives associated with factoring, and it should almost always be viewed as a stopgap or temporary measure. The primary negative associated with factoring is that factoring is very expensive. At 2 to 4 percent per 30-day period, the annual cost of factoring is between 24 and 48 percent interest. There are very few businesses that can generate returns at these levels for sustained periods of time. Factors also typically prefer to engage in longer-term contracts. Finally, a company's existing debt covenants may forbid it from using this source of capital because it involves the selling of assets.

How can an entrepreneur find a factor? Usually the factor will find you. Once you go into business, factors will begin mailing you unsolicited requests to use their services. The postcard or letter will not call it factoring; instead, it will call it working capital or inventory financing.

There are hundreds of factoring firms in the country. Some online resources on factoring include Factors Chain International (www.factor-chain.com) and the International Factoring Association (www.factoring.org). Also, Alana Davidson, the principal of IBC Funding, a factoring broker, has written a paper entitled "Ten Frequently Asked Questions about Factoring." It can be obtained free of charge by writing to IBC Funding, 3705 Ingomar Street, NW, Washington, D.C. 20015.[35]

Advice for Using Factors

- Factors are ideal for businesses in industries with inherent long cash gaps, such as the health-care industry, where insurance companies are notoriously slow in paying claims, or the apparel industry, where producers must buy fabric 6 to 9 months before they use it.
- Factors are also ideal for companies that are experiencing or forecasting rapid growth.
- Factors are also ideal for companies that are first experimenting with exporting goods to foreign countries with unfamiliar regulations.
- They are ideal for companies that cannot get capital from anywhere else.
- However, factors should be used only by companies that have included the cost of factoring in their prices. Otherwise, the cost of factoring could eliminate all of the company's profits. In fact, one factor suggested that the only firms that should use this financing method are those with at least 20 percent gross margins.[36]
- Companies with many small customers should not use factoring, as it is cumbersome to deal with checking the credit of so many customers.
- Ultimately, cheaper forms of capital should replace factor financing. It is too expensive to use on a long-term basis.

Customer Financing

The idea that a customer could be a provider of debt may seem odd, but it is indeed possible and has happened many times. Customers are willing to provide capital to suppliers who provide them with a high-quality or unique product that they may not be able to buy somewhere else. This financing can be a direct loan or a down payment on a future order. That is the financing that Robert Stockard, the owner of Sales Consultants of Boston (SCB), an executive recruiting firm, received from his largest customer, MCI. When the telecommunications giant needed a temporary sales force of 1,200 people to launch its new calling plan, Friends and Family, nationally, it hired SCB. Rather than approach a bank for additional working capital to finance this larger-than-usual job, Stockard persuaded MCI to make a 10 percent down payment on the $2.5 million contract.[37]

Entrepreneurs like Stockard who successfully procure working capital from customers show that anything is possible if you simply ask. An investor who is also a customer is a value-added investor.

But raising capital from a customer has a few drawbacks that should be considered first. One is that you may risk losing customers who are competitors of your investor. Another is that, as an investor, your customer could get access to key information about your company and use it to become your competitor.

Still another negative is that once a customer is an investor, the customer knows more about the true state of the company's operations. This exposure to the company's internal operations may cause the customer to seek another supplier if the customer thinks the company is poorly managed.

Finally, the additional insight that a customer has may make it tough for a supplier to increase prices, since the customer now knows the cost of the product. Therefore, be careful when accepting capital from customers.

Supplier Financing

Suppliers are automatically financiers if they give their customers credit. The simplest way for entrepreneurs to improve their supplier financing is by delaying the payment of their bills. This is called "involuntary extended supplier financing." But sometimes a supplier will graciously agree to extend its invoice terms to help a customer finance a large order that, in turn, helps the supplier sell more goods.

And there are other instances where a supplier will give a direct loan to a customer. That was the case when Rich Food Holdings, a grocery wholesaler in Richmond, Virginia, loaned $3 million to Johnny Johnson, a grocery chain owner, "to buy my buildings, equipment and groceries. In exchange, I agreed to purchase 60% of my inventory from them."[38]

Like customer financing, supplier financing has a few negative aspects. The first is that the supplier may require you to purchase most or all of your products from it. This causes a problem when the supplier has poor delivery, poor quality, and higher prices.

Another problem may be that because your supplier is an investor, other suppliers that are the supplier's competitors may refuse to continue to do business with you.

Purchase Order Financing

Although they may seem alike, factoring and purchase order financing are two different things. The first provides financing after the order has been produced and shipped. The latter provides capital at a much earlier stage—when the order has been received. There are many businesses that have orders that they cannot fill because they cannot buy inventory. This working capital is used to pay for the inventory needed to fill an order. It is a great resource for companies that are growing fast but do not have the capital to buy additional inventory to maintain their growth.

That was the case with Jeffrey Martinez, the president of Ocean World Fisheries USA in Florida. His company is an importer of shrimp and crab from Latin America. His customers were giving him purchase orders at a rapid pace. He, in turn, was generating orders to his supplier faster than he was collecting receivables, which created a cash shortage and diminished the speed with which he could buy more inventory. In addition, his suppliers expected to be paid immediately upon delivery. He had to pay for inventory before he got paid. Martinez explained his working capital problem this way: "We're able to sell all the shrimp and crab we could import and more. But when suppliers put the product in a container, they expect to be paid immediately."[39] His solution? He procured inventory using purchase order financing from Gerber Trade Finance in New York, which allowed him to pay for his inventory upon delivery.

This type of financing is designed for companies that cannot get a traditional loan from a bank or finance company, perhaps because they are carrying too much long-term debt. It is ideal short-term financing for companies that do not hold inventory for long, such as importers, wholesalers, and distributors.

Like factoring, purchase order financing is not cheap. The lender charges fees that range from 5 to 10 percent of the purchase order's value, and payment is due in 30 to 90 days.[40]

Purchase order financing is riskier than factoring because the collateral is inventory, which may get damaged, be poorly produced, or get spoiled. Therefore, banks and other traditional financiers have not wholeheartedly embraced this type of debt financing.

In addition to Gerber, two additional purchase order financiers are Bankers Capital and Transcap Trade Finance. Both are located in Northbrook, Illinois.

Credit Cards

The final source of debt working capital is from credit cards. But before proceeding, let me offer a stern warning about using credit cards. *Be careful!* The abuse of credit cards can be one of the entrepreneur's easiest and quickest ways to go out of business.

Americans owe more than $2 trillion on their credit cards.[41] The top four cards are Visa, MasterCard, American Express and Discover, which collectively hold approximately 70 percent of market share. It is estimated that 88 million U.S. households have at least one credit card. In 2004, the Federal Reserve Survey of Consumer Finances found that the median balance for household credit card debt was $5,100. Americans for Fairness in Lending reports that the credit card industry is cashing in on this debt, with $36.8 billion in profits in 2006, up nearly 80 percent from $20.5 billion in 2000. Not surprisingly, with all this money to be made, the number of credit card offers has skyrocketed. The number of credit card solicitations in the mail has increased from 1.1 billion in 1990 to over 6 billion in 2005. There areapproximately 280 million men, women, and children in the entire country. This is equivalent to 21 solicitations for every person in the country!

One group that has been receptive to these solicitations is entrepreneurs. A 2007 survey done by the National Small Business Association showed that credit cards were the most common financing option that entrepreneurs used to meet their capital needs. Entrepreneurs have embraced credit card use for several reasons. First and foremost, credit cards are very easy to get, as proved by the statistics just cited. Second, the card allows easy access to as much as $100,000 in cash advances without having to explain how the money will be spent. Small businesses that don't qualify for bank loans also look to credit cards to finance their growth. The final reason is that if they are used methodically and strategically, credit cards can provide inexpensive capital. Regarding this final point, there are two ways in which the capital can be cheap. The first is by using cards that offer introductory rates as low as 3.9 percent. The second is a situation where the capital can be provided as an interest-free short-term loan. That occurs when the bill is paid off each month during the grace period.

This second method highlights one of several negative aspects of using credit cards for working capital: one large bill comes due every month, as opposed to small bills from many suppliers when you pay by check. When cash is short, it is easier to juggle the payments of a number of small bills than one large bill.

This problem leads to the next issue, and that is the assessment of expensive late-payment penalties. In 1997, the government lifted restrictions on maximum penalty charges, resulting in credit card issuers charging whatever late fee they wanted, even if the bill was paid only one day after the grace period. Until that ruling, most banks charged an annual fee of about $25, fixed rates to all borrowers, and late fees of $10 or less. Furthermore, most cards came with a grace period. Since that ruling, late fees have jumped to $39, and in some cases the grace period has been eliminated. Moreover, credit card companies have begun increasing rates on borrowers for reasons ranging from being late on a house payment to using too much of their available credit.

One thing that has not changed is the high interest rates. While many credit card companies use low introductory rates to lure new customers, once these rates expire in 3 to 6 months, the traditionally high credit card rates of 12 to 20 percent or even more take effect. This is very expensive money because of the high rates and the fact that the interest charges are compounded. Getting behind on credit card payments can put an entrepreneur in a deep financial hole. The worst is when the debt is so far past due that the interest costs are being compounded and late penalties are being added, so that payments never decrease the principal. A situation like this can harm the entrepreneur's personal credit because she is liable, not the business.

Another challenge in using credit cards other than for cash advances is finding suppliers that will accept them. Suppliers that might have credit card payment capabilities have an aversion to accepting credit cards because the suppliers have to pay the issuing institution 1.5 to 3.0 percent. This in effect reduces the price they charge you.

The final negative is that the use of personal credit cards for business purposes is a violation of the customer-cardholder agreement that you sign.

If you are not dissuaded from using a credit card, here are a few suggestions:

- Pay the entire bill before the end of the grace period to eliminate interest charges or late fees. Payment means that the money must actually be received, not simply be "in the mail."
- Not all cards have grace periods. Use only those that do.
- Know how long your grace period is. That is the amount of time a lender allows before charging interest on the balance due. Some grace periods are as few as 20 days. If the bill is paid in full before the end of the grace period, no interest is charged. You should know that federal law says that credit card bills must be received no later than 14 days before the grace period ends.
- Refrain from getting cash advances if interest is charged immediately after the money is given, regardless of whether the account is paid in full during the grace

period. In addition to interest charges, most credit card
companies charge a fee of 2 to 5 percent of the total cash
advance. Use only cards that treat cash advances like other
charges that you make.

- Find out the closing date of your credit card statement.
  This is the date in every month when billing for that
  month ends. For example, if your statement closing date is
  the tenth of every month and you have a 20-day grace
  period, complete payment must be made and received by
  the thirtieth of the month in order to avoid interest
  charges.

- When using the card to pay suppliers, get an agreement
  with them that no matter when you make the actual
  purchase, they will bill the credit card on the day
  following your statement closing date. Using the example
  in the previous item, that date would be the eleventh of
  the month. Therefore, that charge will not show up until
  you receive the bill that closed on the tenth of the next
  month. With a 20-day grace period added to that, you
  could get a 50-day interest-free loan.

  Let's use a more detailed example to illustrate this point.
  The Perkins Company purchases 60 widgets from the
  Steinharter Company for $1,000 on October 14. The Perkins
  Company's closing statement date is the twenty-ninth of
  each month. Therefore, the Steinharter Company submits
  the charge on October 30. On November 29, the charge is
  sent to the Perkins Company by the issuer. The 20-day
  grace period ends December 18. The Perkins Company
  pays the entire bill at the bank on December 17. The result
  is that the Perkins Company received an interest-free
  $1,000 loan for 62 days, from October 14 to December 17.

In closing—*be careful!* Credit card companies are constantly
changing things. One such change could be your closing statement
date or the number of days in your grace period. Unnoticed
changes in either could result in your owing a complete month's
worth of interest because your payment was one day late. Finally,
just as with any other contract, make sure to read the fine print and
know what obligations you and your business must fulfill.

NOTES

1. *Time*, January 13, 1997, p. 49.
2. Microsoft, Inc., 2007 Annual Report, Microsoft home page, http://www.microsoft.com/msft/reports/ar07/staticversion/10k_fh_fin.html.
3. SBA Office of Advocacy, "Small Business and Micro Business Lending in the United States for Data Years 2003–2004," November 2005.
4. Barnes and Thornburg, "M&A Trends 2006."
5. Global Entrepreneurship Monitor, "2006 Financing Report."
6. Andrew J. Sherman, "Raising Money in Tough Times: An Entrepreneur's Guide to Bootstrapping," www.eventuring.org, January 1, 2003.
7. James Geshwiler, Marianne Hudson, John May, "State of Angel Groups: A Report on ACA and ACEF," April 27, 2006.
8. Jeffrey Sohl, "The Angel Investor Market in 2006: The Angel Market Continues Steady Growth," University of New Hampshire Center for Venture Research.
9. Ewing Marion Kauffman Foundation, "Business Angel Investing Groups Growing in North America," October 2002.
10. Geshwiler, Hudson, and May, "State of Angel Groups."
11. *Crain's Chicago Business*, November 6, 1996.
12. Chronicle of Philanthropy, "Slow Growth at the Biggest Foundations," March 23, 2006.
13. *Inc.*, February 1998, p. 80.
14. Milken Institute's Los Angeles Economy Project, Section 6, October 2005.
15. Ibid.
16. Entrepreneur.com, "SBA-Guaranteed Loans"; accessed August 24, 2007.
17. Small Business Administration, 2006.
18. Small Business Administration, "Information on Basic 7(a) Loan Program."
19. Small Business Administration, Office of Entrepreneurial Development, "An Introduction to the U.S. Small Business Administration," 2007.
20. Ibid.
21. *Crain's Chicago Business*, August 13, 2001.

22. Small Business Administration, "Banking and SME Financing in the United States," June 2006.

23. Federal Reserve Bank of New York, "The Credit Process: A Guide for Small Business Owners."

24. Entrepreneur.com, "Bank-Term Loans."

25. "The State of Small-Business Funding," *Entrepreneur* July 2006.

26. "How Small Firms Can Weather a Credit Crunch," *Wall Street Journal*, August 7, 2007, p. B9.

27. *Nation's Business*, July 1996, p. 45R.

28. *Inc.*, June 1987, p. 150.

29. *Crain's Chicago Business*, December 1996, p. 22.

30. Maureen Farrell, "Banking 2.0: New Capital Connections for Entrepreneurs," Forbes.com, February 2008.

31. Alex Salkever, Inc., "Brother, Can You Spare a Dime?" August 2006.

32. Farrell, "Banking 2.0."

33. Ibid.

34. "Fast Money," *Wall Street Journal* August 20, 2007, p. R7.

35. *Nation's Business*, September 1996, p. 21.

36. *Black Enterprise*, July 1999, p. 40.

37. *Forbes*, December 28, 1998, p. 91.

38. *Black Enterprise*, March 1998, p. 84.

39. *Chicago Sun-Times*, July 17, 2001, p. 47.

40. *Crain's Chicago Business*, March 13, 2000.

41. Federal Reserve Statistical Release, "Consumer Credit."

CHAPTER 10

Equity Financing

INTRODUCTION

Equity capital is money provided in exchange for ownership in the company. The equity investor receives a percentage of ownership that ideally appreciates as the company grows. The investor may also receive a portion of the company's annual profits, called dividends, based on his ownership percentage. For example, a 10 percent dividend yield or payout on a company's stock worth $200 per share means an annual dividend of $20.

Before deciding to pursue equity financing, the entrepreneur must know the positive and negative aspects of this capital.

Pros

- No personal guarantees are required.
- No collateral is required.
- No regular cash payments are required.
- There can be value-added investors.
- Equity investors cannot force a business into bankruptcy.
- On average, companies with equity financing grow faster.

Cons

- Dividends are not deductible.
- The entrepreneur has new partners.
- It is typically very expensive.
- The entrepreneur can be replaced.

SOURCES OF EQUITY CAPITAL

Many of the sources of debt capital can also provide equity capital. Therefore, for those common sources, what was said about them earlier in the book also applies here. When appropriate, a few additional issues might be added in this discussion of equity. Otherwise, please refer to Chapter 9.

Personal Savings

When an entrepreneur personally invests money in the company, it should be in the form of debt, not equity. This will allow the entrepreneur to recover her investment with only the interest received being taxed. The principal will not be taxed, as it is viewed by the IRS as a return of the original investment. This is in contrast to the tax treatment of capital invested as equity. Like interest, the dividend received would be taxed, along with the entire amount of the original investment, even if no capital gain is realized.

The entrepreneur's equity stake should come from her hard work in starting and growing the company, not her monetary contribution. This is called sweat equity.

Friends and Family

Equity investments are not usually accompanied by personal guarantees from the entrepreneur. However, such assurances may be required of the entrepreneur when he receives capital from friends and family in order to maintain the relationship if the business fails.

But this may be a small price to pay in order to realize an entrepreneurial dream. Start-up capital is virtually impossible to obtain except through friends and family. Dan Lauer experienced this firsthand when he was starting his company, Haystack Toys, in 1988. He raised $250,000 from family and friends after quitting his job as a banker. He went to family and friends after 700 submission letters to investors went unanswered.[1]

Angel Investors

Wealthy individuals usually like to invest in the form of equity because they want to share in the potential growth of the company's valuation. There is presently and has always been a dearth of capital for the earliest stages of entrepreneurship—the seed or start-up stage. Angel investors have done an excellent job of providing capital for this stage. Their investments are typically between $25,000 and $150,000. In exchange, they expect high returns (a minimum 38 percent IRR), similar to what venture capitalists get. Since they are investing at the earliest stage, they usually also get a large ownership position in the company because the valuation is so low.

As was stated in Chapter 9, many angel investors are former successful entrepreneurs. One of the prominent former entrepreneurs who has gone on to become an angel investor is Mitch Kapor, who in 1982 founded Lotus Development, the producer of Lotus 1–2–3 software, which is now a division of IBM. Since he became an angel in 1994, one of his most successful investments was in UUNet, the first Internet access provider.

But angel investing has never been limited to former entrepreneurs. In fact, Apple Computer got its first outside financing from an angel who had never owned a company. He was A. C. "Mike" Markkula, who gained his initial wealth from being a shareholder and corporate executive at Intel. In 1977 he invested $91,000 in Apple Computer and personally guaranteed another $250,000 in credit lines. When Apple went public in 1980, his stock in the company was worth more than $150 million.[2]

This is one of several reasons why the number of angel investors increased so dramatically during the 1990s: *returns*. The publicity surrounding successful entrepreneurial ventures often included stories about the returns that investors received. These stories, coupled with research, led many wealthy individuals to the private equity industry. And while the anecdotal stories themselves are quite impressive, the more seductive story is empirical research that compares the returns of private equity firms with returns on several other investment options. As Table 10-1 shows, June 2008 information from Thomson Financial and the National Venture Capital Association determined that over all investment windows, average annual returns for private equity firms were greater than those for all other investment options.

T A B L E   10-1

Average Annual Returns, 1945–1997

Sector	Returns, %
Private equity	16.7
Emerging market stocks	15.6
Small stocks	14.9
S&P 500	12.9
International stocks	11.4
Real estate	8.0
Commodities	7.8
Corporate bonds	5.8
Long-term bonds (Treasuries)	5.5
Silver	5.0

The second reason for the increase in angel capital was an increase in the number of wealthy people in the country who had money to invest. For example, from 1995 to 2000, the number of millionaires in America increased from 5 million to 7 million people. Many of these millionaires gained their wealth through successful technology entrepreneurial ventures.

The final reason for the explosion in angel capital was the change in federal personal tax laws. In 1990, the capital gains tax was decreased from a maximum of 28 percent to 20 percent. Thus people were able to keep more of their wealth, and they used it to invest in entrepreneurs.

Interestingly, it was rumored that one of the groups that lobbied strongly against this change was institutional investors. These are private equity firms, not individual investors. They challenged the change because they correctly predicted that it would hurt their business. They believed that as more money became available to entrepreneurs, a company's valuation would inevitably increase and there would be more competition. Rich Karlgaard, the publisher of *Forbes* magazine, made this same point:

> In my cherubic youth I used to wonder why so many venture capitalists opposed a reduced capital gains tax. Then I woke up to the facts. Crazy as it sounds, even though venture capitalists stand to benefit individually by reduced capital gains taxes, the reduced rates would also lower entry barriers for new competition in the form of corporations and angels. That might lead to—too much venture capital.[3]

Even though the amount of capital invested by venture capitalists and angel investors is traditionally on a similar scale, according to the Center for Venture Research at the University of New Hampshire, there were significantly fewer companies funded by venture capital firms (4,000) than by angel investors (51,000). In 2005, there were an estimated 234,000 active angel investors. The current yield on angel investments, or the percentage of investments shown that ultimately receive investments by angels, is 20.1 percent. This is down from 23 percent in 2000 but up from the 10 percent yield after the Internet bubble burst in 2000. In 2006, 21 percent of angel investments were directed to health services and medical devices and equipment, 18 percent to software, and 18 percent to biotechnology firms.

Despite private equity firms' complaints, the increase in available capital was clearly a huge positive for entrepreneurs. A few other positive aspects of angel equity capital for entrepreneurs are as follows:

- Seed capital is being provided. Most institutional investors do not finance this early stage of entrepreneurship.
- Many of the angels have great business experience and therefore are value-added investors.
- Angel investors can be more patient than institutional investors, who have to answer to their limited partner investors.

But there are also a few negative aspects to raising money from angels:

- Potential interference. Most angels want not only a seat on the board of directors, but also a very active advisory role, which can be troublesome to the entrepreneur.
- Limited capital. The investor may be able to invest only in the initial round of financing because of limited capital resources.
- The capital can be expensive. Angels typically expect annual returns in excess of 25 percent.

Regarding this final point, here is what an angel investor said about his expectations:

> I expect to make a good deal of money—more than I would make by putting my capital into a bank, bonds, or publicly traded stocks. My goal, after getting my principal back, is to earn 33% of my initial investment every year for as long as the business is in operation.
>
> My usual understanding is that for my investment I own 51% of the stock until I am paid back, whereupon my stake drops to 25%. After that we split every dollar that comes out of the business until I earn my 33% return for the year.[4]

Despite the drawbacks, most entrepreneurs who raise angel capital successfully do not regret it. As one entrepreneur said, "Without angel money, I wouldn't have been able to accomplish what I have. Giving up stock was the right thing to do."[5]

Gaining access to angel investors is not an easy task. Cal Simmons, an Alexandria, Virginia–based angel investor and coauthor of *Every Business Needs an Angel*, says, "You need to have networks. If someone I know and respect refers me, then I'm going to always take the time to take a meeting." Angel groups are another mechanism for getting access to angel investors. There are currently 94 angel groups in operation, and they accept applications to present to their angels. Some of these groups charge entrepreneurs a nominal fee of $100 to $200 to present.

There are forums in almost every region of the country similar to the Midwest Entrepreneurs Forum in Chicago. At this event, held the second Monday of each month, entrepreneurs make presentations to angel investors. There are also several angel-related Web sites, including the Angels Forum (www.angelsforum.com) in Silicon

Valley, SourceCapitalnet.com (www.sourcecapitalnet.com) in New York, and Angel Investor News (www.angel-investor-news.com). The SBA started ACE-NET (www.ace-net.org) in 1998 to help bring entrepreneurs and angels together online. Its official name is now Active Capital, which reflect its desire to provide a proactive approach to helping small businesses obtain private capital. The Ewing Marion Kauffman Foundation also manages the Angel Capital Association (www.angelcapitalassociation.org), which is an angel capital industry trade group with nearly 150 members.

PRIVATE PLACEMENTS

When entrepreneurs seek financing, be it debt or equity, from any of the sources mentioned up until now, that financing is called a *private placement offering*. That is, capital is not being raised on the open market via an initial public offering, which will be discussed later in this chapter. The capital is being raised from select individuals or organizations that meet all of the standards set by Section 4(2) of the U.S. Securities Act of 1933 and Regulation D, an amendment to this act that clarified the rules for those seeking a private placement exemption. The rule says, "Neither the issuer nor any person acting on its behalf shall offer or sell the securities by any form of general solicitation or general advertising. This includes advertisements, articles or notices in any form of media. Also, the relationship between the party offering the security and the potential investor will have been established prior to the launch of the offering."[6] All of this simply means that an entrepreneur cannot solicit capital by standing on the corner trying to sell stock in his company to any passersby. He also cannot put an ad in a newspaper or magazine recruiting investors. He must know his investors, directly or indirectly. Potential investors in the latter category are known through the entrepreneur's associates, such as his attorney, accountant, or investment banker.

The final part of the regulation says that fund-raising efforts must be restricted to "accredited investors only." These investors are also known as sophisticated investors. Such an investor has to meet one of the following three criteria:

- An individual net worth (or joint net worth with spouse) that is greater than $1 million

- An individual income (without any income of a spouse) in excess of $200,000 in each of the two most recent years and reasonably expects an income in excess of $200,000 in the current year
- Joint income with spouse in excess of $300,000 in each of the two most recent years and reasonably expects to have joint income in excess of $300,000 in the current year

Prior to accepting investments, the entrepreneur must get confirmation of this sophisticated investor status by requiring all the investors to complete a form called the Investor Questionnaire. This form must be accompanied by a letter from the entrepreneur's attorney or accountant stating that the investors meet all of the accreditation requirements.

Violation of any part of Regulation D could result in a 6-month suspension of fund-raising or something as severe as the company's being required to immediately return all the money to the investors. Therefore, the entrepreneur should hire an attorney experienced with private placements before raising capital. Figure 10-1 summarizes the Regulation D rules and restrictions.

As stated earlier, sources of capital for a private placement are angel investors, insurance companies, banks, family, and friends, along with pension funds and private investment pools. There are no hard-and-fast rules regarding the structure or terms of a private placement. Therefore, private placements are ideal for high-risk and small companies. The offering can be for all equity, all debt, or a combination of debt and equity. The entrepreneur can issue the offering or use an investment banker.

The largest and most prominent national investment banks that handle private placements are Merrill Lynch, JPMorgan, and Credit Suisse First Boston. These three bankers raise a total of over $30 billion annually for entrepreneurs. Regional investment bankers are better suited for raising small amounts of capital.

When hiring an investment banker, the entrepreneur should expect to pay either a fixed fee or a percentage of the money raised (which can be up to 10 percent) and/or give the fund-raiser a percentage of the company's stock (up to 5 percent). One important piece of advice is that the entrepreneur should be extremely cautious about using the same investment banker to determine the amount of capital

F I G U R E   10-1

Regulation D Rules Restrictions

	Amount of Offering		
	$1 million	$1 million–$5 million	Unlimited (Emphasis on Nonpublic Nature, Not Small Issue!)
Number of Investors	Unlimited	35 plus unlimited accredited investors	35 plus those purchasing $150,000
Investor Qualification	None required (no sophistication requirement)	■ Accredited— presumed qualified ■ 35 nonaccredited— no sophistication requirement	Nonaccredited purchasers must be sophisticated—must understand risks and merits of investment; accredited presumed to be qualified
Manner of Offering	General solicitation permitted	No general solicitation	No general solicitation
Limitations on resale	No restrictions	Restricted	Restricted
Issuer Qualifications	No reporting companies; no investment companies; no "blank-check" companies; no "unworthy issuers"	No investment companies; no issuers disqualified under Reg. A; no "unworthy issuers" (Rule 507)	None (except for Rule 507 "unworthy issuer")
Information Requirements	No information specified	If purchased solely by accredited, no information specified; for nonaccredited—info required: (a) Nonreporting companies must furnish information similar to that in a registered offering or Reg. A offering, but modified financial statement requirements (b) Reporting companies must furnish specified SEC documents, plus limited additional information about the offering	
SEC rules	Rule 504	Rule 505	Rule 506

needed and to raise the capital. There is a conflict of interest when the investment banker does both for a variable fee. Whenever only one investment banker is used for both assignments, the fee should be fixed. Otherwise, use different companies for each assignment.

Shopping a Private Placement

After the private placement document has been completed, it must be "shopped" to potential investors. The following describes the process of shopping a private placement:

1. Make an ideal investor profile list (have net asset requirement).
2. Identify whom to put on the actual list:
   - Former coworkers with money
   - Industry executives and salespeople who know your work history
   - Past customers
3. Call the candidates and inform them of the minimum investment amount.
4. Send a private placement memorandum outlining the investment process only to those who are not intimidated by the minimum investment indicated during the call.
5. Contact other companies where your investors have invested.

CORPORATE VENTURE CAPITAL

In the late 1990s, large corporations embraced entrepreneurship with the same interest as individuals. This was surprising because it was assumed that corporations, with their reputations for stodgy bureaucracy and conservatism, were "anti-entrepreneurship." Their primary relationship with the entrepreneurship world came as investors. This began to change in the late 1990s as corporations began to realize the opportunities associated with investing in companies with products or services related to their industry. Such strategic investments became a part of corporations' research and development programs as they sought access to new products, services, and markets. For example, cable television operator Comcast Corp. established a $125 million fund to invest in companies that would "help it understand how to capitalize on the Internet." Comcast wanted to bring its cable TV customers online and also saw the potential to put its QVC shopping channel on the Internet.[7]

The final reason that such prominent corporations as Intel, Cisco, Time Warner, and Reader's Digest created their funds was to find new customers. As one person described it, "Corporations are using their venture-backed companies to foster demand for their own products and technologies."[8] Two companies implementing that strategy were Andersen Consulting and Electronic Data Systems. Both companies invested in customers that used their systems integration consulting services.

Traditional venture capitalists love it when their portfolio companies receive financing from corporate venture capitalists. The primary reason is that the latter are value-added investors. In fact, three of the most successful venture capital firms—Accel Partners, Kleiner Perkins Caufield & Byers (KPCB), and Battery Ventures—have wholeheartedly endorsed the use of corporate funds. This point was made by Ted Schlein, a partner with KPCB, who said, "Having a corporation as a partner early on can give you some competitive advantages. The portfolio companies are after sales and marketing channels."[9]

When the stock market crashed in 2000, corporate venture capital dried up. Total investment dollars dropped from $16.8 billion in 2000 to under $2 billion in 2002. This 88 percent drop was faster than the 75 percent drop in the overall markets. This faster rate of decline makes sense. Venture capital is not the primary business of corporations, and in times of economic hardship, it can be expected that these firms will pull back their financing. Moreover, many of these firms need to manage short-term earnings expectations, so investment funding gets cut when quarterly earnings figures are threatened. Table 10-2 shows corporate venture capital investments from 1999 through early 2006.[10]

PRIVATE EQUITY FIRMS

Many of the sources of equity financing that have been discussed up to this point are from individuals. But there is an entire industry filled with "institutional" investors. These are firms that are in the business of providing equity capital to entrepreneurs, with the expectation of high returns.

This industry is commonly known as the venture capital industry. But venture capital is merely one aspect of private equity.

T A B L E   10-2

Corporate Venture Capital Investment, 1999 to 2006
(First Half)

Year	Number of Companies Receiving CVC Dollars	Percent of All Companies Receiving CVC Dollars	Total CVC Investment (Millions of Dollars)	Percent of All VC Dollars
1999	1,153	26.6%	8,289.2	15.5%
2000	1,960	31.2%	16,772.2	16.1%
2001	955	25.4%	4,967.3	12.3%
2002	539	20.7%	1,914.0	8.8%
2003	437	18.1%	1,291.0	6.6%
2004	516	20.2%	1,460.1	6.6%
2005	535	20.4%	1,535.3	6.8%
2006	358	22.1%	1,044.7	8.2%
Total	7,667	21.3%	41,247.4	11.6%

The phrase *private equity* comes from the facts that money is being exchanged for equity in the company and that it is a private deal between the two parties—investor and entrepreneur. For the most part, all the terms of the deal are dependent on what the two parties agree to. This is in contrast to public equity financing, which occurs when the company raises money through an initial public offering. In that case, all aspects of the deal must be in accordance with Securities and Exchange Commission (SEC) rules. One rule is that the financial statements of a public company must be published and provided to the investors quarterly. Such a rule does not exist in private equity deals. The two parties can make any agreement they want, i.e., financial statements sent to investors every month, quarterly, twice a year, or even once a year.

Private Equity: The Basics

It is important to note that the owners of private equity firms are also entrepreneurs. These firms are typically small companies that happen to be in the business of providing capital. Like all other entrepreneurs, they put their capital at risk in pursuit of exploiting an opportunity and can go out of business.

Legal Structure

Most private equity firms are organized as limited partnerships or limited liability companies. These structures offer advantages over general partnerships by indemnifying the external investors and the principals. They also have advantages over C corporations because they limit the life of the firm to a specific amount of time (usually 10 years), which is attractive to investors. Furthermore, the structures eliminate the double taxation on distributed profits.

The professional investors who manage the firm are the general partners (GPs). The GPs invest only 1 to 5 percent of their personal capital in the fund and make all the decisions. External investors in a typical private equity partnership are called limited partners (LPs). During the fund-raising process, LPs pledge or commit a specified amount of capital for the new venture fund. For most funds formed today, the minimum capital commitment from any single LP is $1 million; however, the actual minimum contribution is completely at the discretion of the firm. The commitment of capital is formalized through the signing of the partnership agreement between the LP and the venture firm. The partnership agreement details the terms of the fund and legally binds the LPs to provide the capital that they have pledged.

Getting Their Attention

GPs rely on their proprietary network of entrepreneurs, friendly attorneys, limited partners, and industry contacts to introduce them to new companies. They are much more likely to spend time looking at a new opportunity that was referred to them by a source they find trustworthy than one referred by other sources. A business plan that is referred through their network is also less likely to be "shopped around" to all the other venture capitalists focused on a particular industry segment. GPs want to avoid getting involved in an auction for the good deals because bidding drives up the valuation. In the course of a year, a typical private equity firm receives thousands of business plans. Less than 10 percent of these deals move to the due diligence phase of the investment.

Business Plan Review

Most firms use a screening process to prioritize the deals they are considering. Generally, associates within a firm are given the responsibility of screening new business plans based on a set of investment criteria, developed over time by the firm. These criteria are grounded in the characteristics of completed deals that have been successful for the firm in the past. Several of the parameters used to screen business plans are:

- Industry
- Growth expectations
- Phase in the life cycle
- Differentiating factors
- Management
- Terms of the deal

An entrepreneur can expedite the process by creating a concise, accurate, and compelling document that addresses an investor's key concerns. The ability of the entrepreneur to effectively communicate her ideas through a written business plan is critical to receiving funding for the project.

Once a deal passes the first screen by meeting a majority of the initial criteria, a private equity firm begins an exhaustive investigation of the industry, the managers, and the financial projections of the potential investment. Due diligence may include hiring consultants to investigate the feasibility of a new product; doing extensive reference checking on management, including background checks; and undertaking detailed financial modeling to check the legitimacy of projections. The entire due diligence process takes from 30 to 90 days in a deal that receives funding.

Management

Most GPs list management as their most important criterion for the success of an investment. The management team is evaluated based on attributes that define its leadership ability, experience, and reputation, including:

- Recognized achievement
- Teamwork

- Work ethic
- Operating experience
- Commitment
- Integrity
- Reputation
- Entrepreneurial experience

GPs use a variety of methods to confirm the information provided by an entrepreneur, including extensive interviews, private detectives, background checks, and reference checks. During the interview process, the entrepreneur must provide compelling evidence of the merits of the plan and of the management team's ability to execute it. Therefore, the management team must clearly and concisely articulate the product or service concept and be prepared to answer a series of in-depth questions. Additionally, the interview process provides an indication to both sides of the fit between the venture capitalist and the entrepreneur. A good fit is critical to the potential success of the investment because of the difficult decisions that inevitably need to be made during the life of the relationship.

Some firms believe in the strength of management so much that they invest in a management team or a manager before a company exists. Often, these entrepreneurs have successfully brought a company to a lucrative exit and are looking for the next opportunity. Some venture firms give these seasoned veterans the title "entrepreneur in residence" and fund the search for their next opportunity.

Ideal Candidate

Again, private equity from institutional investors is ideal for entrepreneurial firms with excellent management teams. These companies should be predicted to experience or be experiencing rapid annual growth of at least 20 percent. The industry should be large enough to sustain two large successful competitors. And the product should have:

- Limited technical and operational risks
- Proprietary and differentiating features

- Above-average gross margins
- Short sales cycles
- Repeat sales opportunities

Finally, the company must have the potential to increase in value sufficiently in 5 to 7 years for the investor to realize her minimum targeted return. Coupled with this growth potential must be at least two explicit discernible exit opportunities (sell the company or take it public) for the investor. The entrepreneur and the investor must agree on the timing of this potential exit and the strategy in advance. For example, an ideal entrepreneurial financing candidate is one who knows that he wants to raise $10 million in equity capital for 10 percent of his company and expects to sell the company to a Fortune 500 corporation in 5 years for 7 times the company's present value. This tells the investor that she can exit the deal in Year 5 and receive $70 million for her investment.

When an entrepreneur goes after private equity funding, he should know what kind of returns are expected. The institutional private equity industry and the targeted minimum internal rates of return are noted in Table 10-3.

T A B L E   10-3

Targeted IRR for Private Equity Investors

Private Equity Investor Type	Targeted IRR
Corporate finance	20–40%
Mezzanine funds	15–25%
Venture capital funds	38–50%

Again, private equity investors make their "real" money when a portfolio company has a liquidation event: the company goes public, merges, recapitalizes, or gets acquired. Depending on the equity firm and its investment life cycle, the fund's investors typically plan to exit anywhere between three and 10 years after the initial investment. Among other things, investors consider the time value of money—the concept that a million dollars today is worth more than a million dollars 5 years from now—when determining what kind of returns or IRR they expect over time. Table 10-4 provides an approximate cheat sheet for the entrepreneur. As the table shows, an investor who walks away with 5 times her initial investment in 5 years has earned a 38 percent IRR.

T A B L E   10-4

Time Value of Money—IRR on a Multiple of Original Investment over a Period of Time

	2×	3×	4×	5×	6×	7×	8×	9×	10×
2 years	41	73	100	124	145	165	183	200	216
3 years	26	44	59	71	82	91	100	108	115
4 years	19	32	41	50	57	63	68	73	78
5 years	15	25	32	38	43	48	52	55	58
6 years	12	20	26	31	35	38	41	44	47
7 years	10	17	22	26	29	32	35	37	39

During the 1990s, there was an explosion in the number of private equity funds formed. According to the National Venture Capital Association (and as seen in Table 7-8), the total number of private equity funds (venture capital, mezzanine, and buyout) in the United States increased substantially, going from 151 in 1990 to 807 in 2000. Why? You know the answer: returns! In 2003, after the dot-com crash, this number fell to only 263. As private equity fundraising returned in the mid-2000s, the number of funds climbed back to over 400, roughly where it sits today. Of those, the National Venture Capital Association reports that 248 are venture capitalists. Table 10-5 shows venture capital fund-raising from 1996 to 2006.

INTERNATIONAL PRIVATE EQUITY

Over the last decade, private equity has exploded around the globe. While North America still represents 41 percent of all private equity dollars, other regions are catching up, and fund-raising is increasing around the world. While much of the capital comes from U.S. investors, foreign investors, including governments such as those of China and Kuwait, have allocated assets to private

T A B L E   10-5

Commitments to Venture Capital Funds

Year	Funds Raised (Billions of Dollars)
1996	12.0
1997	17.3
1998	26.7
1999	57.4
2000	83.2
2001	50.0
2002	13.1
2003	9.9
2004	18.4
2005	24.9
2006	24.3

Source: Dow Jones Venture Source, "Venture Capital Industry Overview," 2006.

equity investing. Within the venture capital world, the United States is still dominant. With a staggering 71 percent of the venture capital raised by G7 nations, the United States remains the center of entrepreneurial activity.

Both the number of funds and the amount of capital that has been raised in Europe, Latin America, and Asia have dramatically increased each year. Most of the money, estimated to be 60 to 70 percent, has come from investors in the United States, including pension funds, insurance companies, endowments, and wealthy individuals. Several of the international funds are highlighted in Figure 10-2. Capital raised in 2007 was $54 billion in Europe [Source: European Private Equity and Venture Capital Association], $51 billion in Asia [Source: Asia Venture Capital Journal] , and $4.4 billion in Latin America and the Caribbean [Source: Emerging Markets private Equity Association].

ADVICE FOR RAISING PRIVATE EQUITY

Derrick Collins, a general partner at Polestar Capital, gives the following advice to entrepreneurs who are interested in obtaining equity capital:

F I G U R E   10-2

Various International Private Equity Firms

Latin America	Europe	Asia
Exxel Capital Partners	Merlin Ventures	SOFTBANK Capital
GP Capital Partners	Early Bird Ventures	Attractor Investors
CVC/Opportunity Equity Partners	3i	Vertex Management

- Do your homework. Seek investors with a proclivity for your deal. Approach only those who are buying what you are selling. Pursue capital from firms that explicitly state in their description an interest in your industry, the size of the investment you want, and the entrepreneurial stage of your company.

- Get an introduction to the investors prior to submitting the business plan. Find someone who knows one of the general partners, limited partners, or associates of the firm. Ask that person to call on your behalf to give you an introduction and endorsement. This action will maximize the attention given to your plan and shorten the response time.

If these steps result in a meeting with a private equity investor, John Doerr, a general partner at KPCB, suggests the following:

> After the first meeting with the venture capitalist, you might say "I'd like a yes or no right now, but I understand you will need more than one meeting. So what's your level of interest, and what's the next step?" Frankly, you'd prefer a swift no to a long drawn-out maybe. Those are death.[11]

INCREASING SPECIALIZATION OF PRIVATE EQUITY FIRMS

There has been an increasing trend toward private equity firms specializing in a particular industry or stage of development. Firms can be categorized as either generalists or specialists. Generalists are more opportunistic and look at a variety of opportunities, from high-tech to high-growth retail. Specialized firms tend to focus on an industry segment or two, for instance, software and communications. Notice that these are still very broad industries.

Specialization has increased for several reasons. First, in an increasingly competitive industry, venture capitalists are competing for deal flow. If a firm is the recognized expert in a certain industry area, then it is more likely that this firm will be exposed to deals in this area. Additionally, the firm is better able to assess and value the deal because of its expertise in the industry. Finally, some specialized firms are able to negotiate lower valuations and better terms because the entrepreneur values the industry knowledge and contacts that a specialized firm can provide. Entrepreneurs should keep this in mind when raising funds. As important as it is for entrepreneurs to target the correct investment stage of a prospective venture capital firm, it is equally important that they consider the industry specialization of the firm.

IDENTIFYING PRIVATE EQUITY FIRMS

One of the best resources for finding the appropriate private equity firm is *Pratt's Guide to Private Equity and Venture Capital Sources*, which lists companies by state, preferred size of investment, and industry interests. Several additional resources are available online:

1. The National Venture Capital Association at www.nvca.org or 703–351–5269
2. VentureOne at ventureone.com
3. New Hampshire Center for Venture Research at http://wsbe2.unh.edu/center-venture-research
4. Ewing Marion Kauffman Foundation at http://www.kauffman.org/resources.cfm

Another online source is the W. Maurice Young Entrepreneurship and Venture Capital Research Centre. It produces the Venture Capital Web Links site. More than 150 Web sites, including 71 sites filled with lists of investors, are highlighted.

The final suggestion is to pursue the opportunity to make a presentation at a venture capital forum such as the Springboard

Conference for female entrepreneurs or the Mid-Atlantic Venture Fair, which is open to entrepreneurs in all industries and at all stages of the business cycle. These are usually 2-day events where entrepreneurs get a chance to present to and meet local and national private equity providers. Typically the entrepreneur must submit an application with a fee of approximately $200. If the investor is selected to make a 10- to 15-minute presentation, an additional fee of $500 or so may be required. The National Venture Capital Association should be contacted to find out about forums and their locations, times, and dates.

SMALL-BUSINESS INVESTMENT COMPANIES

The federal government, through the SBA, also provides equity capital to entrepreneurs. Small-business investment companies (SBICs) are privately owned, for-profit equity firms that are licensed and regulated by the SBA. SBICs invest in businesses employing fewer than 500 people and showing a net worth not greater than $18 million and after-tax income not exceeding $6 million over the two most recent years. There are more than 418 SBICs in the country with over $23 billion nationwide. In 2006, the SBIC program firms invested $2.9 billion in equity and debt capital. The firms made approximately 4,000 investments in 2,121 different small businesses. Investments range from $150,000 to $5 million.

SBICs were created in 1957 for the purpose of expanding the availability of risk capital to entrepreneurs. Many of the first private equity firms were SBICs. And many of the country's successful companies received financing from an SBIC. These include Intel, Compaq Computer, and Outback Steakhouse. They also include some notable debacles like the venture begun by Susan MacDougal, who used her $300,000 to invest in a little real estate project called the Whitewater Development Corporation.

In most ways, SBICs are similar to traditional private equity firms. The primary difference between the two is their origination and their financing. Anyone can start a traditional private equity firm as long as he can raise the capital. But someone who is interested in starting an SBIC firm must first get a license from the SBA. Interest in creating an SBIC comes from the attractive financing arrangement: for every dollar raised by the general partners for the fund, the SBA will invest $2 at a very low interest rate, with no payments due for either 5 or 10 years. Therefore, if the general partners obtain $25 million in commitments from private sources, the SBA will invest $50 million, making it a $75 million fund.

SBICs invest $150,000 to $5 million in each deal. They tend to focus on growth-stage companies rather than pure start-ups.

Included under the SBIC program are specialized small-business investment companies (SSBICs). They are similar to SBICs in every way except that they tend to make smaller investments and, most importantly, they are created specifically to provide investments in companies owned by socially and economically disadvantaged entrepreneurs.

Although they are not technically part of the SBIC program, the New Markets Venture Capital Program and Rural Business Investment Program are modeled on the SBIC program. The two programs combined provide equity capital to entrepreneurs with companies in rural, urban, and specially designated low- and moderate-income (LMI) areas.[12]

Clearly, the comprehensive SBIC program has been a strong contributor to the emergence and success of entrepreneurship in America. It has increased the pool of equity capital for entrepreneurs, as well as made equity capital available to underserved entrepreneurs. The general private equity industry has a reputation for being interested only in investments in technology entrepreneurs. In contrast, SBICs have a reputation for doing "low-tech" and "no-tech" deals. Both reputations are unfounded. Traditional private firms such as Thoma Cressey Equity Partners invest in later-stage, "no-tech" companies, and SBICs such as Chicago Venture Partners invest in technology companies. In fact, 11 of the top 100 companies on the 2005 *Inc.* 500 list of America's fastest-growing companies received SBIC financing, as did 8 of the top 100 "Hot Growth Companies for 2005" featured in *BusinessWeek.*[13] Figure 10-3 lists a sample of successful SBIC-backed companies.

A free directory of operating SBICs can be obtained by calling the SBA Office of Investments at 202–205–6510 or going online at http://www.sba.gov/aboutsba/sbaprograms/inv/inv_directory_sbic.html. There is also a national SBIC trade association. Its directory can be accessed free and SBICs can be sorted by criteria at www.nasbic.org.

F I G U R E   10-3

SBIC-Backed Companies

America Online	Leap Into Learning, Inc.
Amgen, Inc.	Metrolina Outreach
Apple Computer	Octel Communications
	Outback Steakhouse
Compaq Computer	PeopleSoft
Costco Wholesale Corp.	Potomac Group, Inc.
Datastream	Radio One
Federal Express	
Gymboree	Restoration Hardware, Inc.
Harman International	Sports Authority
Healthcare Services of America	Staples
Intel	Sun Microsystems
Jenny Craig Inc.	Telesis
La Madeleine Inc.	Vertex Communications Co.

Source: Small Business Administration, www.sba.gov/aboutsba/sbaprograms/inv/INV_SUCCESS_STORIES.html.

INITIAL PUBLIC OFFERINGS

Every year, hundreds of entrepreneurs raise equity capital by selling their company's stock to the public market. This process of selling a typical minimum of $5 million of stock to institutions and individuals is called an initial public offering (IPO) and is strictly regulated by the SEC. The result is a company that is "publicly owned." For many entrepreneurs, taking a company public is the ultimate statement of entrepreneurial success. They believe that entrepreneurs get recognized for one of two reasons: having a company that went bankrupt or having one that had an IPO. Timing is everything with an IPO issue. The late 1990s were record-breaking days of glory, the early 2000s were miserable, and IPOs have lately begun to rebound to pre-dot-com levels. .

When a company "goes public" in the United States, it must meet a new standard of financial reporting, regulated by the Securities and Exchange Commission. All the financial information of such a company must be published quarterly and distributed to the company's shareholders. Therefore, because of the SEC's public disclosure rules, everything about a publicly owned company is open to potential and present shareholders. Information such as the president's salary and bonus, the company's number of employees, and the company's profits are open to the public, including competitors.

This source of capital was extraordinarily popular during the 1990s. From 1970 to 1997, entrepreneurs raised $297 billion through IPOs. More than 58 percent of this capital was raised between 1993 and 1997.[14] In 1999 and 2000, entrepreneurs were the highly sought-after guests of honor at a record private equity feast. The money flowed, and entrepreneurs could, in essence, auction off their business plans to the highest bidders. Average valuations of high-tech start-ups rose from about $11 million in 1996 to almost $30 million in 2000.[15] But by the summer of 2000, as the Nasdaq began to crash, venture capital investments began to slow dramatically. As Table 10-6 shows, the boom began to end in 2000 when the public markets became less interested in hyped technology companies that had no foreseeable chances of making profits. According to research by PricewaterhouseCoopers, in the first three months of 2001, venture capitalists reduced their investments in high-tech start-ups by $6.7 billion—a 40 percent drop from the previous quarter. In the first quarter of 2001, only 21 companies went public compared with 123 in the same quarter a year earlier. And by late 2001, the IPO market was down dramatically.

For firms that are still committed to going public with an IPO issue during sluggish times, patience had better be a core competency. Venture Economics, a research firm that follows the venture capital industry, studied the time it takes a company to go from its first round of financing to its initial public offering. In 1999, a company took an average of 140 days; 2 years later, that average had surged to 487 days—a jump of 247 percent.

1990s IPO Boom

The stock market boom of the 1990s was historic. In 1995, Netscape went public despite the fact that it had never made a profit. This was the beginning of the craze of companies going public even though they had no profits. In the history of the United States, there has never been another decade that had as many IPOs or raised as much capital. *Barron's* called it one of the greatest gold

T A B L E   10-6

Number of Initial Public Offerings

	Annual U.S. IPO Volume	
	Amount Raised, Billions of Dollars	Number of IPOs
1990	5.3	154
1991	17.0	331
1992	26.8	524
1993	46.2	703
1994	28.0	585
1995	36.9	571
1996	51.4	823
1997	44.3	590
1998	40.4	368
1999	70.8	512
2000	71.2	396
2001	37.7	103
2002	28.1	94
2003	15.8	85
2004	48.9	250

Source: Dealogic; Thomson Financial.

rushes of American capitalism.[16] Another writer called it "one of the greatest speculative manias in history."[17]

The frothy IPO market was not limited to technology companies. On October 19, 1999, Martha Stewart took her company public and the stock price doubled before the end of the day. Vince McMahan, the owner of the World Wrestling Federation, took his company public the same day. Disappointingly, the results were not as good as Martha's. The stock increased only a puny 48.5 percent by the day's end! In 2000, when many Internet companies were canceling their initial public offerings, Krispy Kreme donuts was the second best-performing IPO of the year.[18]

Because the public markets were responding so positively to IPOs in the 1990s, companies began racing to go public. Before 1995, it was customary for a company to have been in business for at least 3 years and have shown four consecutive quarters of increasing profits before it could do an IPO. The perfect example was Microsoft. Bill Gates took it public in 1986, more than a decade after he founded it. By the time Microsoft went public, it had recorded several consecutive years of profitability.

But as stated earlier, the Netscape IPO in August 1995 changed things for the next 5 years. In addition to having no profit, Netscape was very young, having been in business for only 16 months. By the end of 1999, the Netscape story was very common.[19] The absurdity was best described by a Wall Street analyst, who said, "Major Wall Street firms used to require four quarters of profits before an IPO. Then it went to four quarters of revenue, and now it's four quarters of breathing."[20]

This IPO euphoria created unparalleled wealth for entrepreneurs, especially those in Silicon Valley's technology industry. At the height of the boom in 1999, it was reported that Silicon Valley executives held $112 billion in stock and options. This was slightly more than Portugal's entire gross domestic product of $109 million.[21]

As all this information shows, entrepreneurs were using IPOs to raise capital for the company's operations as well as to gain personal wealth.

PUBLIC EQUITY MARKETS

After a company goes public, it is listed and traded on one of several markets in the United States. More than 13,000 companies are listed on these markets. The three major and most popular markets are the New York Stock Exchange (NYSE), the American Stock Exchange (AMEX), and the National Association of Securities Dealers Automated Quotations (Nasdaq). Let's look at each in greater detail.

NYSE

With its start in 1792, the New York Stock Exchange is the oldest trading market in the world. It also has the largest valuation. These two facts are the reason the NYSE that is called the "Cadillac of securities markets." Companies listed on this market are considered the strongest financially of companies on the three markets. In order to be listed on the NYSE, the value of the company's outstanding shares must be at least $18 million, and its annual earnings before taxes (EBT) must be at least $2.5 million. Companies listed on this market are the older, more venerable companies, such as General Electric, Sears, and McDonald's. In 2000 Microsoft moved to the NYSE from the Nasdaq.

AMEX

The American Stock Exchange is the world's largest market for foreign stocks and the second-largest trading market. The market value of a listed company must be at least $3 million, with an annual EBT of $750,000. In this market, traders buy and sell stocks, options, and derivatives in person at auctions. In 1998 the AMEX and Nasdaq markets merged and took the name Nasdaq-Amex Market Group. At the time, the total market value of all companies listed on both markets was $2.2 trillion, compared with $11.6 trillion for the NYSE.[22]

Nasdaq

The Nasdaq market opened in 1971 and was the first electronic stock market. More shares (an average of 1.8 billion per day) are traded over this market than over any other in the world.[23]

The minimum market value for companies listed on this market is $1 million. There is no minimum EBT requirement. That is why this market, with over 5,000 listings, is the fastest-growing market in the world. The Nasdaq is heavily filled with tech, biotech, and small-company stocks. Trading on this market occurs via telephone and computer. All the technology companies that went public since 1995 did so on the Nasdaq market.

Reasons for Going Public

Entrepreneurs take their companies public for several reasons. The first is to raise capital for the operations of the company. Because the money is to be used to grow the company rapidly, the equity capital provided through an IPO may be preferred over debt. In the instances of the tech companies in the 1990s that had negative cash flow, they could not raise debt capital. Only equity financing was available to them.

Even if a company can afford debt capital, some entrepreneurs prefer capital from an IPO because it can be relatively cheap. In fact, the cost of the capital can be lower than that of debt. The explanation is very simple math.

Over the history of the Dow Jones Industrial Average, the average P/E ratio is 14. This means that investors are willing to pay $14 for every $1 of earnings. Therefore, the cost of this capital is only 7 percent ($1/$14)—about 2 percentage points less than the cost of debt today, which at prime plus 2 is approximately 9 percent.

Another reason for going public is that it can be easier to recruit and retain excellent employees by combining publicly traded stock with their salaries. This allows employees to benefit personally when the value of the company increases as a result of their hard work.

Still another good reason is that an IPO provides the entrepreneur with another form of currency that can be used to grow the company. In the 1990s, companies' stock was being widely used as currency. Instead of buying other companies with cash, many buyers paid the sellers with their stock. The seller would then hold the stock and benefit from any future increases in its value. In fact, many deals did not close or were delayed in closing because the seller wanted the buyer's stock instead of cash. This was the case when Disney purchased the ABC network. Disney wanted to pay cash, but the members of the ABC team held out until they received Disney stock. Their reasoning was that $1 worth of Disney's stock was more valuable than $1 cash. They were willing to make the assumption that, unlike cash, which depreciates as a result of inflation, the stock would appreciate.

The final reason for going public is to provide a liquidity exit for the stockholders, including employees, management, and investors.

Reasons for Not Going Public

Taking a company public is extremely difficult. In fact, less than 20 percent of the entrepreneurs who attempt to take a company public are successful.[24] And the process can take a long time—as long as 2 years.

Also, completing an IPO is very expensive. The typical cost is approximately $500,000. Then there are additional annual costs that must be incurred to meet SEC regulations regarding public disclosure, including the publication of the quarterly financial statements.

By the time most companies go public, they have received financing from family and friends, angels, and at least two rounds from institutional investors. As a result, most founders will be lucky if they retain 10 percent ownership. The exception to this rule is Bill Gates, who owns approximately 20 percent of Microsoft.[25] Another is Jeff Bezos, who owns 41 percent of Amazon.com. In late 2001, with his company's stock tanking, that stake was worth just under $1 billion.

One of the greatest problems with going public is that most of the stock is owned by large institutional investors, which have a short-term focus. They exert continual pressure on the CEO to deliver increasing earnings every quarter.

The final reason for not going public is that while funds received when stock is sold by the company can be immediately used for operations, stock owned by the key management team cannot be sold immediately. SEC Rule 144 says that all key members of the company cannot sell any of their stock. These key members are officers, directors, and inside shareholders, including venture capitalists, who own "restricted stock." This is stock that was not registered with the SEC. This is in contrast to the shares of stock issued to the public at the IPO. These stocks are unrestricted.

The holding period for restricted stock is 2 years from the date of purchase. At that time, the restricted stockholders may sell their stock as long as they do not sell more than 1 percent of the total number of shares outstanding in any 3-month period.[26] For example, if the entrepreneur owns 1 million of the 90 million shares of outstanding common stock, she may not sell more than 900,000 shares of the stock in a 3-month period.

Control

One negative myth about going public is that if the entrepreneur owns less than 51 percent of the company, he loses control. This is not true. Founders including Bill Gates, Jeff Bezos, and Michael Dell own less than 51 percent of their companies, but they still have control. The same is true of the Ford family, which owns only 6.5 percent of Ford Motor Company. The key to having control is having influence on the majority of the voting stock. Some stock may be nonvoting stock, a.k.a. capital stock. The entrepreneur, his family, and board members may own virtually none of the nonvoting stock but a majority of the voting stock. This fact, along with the entrepreneur's being in a management position and being the one who determines who sits on the board of directors, keeps him in control.

THE IPO PROCESS

As has been stated earlier, taking a company public can be expensive and time-consuming for the entrepreneur. But when it is done right and for the correct reasons, it can be very rewarding.

While it can take up to 24 months to complete an IPO, investment banking firm William Blair & Company said that 52 to 59 weeks is the norm.

Bessemer Venture Partners, a leading venture capital firm, accurately described a simplified step-by-step IPO process:

1. The entrepreneur decides to take the company public to raise money for future acquisitions.
2. He interviews and selects investment banks (IBs).
3. He meets with the IBs that will underwrite the offering.
4. He files the IPO registration with the SEC.
5. The SEC reviews and approves the registration.
6. The IBs and the entrepreneur go on a "road show."
7. The IBs take tentative commitments.
8. IPO.

Let's discuss these steps in more detail.

The IPO Decision

The entrepreneur's decision to do an IPO can be made almost the day the person decides to go into business. Some entrepreneurs articulate their plans for going public in their original business plan. In starting the business, one of their future objectives is to own a public company.

Others may decide to go public when they get institutional financing. The venture capitalist may provide them with financing only if they agree to go public in 3 to 5 years. In such a case, the entrepreneur and the investor may make the decision.

Other entrepreneurs may decide to go public when they review their 3- to 5-year business plan and realize that their ability to grow as fast as they would like will be determined by the availability of outside equity capital—more than they can get from institutional investors.

Interviews and Selection of Investment Banks

Once the decision to go public has been made, the entrepreneur must hire one or more investment banks to underwrite the offering. This process of selecting an IB is called the "bake-off." Ideally, several IBs that are contacted by the entrepreneur will quickly study the company's business and afterwards solicit, via presentations and meetings, the entrepreneur's selection of their firms. The IB's compensation is typically no more than 7 percent of the capital raised.

Underwriter(s) Meetings

After the IBs are selected, the entrepreneur will meet with the underwriters to plan the IPO. This process includes determining the company's value, the number of shares that will be issued, the selling price of the shares, and the timing of the road show and the IPO.

In typical public offerings, the underwriters buy all of the company's shares at the initial offer price and then sell them at the IPO. When underwriters make this agreement with the entrepreneurs, this is called a firm commitment.

There are also underwriters that make "best-efforts" agreements. In this case, they will not purchase the stock but will make every effort to sell it to a third party.

IPO Registration

The entrepreneur's attorney must file the registration statement with the SEC. This is a two-part document. The first part is called a prospectus and discloses all the information about the company, including the planned use of the money, the valuation, a description of management, and financial statements. The prospectus is the document given to potential investors.

The first printing of this prospectus is called a *red herring* because it contains warnings to the reader that certain things in the document might change. These warnings are printed in red ink.

The second part of the document is the actual registration statement. The four items disclosed are:

- Expenses of distribution
- Indemnification of directors and officers
- Recent sales of unregistered securities
- Exhibits and financial statement schedules[27]

SEC Approval

The SEC reviews the registration statement in detail to determine that all disclosures have been made and that the information is correct and easy to comprehend. The reviewer can approve the statement, allowing the next step in the IPO process to commence; delay the review until changes are made to the statement that satisfy the reviewer; or put a "stop order," which terminates the statement registration process with a disapproval decision.

The Road Show

Once approval of the registration statement has been obtained, the entrepreneur and the IB are free to begin the process of marketing the IPO to potential investors. This is called the road show, where the entrepreneur makes presentations about the company to the potential investors that the IB has identified.

Investment Commitments

During the road show, the entrepreneur makes a "pitch" for why the investors should buy the company's stock. After each presentation, the IBs will meet with the potential investors to determine their interest. The investors' tentative commitments for an actual number of shares are recorded in the "book" that the IB takes to each road show presentation.

The IB wants to accumulate a minimum number of tentative commitments before proceeding to the IPO. IBs like to have three tentative commitments for every share of stock that will be offered.[28]

The IPO

On the day when the IPO will occur, the investment bank and the entrepreneur determine the official stock selling price and the number of shares to be sold. The price may change between the time they began the road show and the day of the IPO, as a result of interest in the stock. If the tentative commitments were greater than a 3-to-1 ratio, then the offering price may be increased. It may be lowered if the opposite occurred. That is exactly what happened to the stock of Wired Ventures, which attempted to go public in 1996. Originally the company wanted to sell 4.75 million shares at $14 each. By the date of the IPO, it made the decision with its IB, Goldman Sachs, to reduce the offering to 3 million shares at a price of $10 per share. One of the reasons for this change was the fact that hours before the stock had to be officially priced for sale, the offer was still undersubscribed by 50 percent. Even at this lower price, though, the IPO never took place. Wired Ventures was not able to raise the $60 million it sought, and it incurred expenses of approximately $1.3 million in its attempt to go public.

Choosing the Right Investment Banker

As the preceding information shows, the ability to have a successful IPO is significantly dependent on the IB. The most critical aspects of an IB are its ability to value the company properly, assist the attorney and entrepreneur in developing the registration statement, help the entrepreneur develop an excellent presentation for the road show, access its database to reach the proper potential investors and invite them to the presentation, and sell the stock. Therefore, the entrepreneur must do as much as possible to select the best IB for her IPO. A few suggestions are as follows:

- Identify the firms that have successfully taken companies public that are similar to yours in size, industry, and amount to be raised. A great resource for finding these companies is *Going Public: The IPO Reporter*, published by Securities Data Publishing (212–765–5311).
- Select experienced firms. At a minimum, the ideal firm has underwritten two deals annually for the past 3 years. The firms that are underwriting eight deals per year, or two each quarter, may be too busy to give proper attention to your deal. Also eliminate those whose deals consistently take more than 90 days to get registration approval.
- Select underwriters that price their deals close to at least the stock's first-day closing. If an underwriter prices the stock too low, so that the stock increases dramatically in price by the end of the first day, then the entrepreneur sold more equity than needed. For example, if the initial offering was 1 million shares at $5 per share and the stock closed the first day at $10 per share, then the stock was underpriced. Instead of raising $5 million for 1 million shares, the entrepreneur could have raised the same amount for 500,000 shares had the underwriter priced the stock better.
- Select underwriters that file planned selling prices close to the actual price at the initial offering. Some underwriters file at a price and then try to force the entrepreneur to open at a lower price so that they can sell the stock and their investors can reap the benefits of the increase. This practice, when it is done, usually occurs a day or so prior to the IPO, when the underwriter threatens to terminate the offering if the price is not reduced. To minimize the chances of this happening, the entrepreneur should select only underwriters that have a consistent pattern of filing and bringing the stock to the market at similar prices.
- Select underwriters that have virtually no experience with failing to complete the offering. Companies that file for an IPO but do not make it are considered "damaged goods" by investors.

- Get an introduction to the investment banker. Never cold-call the banker. The company's attorney or accountant should make the introduction.[29]

THE FINANCING SPECTRUM

There's an old dog food commercial that features a frolicking puppy changing before our eyes into a mature dog. The commercial reminds pet owners that as their dogs grow, the food that fuels them needs to change too. Businesses are the same way with equity financing. As a business evolves from an idea into a mature company, the type of financing it requires changes. At the end of Chapter 8, the steps through which many successful high-growth entrepreneurs raised their equity capital were highlighted in the financing spectrum.

An actual entrepreneur who raised money from almost all the sources of capital on that spectrum was Jeff Bezos. Figure 10-4 shows when Bezos raised capital and from whom.

F I G U R E   10-4

Jeff Bezos's Financing Spectrum

July 1994	October 1994 and February 1995	December 1995	1996	May 1997
Amazon.com concept	Amazon.com incorporation and launch	Amazon.com operating	Amazon.com growing	Amazon.com exponential growth
↓	↓	↓	↓	↓
Capital from personal savings	Capital from mother and father	Capital from angels	Capital from venture capitalist	Capital from IPO
■ $15,000 interest-free loan	■ 582,528 shares of common stock sold to father for $100,000	■ Raised $981,000 at a $5 million premoney valuation	■ $8 million from KPCB at a $52 million premoney valuation	■ Raised $54 million
■ $10,000 equity invest-ment for 10 million shares of common stock	■ 847,716 shares of common stock sold to mother for $144,000			

DIRECT PUBLIC OFFERINGS

In 1989, the SEC made it possible for companies seeking less than $5 million to raise it directly from the public without going through the expensive and time-consuming IPO process described earlier. This direct process is aptly called a direct public offering, or DPO. In a DPO, shares are usually sold for $1 to $10 each without an underwriter, and the investors do not face the sophisticated investor requirements. Forty-five states allow DPOs, and the usual legal, accounting, and marketing fees are less than $50,000.

There are three DPO programs that have been used by thousands of entrepreneurs. The programs are:

1. Regulation D, Rule 504, which is also called the Small Corporate Offering Registration, a.k.a. SCOR
2. Regulation A
3. Intrastate

The SEC has a free pamphlet entitled "Q & A: Small Business and the SEC—Help Your Company Go Public" available on its web site at www.sec.gov. Let's discuss each DPO program in more detail.

- *Small Corporate Offering Registration.* In the Small Corporate Offering Registration, or SCOR, program, the entrepreneur has 12 months to raise a maximum of $1 million. Shares can be sold to an unlimited number of investors throughout the country via general solicitation and even advertising. One entrepreneur who accessed capital via a DPO was Rick Moon, the founder of Thanksgiving Coffee Co. Rick raised $1.25 million in 1996 for 20 percent of his coffee and tea wholesaling company, which had annual revenues of $4.6 million. He aggressively advertised the offering to his suppliers and customers on his Web site, in his catalog, on his coffee-bean bags, and on the bean dispensers in stores.[30]
- *Regulation A offering.* Under the Regulation A program, an entrepreneur can raise a maximum of $5 million in 12 months. Unlike offerings under SCOR, where no SEC filings are required, this offering must be filed with the SEC. Otherwise, all the attributes assigned to SCOR are applicable to Regulation A. Dorothy Pittman Hughes, the

founder of Harlem Copy Center, with $300,000 in annual revenues in 1998, began raising $2 million under this program by offering stock for $1 per share. The minimum number of shares that adults could buy was 50; for children, the minimum was 25.[31]

- *Intrastate program.* The intrastate program requires companies to limit the sale of their stock to investors in one state. This program has other significant differences from SCOR and Regulation A. First, there are no federal laws limiting the maximum that can be raised or the time allowed. These two items vary by state. The other difference is that the stock cannot be resold outside the state for 9 months.

The DPO is best suited for historically profitable companies with audited financial statements and a well-written business plan. Shareholders are typically affinity groups that are somehow tied to the company, such as customers, employees, suppliers, distributors, and friends. After completing a DPO, the company can still do a traditional IPO at a later date. Real Goods Trading Company did just that. In 1991, it raised $1 million under SCOR. Two years later, it raised an additional $3.6 million under Regulation A. Today its stock is traded on the Nasdaq market.

DPOs have a few negative aspects. First, it is estimated that over 70 percent of those who register for a DPO fail, for various reasons. But the greatest drawback is the fact that there is no public market exchange like the NYSE for DPO stock. This type of exchange brings sellers and buyers together, and that does not exist for DPOs. Therefore, the ability to raise capital is negatively affected by legitimate concerns on the potential investors' part that their investment cannot be made liquid easily. Another problem is that the absence of a market leaves the market appreciation of the stock in question. One critic of DPOs said, "There is no liquidity in these offerings. Investors are stepping into a leghold trap."[32] As a result, DPO investors tend to be long-term-focused. Trading in the stock is usually arranged by the company or made through an order-matching service that the company manages. The shareholders can also get liquid if the company is sold, the owners buy back the stock, or the company does a traditional IPO.

Because this is a book about finance, not about law, we have intentionally avoided a long discussion of the legal aspects of entrepreneurship. That doesn't mean that you should ignore the legal ins and outs of running a business or getting one started. One great resource that comes highly recommended from my students is the book *The Entrepreneur's Guide to Business Law* by Constance Bagley and Craig Dauchy.

NOTES

1. *BusinessWeek*, January 8, 2001, p. 55.
2. *Forbes ASAP*, June 1, 1998, p. 24.
3. *Forbes*, January 10, 2000, p. F.
4. *Inc.*, July 1997, p. 48.
5. *Crain's Chicago Business*, March 9, 1999, p. SB4.
6. *BUYOUTS*, February 8, 1999, p. 23.
7. *Private Equity Analyst*, August 1999, p. 36.
8. Ibid., p. 34.
9. Ibid.
10. PricewaterhouseCoopers/National Venture Capital Association, "Corporate Venture Capital Activity on the Rise in 2006."
11. *Fast Company*, February 1998, p. 86.
12. Small Business Administration.
13. National Association of Small Business Investment Companies, February 2006.
14. *Directorship Inc.*, Fall 1998, p. 1.
15. *The Economist*, May 3, 2001.
16. *Fast Company*, January 2000, p. 50.
17. Edward Chancellor, *Devil Take the Hindmost: A History of Financial Speculation* (New York: Farrar, Straus, Giroux, 1999).
18. *Boston Globe*, February 21, 2001.
19. *USA Today*, June 22, 2000.
20. *USA Today*, December 23, 1999.
21. *Time*, September 27, 1999.
22. *Chicago Sun-Times*, November 3, 1998, p. 45.
23. *Chicago Sun-Times*, September 3, 2000, p. 47A.
24. *Wall Street Journal*, April 6, 2001, p. C1.

25. *USA Today*, January 21, 1999.
26. *The Entrepreneur's Guide to Going Public*, p. 297.
27. Ibid., p. 202.
28. *Inc.*, February 1998, p. 57.
29. *Success*, January 1999, p. 20.
30. *Inc.*, December 1996, p. 70.
31. *Essence*, May 1998, p. 64.
32. *USA Today*, April 29, 1997, p. 4B.

CHAPTER 11

Financing for Minorities and Women

INTRODUCTION

As noted in the beginning of the book, minority- and women-owned firms are fast becoming powerful economic forces in the small-business world. Minority-owned businesses grew more than 3 times as fast as U.S. firms overall between 1997 and 2002, increasing from 3.1 million to 4.1 million firms.[1] The following statistics come from a report by the Small Business Administration in 2007 and are worth considering:

- Minority-owned firms generated $694 billion in annual revenue.
- While Hispanics controlled the largest share of firms owned by minorities and constituted the largest minority business community, Asian- and Pacific Islander–owned firms had the largest share of minority-owned business revenues—49 percent.
- Black-owned firms experienced explosive growth. The total number of black-owned firms grew 45 percent, while their total receipts grew 25 percent.
- The number of employees declined by 6 percent for white-owned firms, while Hispanic firms saw the highest employment growth—11 percent.

- Women owned 17 percent of all private firms with employees in the United States; Native Americans women owned 30 percent of all businesses with employees owned by Native Americans, the highest percentage among all ethnic groups.

As I also mentioned at the beginning of the book, my mother, Ollie Mae Rogers, was the first entrepreneur I ever met, and accordingly, I have a tremendous amount of respect for women entrepreneurs. As noted earlier, women-owned businesses total over $1.9 trillion in annual sales and have more than 12.8 million employees nationwide.[2] Between 1997 and 2006, the number of majority women-owned firms increased from 5.4 million to 7.7 million, an increase of 42 percent, almost double that of all firms.[3] Between 1997 and 2004, the number of privately held firms that are more than 50 percent owned by women of color grew 6 times as fast as the total number of privately held firms.[4]

Needless to say, minority and women entrepreneurs have played the game of catch-up brilliantly, and they have forced the traditional small-business infrastructure to change. Thank God we are past the era when women could not get a loan without their husband's signature and it was legal to reject a loan application from a person simply because of his ethnicity or race! The laws that made such gender and racial discrimination legal had a profound effect on minority and women entrepreneurship. The inability to access capital from other than personal savings, family, friends, and angels retarded the growth of most entrepreneurs from these two sectors. Given the absence of growth capital from financial institutions, these entrepreneurs, in essence, were involuntarily relegated to a life as mom-and-pop, or lifestyle, entrepreneurs. The legacy is that we have virtually no major corporations that were founded by minorities or women.

Recent research from the SBA also indicates that race is a significant predictor of the likelihood of opening a business and that the odds of a minority person opening a business are 55 percent lower than those for a nonminority. The data in Table 11-1 show the composition of the total U.S. population side by side with a breakdown of U.S. business receipts by race. While the situation continues to improve, these data clearly indicate that the process is still ongoing.

T A B L E 11-1

Composition of U.S. Population versus Share of Business Receipts

Group	Share of Population	Share of Business Receipts
White	68.2%	92.5%
Hispanic	13.5%	2.5%
Black	11.8%	1.0%
Asian/Pacific Islander	4.1%	3.7%
Native American/Other	2.4%	0.3%

Source: Small Business Administration.

And while there are federal laws that prohibit gender and racial discrimination in debt and equity financing, it is sad to report that even today, minority and women entrepreneurs are receiving a pittance of all the capital provided to entrepreneurs.

Still, there are an increasing number of investment firms that are focusing on all kinds of niches, and these firms are an important resource. For example, there are specialized firms that target entrepreneurs who are female, are minorities, or are in industries such as consumer goods, food products, banking, and sports. There are even firms that will invest only in companies in certain geographic regions, such as the New England region or rural areas. A few of these specialized firms are listed in Figure 11-1.

F I G U R E 11-1

Niche Equity Investment Firms

Name	Targeted Investments
Belvedere Capital Partners	Community banks in California
IMG/Chase Sports Capital	Sports-related companies
Village Ventures	Underserved areas, nonmajor cities
Bastion Capital	Hispanic entrepreneurs
Capital Across America (CXA)	Women-owned businesses
Ceres	Women-owned businesses

MINORITIES — DEBT FINANCING

The history regarding the success rate of minority entrepreneurs in raising institutional equity and debt capital is worse than that of women. Research by the Small Business Administration showed that minorities face significantly higher rejection rates for credit than firms owned by white males. The data in Table 11-2 show denial rates for minority owned firms.

T A B L E   11-2

Denial Rates for Business Lending

African Americans	53%
Asian	36%
Hispanic	47%
All minority-owned	47%
All firms	21%

The result of this high rejection rate is that minority-owned companies use personal financing more. SBA data suggest that only 9.5 percent of white-owned businesses use a credit card in their business, whereas 20.6 percent of Islander-owned, 15 percent of black-owned, and 13 percent of Hispanic-owned business do.

Advice

Minority entrepreneurs who are seeking debt capital should approach the institutions that are friends to minorities. Those firms include community development banks and large finance companies such as CIT Group, the large middle-market-focused financial services firm (which is unrelated to the more widely known bank holding company Citigroup, Inc.). The CIT Small Business Lending Corporation has been the nation's leading SBA lender to women-, veteran-, and minority-owned businesses for the past four years. CIT provided $440 million to these groups during 2005–2006.

Another excellent source of debt financing is SBA lenders. The number of SBA loans has increased from 37,528 to 88,912 between 2001 and 2005. During this period, the share of total loans to minorities has increased from 25 percent to 29 percent. Large financial institutions that have increased their lending to minority firms include Wells Fargo, which has committed to lend $3 billion to Asian-owned businesses, $5 billion to Latino businesses, and $1 billion to black-owned businesses. Other sources of funding for minority-owned businesses are Accion USA, the largest business lender of its kind in the United States, making loans from $500 to $25,000. Also, the National Minority Business Council Micro-Loan Fund provides short-term loans of $1,500 to $2,500 to minority-owned small businesses.

MINORITIES—EQUITY FINANCING

Less than 1 percent of all equity capital provided by institutional investors has gone to minority entrepreneurs. Part of the problem is participation rates. For example, minority entrepreneurs represented only 6.9 percent of entrepreneurs that presented their business concepts to angels. Strong evidence suggests that the problem is a lack of opportunity. The yield, or percentage of approved investments, for minority-owned firms was 7.1 percent, or close to two-thirds the general yield rate. This makes no sense in light of the fact that from 1991 to 2001, investment firms targeting minorities returned an average of 23.9 percent compared to 20.2 percent for all private equity firms.[5]

Virtually all of that capital has come from firms that are associated with the National Association of Investment Companies (NAIC). These NAIC-related firms explicitly target investments in minority-owned companies and work together extensively to find minority investments. As proof, a survey of these firms indicated that 100 percent of them had participated in syndicated deals. Some also invest proactively in women entrepreneurs. There are more than 50 NAIC firms in the United States that have invested over $2.5 billion in approximately 20,000 ethnically diverse businesses. By 2003, these firms had a collective $5 billion of capital under management.[6]

Almost every high-growth, successful, minority-owned company has received financing from an NAIC-affiliated firm. A few of the equity capital recipients are listed in Figure 11-2.

F I G U R E   11-2

Various Equity Investments from NAIC Member Firms

Company	Minority	Description	NAIC Member
Radio One	Black	Public company (Nasdaq: ROIA). Largest station targeting African Americans	TSG Capital
Black Entertainment Television	Black	Former public company (NYSE: BTV). Acquired by Viacom	Syncom
Z-Spanish Media	Hispanic	Largest Spanish-language media network	TSG Capital
Watson Pharmaceuticals	Asian	Public company (NYSE: WPI)	Polestar Capital
BioGenex Laboratories	Indian		Pacesetter

Equity capital has also been made available to minority entrepreneurs by angel investors. One such group is called the Access to Capital Group. It is a Dallas-based group of minority investors that can be contacted at 877–408–1ACG.

Advice

Minority entrepreneurs who are seeking equity capital should contact the NAIC at www.naicvc.com to get a complete listing of the member funds. A few are presented in Figure 11-3.

F I G U R E   11-3

Various NAIC Members

NAIC Member	Location	Phone
Black Enterprise/Greenwich Street Equity Fund	New York, New York	212-816-1189
Opportunity Capital Partners	Fremont, California	510-795-7000
Hispania Capital	Chicago, Illinois	312-697-4611

WOMEN — DEBT FINANCING

Throughout history, women have always had a tough time getting debt capital from institutions such as banks. Fortunately, that situation has begun to improve in recent years. A new study by Wells Fargo showed that 70 percent of women express satisfaction with their access to credit. That figure is up from 50 percent 10 years ago.[7] Moreover, women business owners' access to commercial credit increased by more than two-thirds between 1996 and 2003, from 20 percent of women using commercial credit in 1996 to 34 percent in 2003.

However, there is still considerable work to be done. An SBA study showed that 32 percent of male-owned businesses had a line of credit, compared to only 23 percent of women-owned businesses. Rejection rates for a bank line of credit for a woman-owned business were higher, at 45 percent versus 32 percent for a male-owned firm. Rejection rates for all credit sources for women-owned firms were 26 percent as compared to 20 percent for all firms. Finally, 22 percent of women view credit as their greatest challenge during their first 2 years in operation, versus 13 percent for men.[8] To compound the problem, the Wells Fargo study showed that many women business owners are not taking advantage of the full range of credit products. For example, 74 percent never considered pledging accounts receivable, 55 percent never considered unsecured personal loans, and 42 percent never considered vendor credit.[9]

Advice

Women who are seeking debt financing should approach institutions that want to do business with women. Those firms include SBA lenders and banks such as Wells Fargo, which in 1994 committed to loan $1 billion to women entrepreneurs. A year later, Wells Fargo became so convinced that financing women entrepreneurs was a great strategy that it increased its commitment to $10 billion to be invested over a 10-year period. In the following 10 years, Wells Fargo lent more than $25 billion through 600,000 loans to women business owners.[10] This additional commitment came after the National Foundation for Women Business Owners published research showing that investing in women entrepreneurs was sound business because they had a better chance of repaying business loans. This fact was proved by information showing that, on average, women-owned companies stay in business longer. Specifically, nearly 75 percent of women-owned firms founded in 1991 were still in business 3 years later, compared with 66 percent for all U.S. firms.[11] Other banks that have actively targeted women-owned businesses include KeyBank, through its Key4Women program, and Wachovia. Both banks have successfully provided more than $1 billion in loans to women.[12]

In addition, the SBA has increasingly supported women's businesses. Between 1990 and 2004, the percentage of U.S. Small Business Administration–backed loans going to women increased from 13 percent to 22 percent. While this increase in activity is to be applauded, it should be noted that there is still room for improvement on SBA loans. From 2000 to 2004, the percentage of loans made to women increased only from 20 percent to 21 percent.[13] A few other institutional sources of debt capital for women entrepreneurs are listed in Figure 11-4.

F I G U R E 11-4

Various Women-Focused Institutional Debt Sources

Source	Description/Contact
Capital Across America	Mezzanine-stage financing
Count-Me-In for Women's Economic Independence	An online lending program
FleetBoston Financial's Women Entrepreneurs' Connection	Small-business-banking program
SBA, Office of Women's Business Ownership	800-8-ASK-SBA
Wells Fargo Bank	800-359-3557, ext. 120
Women, Inc.	$150 million loan fund, 800-930-3993

WOMEN—EQUITY FINANCING

The year 2000 was the first year in which women received more than 2 percent of institutional equity capital. In 2000, they received 4.4 percent.[14] In 2003, only 4 percent of women business owners with revenues of $1 million or more obtained or intended to seek equity investment, compared with 11 percent of men-owned firms. In that year, 4.2 percent of venture capital went to women entrepreneurs.[15] According to a study commissioned by the Center for Women's Business Research (formerly National Foundation for Women Business Owners), women entrepreneurs who seek or have obtained equity capital find their sources of funding in three ways: word of mouth (60 percent of recipients, 49 percent of seekers), their own networks of business consultants (50 percent of recipients, 42 percent of seekers), and investors who have sought them out (38 percent of recipients, 39 percent of seekers).[16]

Advice

My advice would be the same as with the debt capital sources: go to sources that are interested in doing business with women. Figure 11-5 lists equity funds that target women entrepreneurs.

FIGURE 11-5

Women-Focused Private Equity Firms

Source	Location	Information
Three Guineas Fund	San Francisco, California	www.3gf.org
Boldcap Ventures, LLC	New York, New York	www.boldcap.com
Ceres Venture Fund	Evanston, Illinois	www.ceresventurefund.com
New Vista Capital	Palo Alto, California	www.nvcap.com
Isabella Capital	Cincinnati, Ohio	www.fundisabella.com

A leader in the campaign to accelerate women's access to equity markets is Springboard Enterprises. Springboard has held 17 forums, involving over 3,500 women, and has raised over $4 billion for women's businesses. Springboard's Web site has a Learning Center that is a good resource for women entrepreneurs.[17]

Another great source of equity capital is angel investors. Figure 11-6 lists those investors who are interested in financing women entrepreneurs.

F I G U R E   11-6

Various Women-Focused Angel Investors

Source	Location	Information
Astia	San Francisco, California	www.astia.org
Seraph Capital Forum	Seattle, Washington	www.seraphcapital.com
Golden Seeds	New York, New York	www.goldenseeds.com
Phenomenelle Angels	Madison, Wisconsin	www.phenomenelleangels.com

In addition to Springboard, there are several other resources and organizations devoted to helping women entrepreneurs. Some of these include:

- The Amber Foundation Biz Plan Competition. This monthly competition awards grants to the best mini-business plans received from women on the Web.[18]
- The SBA's Online Women's Business Center. The SBA's Office of Women's Business Ownership (OWBO) promotes the growth of women-owned businesses through various programs that address business training and technical assistance and provide access to credit and capital, federal contracts, and international trade opportunities. Every SBA district office has a women's business ownership representative, providing a national network of resources for women entrepreneurs.
- WomenBiz.gov. WomenBiz.gov is a Web gateway for women-owned businesses that sell to the federal government and helps a woman business owner explore whether the federal government is the right customer for her.
- Center for Women's Business Research. The Center for Women's Business Research was originally founded as the National Foundation for Women Business Owners. It is a premier source of knowledge about women business owners and their enterprises.
- National Association of Women Business Owners. The National Association of Women Business Owners (NAWBO), headquartered in the Washington, D.C.,

metropolitan area, is the only dues-based national organization representing the interests of all women entrepreneurs in all types of businesses. The organization currently has more than 75 chapters and is represented in 35 countries.

- Center for Women & Enterprise. CWE is the largest regional entrepreneurial training organization in Boston and Worcester, Massachusetts, and Providence, Rhode Island. Its mission is to empower women to become economically self-sufficient and prosperous through entrepreneurship.

- Women's Business Development Center. The WBDC offers a full-service approach to launching emerging businesses and strengthening existing businesses owned by women in the Chicago area. Services of the WBDC include workshops and one-on-one counseling on all aspects of business development, including marketing, finance, business management, technology integration, and more. The WBDC has consulted with more than 35,000 women entrepreneurs, helping them to start and grow their businesses, and facilitated the receipt of over $24 million in loans to women business owners.

While things are improving for both women and minorities, it is not happening fast enough. Poor access to capital for these two groups is hurting America. Former SBA chief Aida Alvarez stated it beautifully when she said: "Businesses owned by women and minorities are multiplying at a faster rate than all other U.S. businesses. If we don't start investing now in the potential of the businesses, we will not have a successful economy in the new millennium."[19]

NOTES

1. U.S. Census Bureau, 2002.
2. Center for Women's Business Research, "Women-Owned Businesses in the United States, 2006: A Fact Sheet," 2006.
3. Ibid.

4. "Women Lead the Startup Stats," *BusinessWeek*, November 29, 2004.
5. Minority Business Development Agency, "Expanding Financing Opportunities for Minorities," 2004.
6. National Association of Investment Companies, www.naivc.com.
7. Center for Women's Business Research, "Capital Choices: Volume Two, The Value of Knowledge," 2006.
8. Center for Women's Business Research, press release, January 25, 2005.
9. Center for Women's Business Research, "Women Business Owners in Nontraditional Industries," 2005.
10. Wells Fargo, press release, May 2, 2006.
11. National Foundation for Women Business Owners, October 17, 1996.
12. *Atlanta Journal-Constitution*, July 4, 2007.
13. Center for Women's Business Research, press release, January 25, 2005.
14. *USA Today.com*, August 14, 2001, http://www.usatoday.com.
15. *Ottawa Business Journal*, November 29, 2004.
16. "Women Entrepreneurs in the Equity Capital Markets: The New Frontier, National Foundation for Women Business Owners, 2000.
17. Springboard Enterprises Web site.
18. Georgia SBDC Network, "New Non Traditional Financial Sources," August 2006.
19. *Chicago Sun-Times*, March 24, 1999, p. 69.

CHAPTER 12

Taking a Job with an Entrepreneurial Firm

INTRODUCTION

Five years ago, the Levy Entrepreneur Institute at Kellogg published the findings of our research regarding Kellogg alums and entrepreneurship. Specifically, we wanted to answer the question, how many of our 45,000 alums have become entrepreneurs? The first stage of this research focused on alums who majored in entrepreneurship from 1997 to 2005, while they were students. We contacted 1,500 alums and got a 36 percent response. We were enormously happy with the findings, which are given in Figure 12-1.

One of the unexpected takeaways from the research was that a large percentage of our alumni who were involved in entrepreneurship were employees in an entrepreneurial firm. They had resigned from their safe job with successful investment banking, consulting, or manufacturing companies and had taken a job with a start-up firm. How does a person make such a decision to leave the security of a well-established, in many instances Fortune 500 company to work for a high-risk venture in its embryonic stages of development?

The following case study, followed by an analysis of the situation, should be used as a template for answering these questions: Should I leave my job to take a job with a start-up? How should I do a financial analysis of the decision?

F I G U R E   12-1

Results of Kellogg Alumni Entrepreneurship Study

CASE STUDY: CONSIDERING A JOB OFFER FROM AN EARLY-STAGE COMPANY

In her Chicago home on a warm Friday afternoon in June, Nailah Johnson, who was graduating from the weekend Executive MBA (EMBA) program at the Kellogg School of Management in 2 weeks, hung up the phone. She was happy. John Paul, founder of AKAR and Johnson's potential future employer, had said as their conversation ended: "Tell me what it would take to get you on board."

For many reasons, Johnson was excited about joining an entrepreneurial firm and possibly much later even buying her own business. She recalled including this goal in the essays that had helped her gain admission to the Kellogg School 2 years earlier. The role Paul wanted Johnson to have at AKAR was appealing: a director of sales and marketing position with significantly more responsibility than Johnson currently had, and with possible promotion to vice president in less than 12 months. Johnson had heard about the many downsides and upsides of positions with an early-stage company. If the company failed, it could result in a direct financial loss because employees at start-ups were paid low salaries. On the other hand, the financial rewards could be lucrative if the employees owned part of the company and its value increased.

Johnson had joined Motorola in 2004 as a director of operations. Recently, based largely on her Kellogg School training and her desire to broaden her on-the-job skills, Johnson had successfully moved to a product marketing manager role. She and her husband enjoyed comfortable professional and social lives in Chicago. Just 2 days earlier, Johnson had informed her husband that she was pregnant with their first child. They expected this new addition to their family to increase their annual budget by $19,000. Early in their marriage, they had envisioned her becoming a full-time mother when the time came.

Still giddy from Paul's call, Johnson sat at her kitchen table, thinking about what he had said: "The sooner we can start you, the better." Until that moment, Johnson would have predicted that she would accept the position with AKAR on the spot, on almost any terms that sounded reasonable; after all, she had invested many months and a great deal of energy in making it happen. But now, as the costs and benefits of the position swirled through her mind, she felt unsure about what terms to request. Johnson owed Paul an answer in 5 days, but she was not sure if she could determine what she wanted even if she had 3 months. She also considered rejecting this opportunity because the risk was too high and the timing was poor. Finally, she wondered, if she took this or any other job, would she ever become an actual entrepreneur, or would she always be simply someone's employee? Should she pursue acquiring her own company instead?

In many ways, Johnson's career was typical for an MBA student. Thus, despite her interest in entrepreneurship, seriously considering an offer from an early-stage company was new territory for her. As Johnson reflected on the offer's pros and cons, she thought back to the path that had led her here.

Walking the Straight and Narrow

Johnson had attended Williams College, graduating near the top of her class (see Figure 12-2 for Johnson's résumé). Immediately after college, she began her career at Sun Microsystems and later moved to Motorola. Although Johnson enjoyed working on mobile devices, she found the business issues related to them even more interesting: Who were their target segments? What were the best ways of distributing and marketing the products? What kinds of new products were most likely to survive?

F I G U R E   12-2

Nailah Johnson's Résumé

Nailah Johnson
EDUCATION:

2005–present **KELLOGG SCHOOL OF MANAGEMENT** Evanston, IL
Executive Master of Business Administration, GMAT 770
- Majors in Management & Strategy, Finance, and Marketing
- Member of NBI team that created a strategic marketing plan for Handi-Ramp Foundation; member of Kellogg team that reached the school finals for AT Kearney Global Prize competition
- Entrepreneurship Club Member; GIM-China participant; logistics director for India Business Conference

1995–1999 **WILLIAMS COLLEGE** Williamstown, MA
BACHELOR OF SCIENCE IN COMMUNICATIONS, GPA: 3.92/4.0
- Financed 100% of education through assistantships
- Selected as key instructor for freshman-level mathematics courses. Taught classes of forty students, consistently receiving high ratings (4.5/5). Selected to teach remedial courses
- Member of school's five-person badminton team. Won the zonal championship in 1996 *Continued on next page*

FIGURE 12-2

Nailah Johnson's Résumé (continued)

EXPERIENCE:

2004–present **MOTOROLA**   Chicago, IL

Senior Director of Sales (2006–present)

- Manage marketing for next-generation mobile video service with expected commercial value of $48 million over 5 years
- Coordinated cross-functional team, including eight experts from different divisions of Motorola, to develop marketing plan for mobile video system
- Independently led research initiative to explore new distribution channel for music and talk shows on cell phones. Market estimated at $2 billion

Director of Global Product Marketing and Director of Operations (2004–2006)

- Selected technical consultant on an 8-month-long project valued at $2 million. The project cemented Motorola's relationship with a major external customer
- Collaborated with six other research experts to develop differentiating technology for the $13 billion home networking market. Technology is showcased in Motorola's Horsham (PA) innovation center
- Selected into Motorola's Applications Research patent committee of ten senior researchers among eight hundred to evaluate the technical and business viability of innovation ideas; authored eight Motorola patent applications and five external publications

1999–2004 **SUN MICROSYSTEMS**   Oak Brook, IL

Senior Product Manager (2002–2004)

- Led eight-person, $2 million platform integration project for new SPARCstation products
- Presented major Sun engineering initiatives to more than one hundred client managers at annual customer meeting
- Selected from more than sixty other project leaders to demonstrate research prototype at WIRED NextFest 2004. More than twenty thousand members of the public attended the exposition

Product Manager (1999–2002)

- Presented research to senior Sun executives. Presentation was subsequently broadcast to more than thirty thousand Motorola engineers
- Awarded "Significant Achievement Award" for integrating third-party location detection system one month ahead of schedule

ADDITIONAL INFORMATION:

- Robot inspector for Midwest regional championship. USFIRST, an organization that aims to increase interest in science and engineering among children, hosted the event
- College lacrosse enthusiast (fanatical supporter of Williams College). Enjoy playing golf and traveling

These interests led to Johnson's application to the Kellogg School. Because she had always had an interest in start-ups, she took several courses in entrepreneurship and joined the entrepreneurship club. As part of these student activities, Johnson enjoyed discussing entrepreneurship, especially the potential for new high-tech products, but her career goals remained focused on larger-company opportunities. In line with this, she pursued a marketing manager position at Motorola and was pleasantly surprised to receive an offer. The new position came with a salary of $115,000 (a 30 percent raise that put her in the 28 percent tax bracket), bonus potential of approximately 25 percent of her salary, and responsibilities for marketing a next-generation mobile video device. Johnson loved the work, and was already in line for a promotion to business development manager.

Taking on the new position a year ago had not been the only change in her life: she married Naeem, her classmate at Kellogg, soon afterward. They purchased a $400,000 two-bedroom condo in Chicago. The Johnsons made a 20 percent down payment (their entire savings) and secured a 30-year fixed-rate mortgage at 6 percent interest. The mortgage and the school loans were their only debts. Monthly assessment, taxes, and insurance were approximately 40 percent of the mortgage. All other household expenses, including telephone, electricity, cable, gas, and groceries, were approximately 35 percent of the monthly mortgage. They owned two cars, which were paid in full.

By the time Johnson was considering a position with AKAR, Naeem had also been promoted at Kraft; his salary was $105,000, with a bonus of approximately 20 percent. His company's health, medical, dental, and vision care insurance were all free. Together, the couple led a busy but enjoyable life, building their career experience, earning their MBAs, and taking vacations. They spent approximately 25 percent of Naeem's monthly salary on recreational activities. Despite some tuition reimbursement from their companies, they amassed significant student debt (see Figure 12-3).

Below is a summary of all loans processed by the financial aid office as of 6/14/2007. The principal amounts listed are the original principal balances. These amounts do not reflect any payments made to these loans. Loans from other institutions are not included on this form.

F I G U R E   12-3

Student Loan Separation Statement

Kellogg School of Management
Office of Financial Aid

June 14, 2007

Nailah Johnson

652 W. Evans Dr.

Chicago, CO 80201

Separation Date: 14-JUNE-2007

School: Kellogg School of Management

Lender	Guarantor	Int.	Loan Type	Amount Borrowed
Kellogg 555 Clark St. Third Floor Evanston, IL 60208	Illinois Student Assistance Co. 500 W. Monroe 3rd Floor Springfield, IL 62704–1876	6.8%	Subsidized Stafford	$17,000.00
Kellogg 555 Clark St. Third Floor Evanston, IL 60208	Illinois Student Assistance Co. 500 W. Monroe 3rd Floor Springfield, IL 62704–1876	6.8%	Unsubsidized Stafford	$22,000.00
Kellogg 555 Clark St. Third Floor Evanston, IL 60208	Kellogg 555 Clark St. Third Floor Evanston, IL 60208	5.0%	Perkins	$12,000.00
Total				**$51,000.00**

The Search for More

While she had walked a successful career path to date, for the last several months, Johnson had found several questions frequently on her mind: Is this all there is, career-wise? How can you keep more of the value that you are creating for yourself? How can you become a millionaire without risking everything? These questions also arose when she recalled how much she had enjoyed her entrepreneurship classes or heard news of others' entrepreneurial accomplishments.

According to the *Kellogg World* alumni magazine, Deniece Grant, a recent alumna from the part-time evening program, had raised $4 million in angel and early-stage venture capital for the company she founded, which provided software that allowed computers to search automatically for information related to documents on which the user was working. Grant gave "put rights" to some of her managers who owned stock in the company. She had originally given these employees restricted stock units (RSUs) when they were hired.

Raymond Robinson, a friend of Johnson in Chicago who had graduated from the full-time day program 2 years earlier, was already a vice president with a 2 percent ownership stake after exercising the stock options given to him when he was hired at a wireless technology company that had just completed a successful initial public offering (IPO). Robinson was now a multimillionaire. His stock options were originally scheduled to vest 20 percent annually after his second year of employment. But the IPO triggered the "change in control" clause, resulting in the immediate full vesting of 100 percent of his options. "That could be me," Johnson thought when she heard such stories.

Four months ago, after the completion of a very challenging project at work, Johnson had decided to stop sitting on the sidelines of entrepreneurship. She began reading entrepreneurship magazines and books, reaching out to friends who she thought would know of opportunities with early-stage companies, scouring the Kellogg School alumni database for people in small firms, and setting up as many informational interviews as she could. Johnson also connected with a recruiter who specialized in placements at early-stage firms and a business broker who could show her businesses for sale. The time she spent on the search, on top of her responsibilities at work and at school, left Johnson with almost no space in her weekly schedule for fitness, social activities, or spending time with Naeem. But it felt like the right thing to do.

Despite Johnson's enthusiasm for the search, months passed without major progress. If anything, like a corporate Goldilocks, she discovered many of the things she was *not* seeking in a new opportunity: what had appeared initially to be several promising positions were rejected as being too risky (a five-person software company in the initial fund-raising stage), not exciting enough (a firm that provided marketing solutions to the paper industry), or too strange (a venture that developed software so proprietary that the founders asked all employees to sign nondisclosure agreements—daily).

But 2 months earlier, Johnson's luck had changed when she met John Paul. Johnson had signed up to meet him through the entrepreneurship center's Entrepreneur-in-Residence program (EIR), through which entrepreneurs and principal investors spent a full day at Kellogg meeting in 30-minute sessions with individual students to answer questions and provide experience-based insights.

AKAR: The Opportunity

John Paul was only 46 years old, but he had already sold two companies. According to an article Johnson had read, AKAR, Paul's most recent venture, was very promising and had received significant industry attention. The article also characterized Paul as a "gambler with great judgment—or maybe great luck."

After dropping out of Grambling University in 1981, Paul had worked as a computer programmer for a series of video game manufacturers before moving into roles in operations and database design. He prided himself on being self-taught in most aspects of business, from finance to marketing: "Best teachers I ever had? Trial and error," he often said. Paul sold his first company, GamerParadize (launched out of his apartment 6 years earlier), one of the first online gaming portals, to Midway Games for $40 million (20 times its revenues) in its third year of operations. Paul owned 60 percent of the company, and the top two levels of management (vice presidents and managers), consisting of nine people, owned 20 percent. At closing, the four vice presidents shared $4 million. The remaining 20 percent went to the investors, who had invested $2 million 5 years earlier.

Paul was much more ambitious for his second company: to fund X-Cell, an Internet design and security firm, he obtained venture backing of $15 million. He had "call rights" agreements with all managers who owned stock in the company, giving him the option to buy the stock back at any time at a multiple of 3 times the original price. Unfortunately, because of a patent-related lawsuit,

X-Cell had to stop marketing its main security product, and Paul and the investors decided to sell off all assets in 2003, losing a portion of their investment.

AKAR was Paul's current company. Based in Chicago, the tech company had been built around a simple idea that Paul had developed with his chief technology officer (CTO), who had worked with Paul at X-Cell: distributing digital information across several geographically dispersed storage sites to store it more securely, reliably, and cost-effectively. AKAR was commercializing this idea as an online data storage service while offering commercial software for firms seeking to build their own storage capabilities. With this value proposition, AKAR was trying to capture share of the $43 billion global data storage management services market, with initial focus on the $3.3 billion U.S. market for automated data backup services.

At the time that Johnson met Paul, AKAR had just launched the commercial version of its backup services. With only a few loyal customers in place, the firm's revenues were minimal, but Paul—and many observers—was confident that that would change soon (see Figure 12-4 for AKAR's pro forma financials). Paul had self-funded much of AKAR, but he had also received round A financing of $3.2 million from one venture capital group in return for 23 percent of AKAR.

FIGURE 12-4

AKAR Financials (Pro Forma)

	Best-Case Scenario				
	Year 1	Year 2	Year 3	Year 4	Year 5
Revenue	$950,000	$5,000,000	$10,000,000	$20,000,000	$40,000,000
	Most-Likely Scenario				
	Year 1	Year 2	Year 3	Year 4	Year 5
Revenue	$950,000	$2,500,000	$5,000,000	$7,500,000	$15,000,000
	Worst-Case Scenario				
	Year 1	Year 2	Year 3	Year 4	Year 5
Revenue	$950,000	$1,500,000	$2,500,000	$3,000,000	$3,500,000

Aside from CEO Paul, AKAR had 14 employees; most of these were engineers with hardware and/or software experience, several of whom had come to AKAR directly from college. None of them, including Paul, was paid a six-figure salary. Paul believed that everyone should sacrifice salary for annual performance bonuses and company stock. The only other senior manager at AKAR was Mark Chin, the CTO. Chin had helped Paul build X-Cell. "My right- and left-hand man," Paul often called him.

From the moment Johnson met Paul, she described the recruiting process as "casual, but intense." For example, the day after the event where they first met, Paul called Johnson and told her how impressed he had been by Johnson's qualifications. "You'd make a heck of a marketing director," Paul said numerous times. In the weeks that followed, the two kept in close contact: three phone calls that lasted late into the night, several strings of e-mail correspondence, and two dinners. During these interactions, they discussed technology trends, the fit between Johnson and AKAR, sports, and Paul's personal life. Johnson learned that Paul had divorced and remarried ("Second time's the charm, so far") and had two elementary school–age stepchildren, a 132-foot yacht ("Want to sail her around the world—hopefully after selling this company"), and Type II diabetes ("For me, they're not doughnuts, they're dough-nots").

One month ago, Paul had invited Johnson to meet the CTO and tour AKAR's office, a hip loft space in the Bronzeville neighborhood of Chicago. The meeting with CTO Chin was similar to Johnson's encounters with Paul: casual but intense. For almost two and a half hours, Chin discussed AKAR's products, mission, and culture, rarely pausing to ask Johnson questions. When he did, it was typically to probe Johnson's level of commitment to AKAR's vision and mission. During the marathon interview, Chin used the phrase "John's way" often, endowing it with an almost mythical quality. After the interview, Paul and Chin introduced Johnson to several of the other employees and took her out to dinner with a customer. On her way home, an exhausted Johnson called Naeem. "It's like I already work there," she told him.

Four days after the meeting, Paul called Johnson with good news: the team wanted to make her an offer. "But first," Paul said, "it would mean a lot to us if you and Naeem came to 'Shut Up and Sing' in 2 weeks." Johnson thought she had misheard Paul, until he explained: Shut Up and Sing was a party that Paul threw twice a year at his house for all AKAR employees and their spouses or partners. The two main ingredients: homemade sangria and karaoke.

Two weeks later, Johnson and her husband attended the party. Paul stayed by Johnson's side most of the night, guiding her around his large lakefront home and introducing her as "guest of honor and future marketing director." For Johnson, the night was a blur of smiling faces, handshakes, and her singing "Girls Just Wanna Have Fun" in front of about 50 people she barely knew. She also could not help but feel that the party had been a final test for her, to see how well she would fit at AKAR.

Four days later, Paul called, as enthusiastic about Johnson as ever. Johnson had expected an offer from Paul, even if only verbal. Instead, Paul had said, "Tell me what it will take to get you on board."

Decisions, Decisions

As Johnson sat at her kitchen table, thinking about Paul's words and the position with AKAR, Naeem returned from work. She smiled at him. "They want to hire me," she said.

"Great news!" Naeem hugged her. "What's their offer?"

CASE STUDY ANALYSIS

The following questions illustrate key items for Nailah to consider as she evaluates the opportunity with AKAR.

Question 1: Should Nailah keep her job?

Yes	No
■ She has a new baby.	■ The new job is an opportunity for entrepreneurial experiences.
■ She has job security with her current position.	■ There is limited financial upside in her current position.
■ Her current company is stable and established.	

Question 2: Should Nailah pursue the AKAR employment opportunity?

Yes	No
▪ They want her	▪ Decrease in salary
▪ More responsibility	▪ Paul's quirky personality
▪ Promotion opportunities	▪ Company could fail
▪ Wealth opportunity	
▪ Nailah's passion for entrepreneurship	
▪ Paul's past success	
▪ Chance to experiment with entrepreneurship	

Question 3: What are Nailah's personal strengths and weaknesses?

Strengths	Weaknesses
▪ Smart	▪ Never been an entrepreneur
▪ Successful business career	▪ No finance experience
▪ Sincerely interested in entrepreneurship:	
▪ Hired specialized recruiter	
▪ Worked with business broker	
▪ Participated in Entrepreneur-in-Residence program	

Question 4: What are John Paul's strengths and weaknesses?

Strengths	Weaknesses
▪ Founded two companies	▪ X-Cell failure
▪ Wealthy	▪ Quirky personality
▪ Willing to share wealth with employees	
▪ Made other people rich (Midway Games), including:	
▪ Investors	
▪ Managers	

Question 5: What was the value of GamerParadize to each stakeholder?

Stakeholder	Total Financial Return
■ Paul	■ $24 million (60% of $40 million)
■ Investors	■ $8 million (20% of $40 million)
	– Original investment: $2 million
	– Time: 5 years
	– Cash-on-cash return: 4×
	– ROI: 300%
	– IRR: 32%
■ Employees	■ $8 million (20% of 40% million)
	– 4 V.P.s: $4 million, or $1 million each.
	– Managers: $4 million, or $800,000 each

Question 6: What is the Johnson family's current maximum income?

	Salary	Bonus	Total
Nailah (salary)	$115,000	$28,750	$143,750
		(25% of salary)	
Naeem (salary)	$105,000	$21,000	
		(20% of salary)	$126,000
Total	$220,000	$49,750	$269,750

Question 7: What is the Johnson family's after-tax cash flow?

	Worst-Case (without bonus)	Best-Case (with bonus)
Nailah and Naeem	$220,000	$269,750
28% tax	−$61,600	−$75,530
Total	$158,400	$194,220

Question 8: What is the Johnson family's current budget?

Expense	Annual	Monthly
1. New baby	$19,000	$1,583.33
2. Household expenses	$8,058	$671.50
(35% of monthly mortgage)		
3. Assessments, taxes, and insurance	$9,209	$767.42
(40% of monthly mortgage)		
4. Recreational activities	$26,250	$2,187.50
(25% of Naeem's monthly salary)		
5. Five school loans (10-year amortization)	$6,913	$576.10
6. Mortgage (principal and interest)	$23,022	$1,918.56
Total	**$92,452**	**$7,704.56**

Question 9: What is the minimum amount of cash that Nailah needs to bring home for the Johnson family to pay their expenses?

Naeem's salary (worst case, without bonus)	$105,000
axes	−$29,400
Naeem's after-tax cash	**$75,600**
Family budget	$92,452
Naeem's after-tax cash	−$75,600
Cash needed from Nailah	**$16,582**

Question 10: What should Nailah propose?

Key Terms to Propose
At least 4% raise annually
Put rights
2–3% ownership
Starting salary $95,000
Change of control clause with immediate vesting
6-week maternity leave with full pay
No termination without cause
3-year contract
Stock options *or* restricted stock units

Question 11: What is the difference between stock options and restricted stock units?

	Stock Options	Restricted Stock Units
Stock-based compensation?	Yes	Yes
Employers required to expense immediately?	Yes	Yes
Taxed when?	At exercise of option	At time of vesting
Employer required to withhold taxes?	No	Yes. Some options: 1. "Same-day sale" 2. "Sell to cover" (sell just enough to cover taxes) 3. "Cash transfer" (you give the employer cash to cover taxes and keep all the shares
Retains value?	Not always. Example: ■ Strike price: $10 ■ Stock price: $8 ■ Has no value ■ "Underwater" ■ Lost 100%	Yes. Example: ■ Given at $10 ■ Stock price at vesting: $8 ■ Lost 20%

Question 12: What is the potential future value of AKAR?

GamerParadize multiple of revenue	20
Best	20 × $40,000,000 = $800 million
Likely	20 × $15,000,000 = $300 million
Worst	20 × $3,500,00 = $70 million

Question 13: How much could Nailah make?

Nailah's potential ownership stake	2%
Best	2% × $800 million = $16 million
Likely	2% × $300 million = $6 million
Worst	2% × $70 million = $1.4 million

Question 14: Is she entitled to 2 percent of the company or 2 percent of the new value of the company?

She's entitled to 2 percent of the company.

Question 15: What is the starting point for Nailah's value?

Equity series	A
Investment	$3.2 million
Premoney valuation	$10,713,043
VC ownership stake	23%
Equation for postmoney valuation	23% $\times$ Y = $3,200,000
Postmoney valuation	$13,913,043

Question 15a: What is the worst case for Nailah?

Worst-case future value of AKAR	$70,000,000
VC ownership	$13,913,043
Remaining equity	$56,086,057
Nailah's ownership stake	2%
Nailah's potential return	$1,121,739

Question 15b: What is the financial difference of staying versus going?

Scenario 1: Remain at job for 5 years with 4% increase annually		
Year	Worst Case (Guaranteed Compensation)	Upside (Bonus)
0	$115,000	$0
1	$119,600	$29,900
2	$124,384	$31,096
3	$129,359	$32,339
4	$134,533	$33,663
5	$139,914	$39,978
Total	$647,790	$161,946
Total value of staying = $809,736		

Scenario 2: Take AKAR job with 4% annual increase		
Year	Worst Case	Equity
0		
1	$95,000	
2	$98,800	
3	$103,740	
4	$107,889	
5	$112,204	$1,121,739
Total	**$517,633**	**$1,121,739**
Total value of taking job = $1,639,372		

Comparison of staying versus going:

Value of staying	$809,736
Value of going	$1,639,372
Difference	$829,636
Percent difference	102.26% better to take job

CHAPTER 13

Intrapreneurship

Joseph Alois Schumpeter, an Austrian-trained economist who taught at Harvard, is considered the chief proponent and popularizer of the word *entrepreneur* in 1911. During the next decade, he made the following statement in support of the idea that entrepreneurship was not limited to small start-up firms, but could also occur within big established firms: "Innovation within the shell of existing corporations offers a much more convenient access to the entrepreneurial functions than existed in the world of owner-managed firms. Many a would-be entrepreneur of today does not found a firm, not because he could not do so, but simply because he prefers the other method."[1]

Thus, the idea of corporate entrepreneurship was born almost 100 years ago. This activity is now commonly referred to as intrapreneurship. While I introduced intrapreneurship in Chapter 1 when discussing the entrepreneurial spectrum, I chose not to discuss it in greater detail because I believe that an entire chapter should be devoted to the subject. I also believe that to really understand intrapreneurship, one must thoroughly understand entrepreneurship, and therefore I wanted the reader to fully digest all the lessons about entrepreneurship in the previous chapters before tackling this subject.

Intrapreneurship is the spirit and act of entrepreneurship in a corporate setting. I have done training sessions on the topic of intrapreneurship at Nike, Hearst Management Institute,

S. C. Johnson, Allstate Insurance Company, the National Association of Broadcasters, and the American Press Institute. These are companies and organizations that know that we live in a world where time is not what it used to be. This is the age of "Internet time," where compared to a decade ago, a year is 6 months, a month a week, and a week a day. Therefore, corporations must know that they cannot rest on yesterday's successes. They also realize that growth can no longer come through simply increasing prices. Today, more than ever before, we live in a global world. Instead of accepting price increases on products or services, customers will go to the Internet to find the same products or services at a lower price. As a result, corporations must continue to remain hungry, with a sense of urgency, creativity, and, most important, vision.

Bob Morrison, the former CEO of Quaker Oats, is a great example of corporate leadership embracing the intrapreneurial spirit. At a company meeting, he announced to his employees, "We must change the mind-set and culture at Quaker. We must think and act like a small, entrepreneurial company."

THE INTRAPRENEURSHIP SPECTRUM

To give greater clarity to the subject of intrapreneurship, I have created the intrapreneurship spectrum in Figure 13-1.

F I G U R E   13-1

Caretaker	Developer	Innovator
Pfizer	SC Johnson	Altoids

Caretaker

While the caretaker is not an intrapreneur, the category is included on the spectrum simply as a point of reference. This is the corporate employee who is the antithesis of the intrapreneur. All things entrepreneurial are anathema to him. He is most satisfied with inheriting an established product line that has a solid customer and employee base with moderate growth.

Developer

This is the intrapreneur who takes a company's existing products or services and pursues high growth by targeting new customers and markets. While the products or services are not new, they have no brand equity with the new targeted markets. For example, Altoids was a 200-year-old British product that was originally used to calm upset stomachs. It has been owned by Kraft Foods, who sold it to Wm. Wrigley Jr. Company, and it is now the most popular breath mint (even more popular than Certs), with over 20 percent of the $300 million U.S. breath mint category.

Another great example is the Pfizer company's introduction of sildenafil, a drug that was initially studied for hypertension. It was patented in 1996. The story goes that when male patients used the drug, their wives complained to the doctors that their husbands were now chasing them around the house like they did during their honeymoon decades earlier. With these data, in 1998, Pfizer decided to target a new market with the same drug, which we all know as Viagra.

Innovator

This is the intrapreneur who pursues high growth for his company through new products, services, and/or business models. The innovator is not a member of the company's R&D department, and therefore creating new products, services, or business models is not her official responsibility.

A great example of an intrapreneur in this category is Sam Johnson, the former CEO of S. C. Johnson. Several decades ago, Sam, the grandson of the company's founder, decided to pursue the development of a new product without the approval of his father, who was the CEO. The company, which now manufactures an entire spectrum of consumer products, including Glade air fresheners, Windex, Scrubbing Bubbles toilet cleaners, and Oust air sanitizer, was primarily a manufacturer of wax cleaners. Sam came to his father and informed him that he had developed a new product, outside of the research and development department. His father's reply was, "That's fine as long as it has wax in it." Sam responded, "No it does not have wax in its ingredients, but if you include it, the product would be less effective." Sam's new product was a pesticide that we all know today as Raid.

INTRAPRENEURSHIP MODELS

Intrapreneurs, whether they are developers or innovators, use different formal or informal models to bring their innovative ideas to fruition. The best descriptions of these models were published in a recent research paper by corporate entrepreneurship expert Robert Wolcott, an outstanding scholar and adjunct professor in the Levy Entrepreneur Institute at Kellogg, and Michael Lippitz, a research fellow at Northwestern. These models are the Opportunist, the Enabler, and the Producer.[2]

The Opportunist

This model basically says to employees, "Do whatever you want to do, because the company does not have any formal systems relative to corporate entrepreneurship." This is a model in which new services or products, like Raid, come from individual champions, not through systems. Ironically, success under this model typically leads an organization to implement a more formal model, such as the Producer or the Enabler.

The Enabler

This model says to employees, "Anybody in the company can come up with a new service or product, but here is the process for developing it." With this model, the company explicitly communicates to its employees the procedures for requesting development capital and the criteria that will be used to determine which projects receive funding. Google is a company that has had major success with this model. For example, its service Google Talk, which is a free system for instant and voice messaging, came from an employee as part of the company's 10 percent program. This innovative program allows all employees to devote 10 percent of their daily working hours to the development of their own ideas. As one Google employee stated, "We're an internal ecosystem for entrepreneurs . . . sort of like the Silicon Valley ecosystem but inside one company."

The Producer

This model openly recognizes and proactively supports the importance of entrepreneurship in a corporate setting. The company creates a separate entity that has the specific task of creating new products or services outside of the present business. Several companies have embraced this model, including Xerox, with its New Enterprises Division; Coca-Cola's Innovation centers in five different locations throughout the world; and Cargill's Emerging Business Accelerator division.

TRAITS OF THE HIGH-GROWTH INTRAPRENEUR

In Chapter 2 we identified 15 common attributes of successful high-growth entrepreneurs. Interestingly, while many of those traits also apply to the intrapreneur, there are a few unique attributes.

Those attributes include:

- Risk taker
- Hard worker
- Has a plan
- Good manager
- Visionary
- Profit focused
- Innovator
- Accepts being managed

Some of these traits are worth discussing in more detail.

Risk Taker

The successful intrapreneur is not a blind risk taker. He has a plan, especially if he works for a company that uses the developer or innovator model, and he executes the plan according to a defined timeline. This is called "planning the work and working the plan." Unlike the entrepreneur, who typically risks his personal assets, the intrapreneur's risk is much less. At the most, he could lose his job if his new ideas or innovations are not commercially successful.

However, while the intrapreneur's risk may be less than the entrepreneur's, he certainly assumes greater risk than the average corporate employee.

Accepts Being Managed

One of the reasons why some people become entrepreneurs is that they want to be as independent as possible. Specifically, they loathe the idea of having a boss. In contrast, the intrapreneur, given his status as an employee, accepts the fact that he answers to a manager above him. He does not have carte blanche to do anything that he wants to do. He must usually seek and receive approval from a higher authority in the company's organization chart. The intrapreneur usually accepts being managed by others as a standard way of doing business.

ACTS OF INTRAPRENEURSHIP

Intrapreneurial activities include acquisitions of other companies and product lines, the introduction of new products outside of the traditional research and development process, the creation of new strategic partners, and changes in a company's business model. Let's review, through anecdotes, each of these activities in greater detail.

Acquisitions of Other Companies and Product Lines

In 1998, McDonald's purchased 90 percent of Chipotle Mexican Grill, a chain of 14 restaurants that was founded in 1993 by Steve Elis, a professional chef trained at the Culinary Institute of America. This acquisition was truly an intrapreneurial act of innovation on McDonald's part. Prior to this acquisition, the company seemingly viewed innovation as simply putting the letters "Mc" on the beginning of any idea. For example, it unsuccessfully experimented with the McDiner, a restaurant serving traditional food, such as meat loaf and mashed potatoes, in a diner.

Introduction of New Products Outside of the Traditional R&D Process

A great example of the intrapreneurship model in which "products emerged from champions rather than systems," a phrase created by Bill Perez, occurred at SC Johnson Wax company with the development of its storage bag product line, which generates in excess of $150 million of annual revenues. The original idea and the development of the prototypes came not from the company's R&D department, but from two marketing department employees. The company had no plans to enter the storage bag category until these two intrapreneurs persuaded management that it was a business that could be grown fast. As Bill Perez, the former CEO of SC Johnson, said about the two employees, "Nobody asked them to do it."

Creation of New Strategic Partners

In 1994, Viacom, a $10 billion entertainment conglomerate that owned Madison Square Garden, MTV Networks, Showtime Networks, numerous theme parks, and dozens of television stations, purchased the 6,000-store Blockbuster video chain for $8 billion. Two years later, Blockbuster's cash flow had dropped 42 percent. Sumner Redstone, the 75-year-old chairman and founder of Viacom, knew that he had to make changes. Rather than simply cutting overhead, he got intrapreneurial.

Redstone knew that videos shown at home provided movie studios with nearly 3 times the revenue of showings in movie theaters. The studios charged Blockbuster a flat fee of $80 per video. In contrast, movie theaters usually did not pay a fixed price; instead, they split the revenues with the studios. Redstone decided that this partnership model between movie studios and theaters should also be applied to Blockbuster. The first studio that he approached with this partnership was Warner Brothers, which rejected the proposal. His next target was Disney, which he successfully convinced that it could make money if it treated Blockbuster as a partner, instead of as a customer. The agreement was that Blockbuster's fixed cost of $80 per video would be reduced to $8 and that Disney would receive 40 percent of the video's rental revenues for up to 26 weeks, at which time Blockbuster could sell the video, thereby recouping its original $8 investment.

The financial results were enormously positive for both parties because they reduced the outlay of capital by Blockbuster while allowing it to increase its stock of the most popular videos. Six other studios followed Disney with a similar strategic partnership with Blockbuster, including Warner Brothers.

Changes in Business Model

Three of America's blue-chip companies, IBM, Best Buy, and Nike, have been wonderfully intrapreneurial by changing their business models. IBM, a company that was seemingly an antiquated, lumbering old has-been by the 1990s, was turned around by a great intrapreneur, Lou Gerstner, the CEO, who did not have a technology background when he came from RJR Nabisco. Gerstner successfully changed IBM from an equipment supplier, as it had been for its entire life, to a solution provider/consultant.

After Wal-Mart, the world's largest retailer, began selling brand-name consumer electronics earlier this decade, it was assumed that Best Buy's revenues would decline dramatically. Instead of acting like a victim, however, Best Buy became intrapreneurial. Five years ago, it changed its model from being exclusively a retailer to being a solution provider, like IBM, by adding installation services and trained salespeople, which Wal-Mart did not offer. Best Buy's revenues increased 16 percent.

Phil Knight, the great entrepreneur who founded Nike in 1974 as an importer of running shoes, later changed its model to an athletic shoe and apparel manufacturer. Today it is also a successful retailer.

SIGNS OF INTRAPRENEURIAL SUCCESS

A company has successfully created an intrapreneurial spirit and program when it is unequivocally clear that it agrees to manage intrapreneurs differently from other employees by encouraging them and giving them the space and freedom to innovate.

Further evidence of intrapreneurship includes the company's acceptance of failure. Google is a great example. In response to an unsuccessful innovation that cost the company several million dollars, Larry Page, one of Google's founders, told the employee who had been in charge of the idea, "I'm so glad you made this mistake, because I want to run a company where we are moving too quickly and doing too much, not being too cautious and doing too little. If we don't have any of these mistakes, we're just not taking enough risk."[3]

The final sign of successful intrapreneurship is when the company proactively encourages employees with creative ideas to step forward. An extreme example is Sealed Air Corporation, which has 14,000 employees. Its employees are encouraged to bring entrepreneurial ideas directly to its CEO.

STANDARD OPERATING PROCEDURES

The ideal intrapreneurship system should be made up of the following processes:

1. *The system should be simple and user-friendly.* The U.S. Forest Service Eastern Region changed its innovation suggestion process from a four-page form to telling its employees, "If you have an idea, tell your supervisor or send an e-mail. If you do not get a response in 2 weeks, as long as the idea is not illegal, go ahead and implement the idea." Before the change, the 2,500 employees submitted, on average, 60 ideas annually. A year after the new procedures were implemented, 6,000 new ideas were submitted!

2. *Reward employees for successful ideas.* Share the wealth. Northwestern University has a results-oriented reward system for anyone who develops an idea that gets commercialized. In 2007, chemistry professor Richard Silverman received his portion of the royalties that the university received from a pharmaceutical firm, Pfizer, which purchased Lyrica, a chronic pain relief drug that had been created by Silverman. The university received more than $700 million. Silverman's portion has not been

publicly disclosed, but it can be assumed that it's many millions of dollars, given the fact that he and his wife are the primary benefactors for the new $100 million Northwestern University building that will "bring together engineering, biology and chemistry for interdisciplinary research." Its name will be the Richard and Barbara Silverman Hall for Molecular Therapeutics and Diagnostics.

3. *All ideas should be reviewed*, and the submitters should be informed of a decision as soon as possible.

4. *Every step in the review process should be transparent and well publicized*, as should the criteria used to approve ideas.

5. *The review and approval process should be managed by more than one person.*

6. *All intrapreneurial success stories should be publicized throughout the company to all employees.*

7. *Employee expectations should be proactively managed.* Employees should be told that in the entrepreneurship world, most new companies do not succeed. And the same applies in the corporate intrapreneurship world, where most ideas will be rejected.

INTRAPRENEURSHIP BLUNDER

The implementation of the procedures just listed will almost guarantee that a company does not duplicate one of the greatest intrapreneurial blunders in corporate history. In the mid-1970s, Steve Wozniak, a college dropout and self-taught electronics engineer, worked at Hewlett-Packard (HP). He offered his employer the chance to develop the idea that he had for a user-friendly personal computer. Hewlett-Packard said no thank you. So with $1,300 derived from selling his van and other assets, he left HP at the age of 26 and, with the help of his friend, Steven Jobs, developed the Apple I computer for their new entrepreneurial start-up, Apple Computer, Inc.

N O T E S

1. Gary Emmon, "Up from the Ashes: the Life and Thought of Joseph Schumpeter," *Harvard Business School Alumni Bulletin,* June 2007, p. 25.
2. Robert C. Wolcott and Michael J. Lippitz, "The Four Models of Corporate Entrepreneurship," *MIT Sloan Management Review,* Fall 2007, p. 77.
3. Adam Lashinsky, "Chaos by Design," *Fortune,* October 2, 2006, p. 88.

Conclusion

My alma mater, the Harvard Business School, recently asked me to sit on a panel to discuss entrepreneurship. All the other panelists were current entrepreneurs, and the questions eventually focused on the future of entrepreneurship: given the tough economic times, was this really the right time to consider starting a business? Everyone else on the panel shook his head no. By now, I think you can guess my answer: of course this is the right time to start a business! In every recession, depression, and downturn that this country has ever seen, entrepreneurship has been the engine of growth.

After the terrorist attack on September 11, 2001, the airline industry alone laid off more than 100,000 workers. Which Fortune 500 company do you think will hire all those pink-slip recipients? If anyone is waiting for the big companies with thousands of employees to fill a cloudy day with sun and turn around these tough times, she is in for a long and disappointing wait. Entrepreneurs hold the keys to the next generation of Fortune 500 companies. Of course capital is constrained, and investors are more skeptical than they have been. In many ways, that's good news. It means that only the best companies—those with the best ideas and the best managers—will get financial backing. I'm a firm believer that good managers make better decisions when times are tough. And tough times make better managers. Expenditures are scrutinized more carefully, cash flow gets a closer look, innovative partnerships are born, and managers learn once again that execution is everything.

Is this the right time for you? Only you can answer that question. Volkswagen has a catchy marketing campaign that tells consumers, "On the road of life, there are drivers and passengers. Drivers wanted." For future entrepreneurs, the worst thing you could do to yourself is to spend your life kicking the tires and wondering whether you should have taken a risk, cut the safety net, and taken the plunge. Entrepreneurship is about passion, vision, focus, and sweat, and no swing of the stock market will ever change that. Around every corner is the next idea, the next dream, and the next business opportunity. I wish you well on your adventure.

Industry Profitability

The following table looks at the national averages for corporate gross profit, net income, and return on equity. The data were compiled by BizStats.com using information from a large variety of sources, including the Internal Revenue Service, U.S. Census Bureau, the U.S. Department of Commerce and the U.S. Department of Labor.

TABLE A-1

Industry Profitability—Corporations

Construction	Cost of Sales, %	Gross Profit, %	Net Income as % of Sales	Interest as % Sales	Taxes as % of Sales	Depr. and Amort. as % of Sales
Building construction	77.33%	22.67%	7.39%	0.69%	1.05%	0.47%
Heavy construction, and land subdivision	70.15%	29.85%	8.81%	1.01%	1.66%	2.29%
Specialty trade contractors	65.99%	34.01%	5.96%	0.46%	2.26%	1.49%

Retail Trade	Cost of Sales, %	Gross Profit, %	Net Income as % of Sales	Interest as % Sales	Taxes as % of Sales	Depr. and Amort. as % of Sales
Motor vehicle and parts dealers	82.95%	17.05%	2.11%	0.70%	0.97%	0.53%
Furniture and home furnishings stores	57.22%	42.78%	4.99%	0.53%	2.24%	1.26%
Electronics and appliance stores	69.38%	30.62%	4.89%	0.49%	1.64%	0.83%
Building materials and garden equipment supply dealers	67.70%	32.30%	8.32%	0.57%	1.95%	1.39%
Food, beverage, and liquor stores	71.82%	28.18%	3.14%	0.85%	1.61%	1.44%
Health and personal care stores	70.72%	29.28%	3.87%	0.59%	1.26%	1.13%
Gasoline stations	88.40%	11.60%	1.58%	0.42%	1.04%	0.92%
Clothing and clothing accessory stores	51.64%	48.36%	8.37%	0.74%	2.23%	1.99%
Sporting goods, hobby, book, and music stores	59.87%	40.13%	4.66%	0.77%	2.08%	1.93%
General merchandise stores	69.47%	30.53%	5.12%	1.00%	1.74%	1.41%
Miscellaneous store retailers	61.97%	38.03%	5.98%	0.88%	1.83%	1.31%
Non-store retailers	67.03%	32.97%	5.66%	0.67%	1.14%	1.10%

Wholesale Trade	Cost of Sales, %	Gross Profit, %	Net Income as % of Sales	Interest as % Sales	Taxes as % of Sales	Depr. and Amort. as % of Sales
Durable goods	77.45%	22.55%	4.28%	0.74%	0.91%	1.47%
Nondurable goods	81.61%	18.39%	4.09%	0.78%	0.92%	0.79%
Electronics markets agents and brokers	0.00%	100.00%	14.70%	1.60%	3.08%	2.03%

Services	Cost of Sales, %	Gross Profit, %	Net Income as % of Sales	Interest as % Sales	Taxes as % of Sales	Depr. and Amort. as % of Sales
Accommodations	11.15%	88.85%	13.57%	7.52%	6.29%	4.48%
Food services and drinking places	37.78%	62.22%	8.58%	1.55%	3.88%	2.46%
Administrative and support services	43.00%	57.00%	7.63%	1.33%	4.16%	1.90%
Waste management and remediation services	39.25%	60.75%	7.98%	4.48%	3.81%	6.31%
Amusement, gambling, and recreation	22.08%	77.92%	12.41%	2.95%	6.32%	4.86%
Other arts, entertainment, and recreation	14.62%	85.38%	14.78%	1.04%	2.60%	2.60%
Educational services	13.47%	86.53%	12.48%	0.81%	3.25%	2.12%
Health practitioners and outpatient health services	8.24%	91.76%	9.37%	0.63%	3.08%	1.34%
Misc. health care and social assistance	18.95%	81.05%	9.38%	1.53%	3.69%	2.61%
Hospitals, nursing, and residential health facilities	8.72%	91.28%	7.96%	2.78%	5.11%	2.99%
Repair and maintenance services	50.50%	49.50%	6.36%	0.85%	3.14%	1.71%
Personal and laundry services	26.70%	73.30%	8.58%	1.48%	3.83%	3.46%
Religious, grant-making, civic, and professional organizations	13.60%	86.40%	4.72%	0.33%	1.92%	1.42%

(continued)

T A B L E   A-1

Industry Profitability—Corporations (continued)

Services	Cost of Sales, %	Gross Profit, %	Net Income as % of Sales	Interest as % Sales	Taxes as % of Sales	Depr. and Amort. as % of Sales
Legal services	6.79%	93.21%	12.73%	0.39%	3.12%	0.84%
Accounting, bookkeeping, tax prep, and payroll services	12.39%	87.61%	9.91%	1.85%	4.24%	1.54%
Architectural, engineering, and related services	40.16%	59.84%	6.81%	0.61%	2.83%	1.29%
Specialized design services	43.09%	56.91%	11.33%	0.57%	2.53%	1.29%
Computer systems design and related services	28.15%	71.85%	9.21%	1.25%	3.75%	2.34%
Management, scientific, and technical consulting services	24.86%	75.14%	10.93%	0.74%	2.78%	1.24%
Scientific research and development services	36.37%	63.63%	11.98%	1.70%	2.47%	2.80%
Advertising and related services	30.09%	69.91%	8.20%	2.73%	2.19%	2.06%
Other professional, scientific, and technical services	23.57%	76.43%	10.33%	1.63%	3.09%	2.32%

Finance, Insurance and Real Estate	Cost of Sales, %	Gross Profit, %	Net Income as % of Sales	Interest as % Sales	Taxes as % of Sales	Depr. and Amort. as % of Sales
Credit intermediation	2.21%	97.79%	12.40%	48.27%	1.38%	1.59%
Non-depository credit intermediation	3.07%	96.93%	10.05%	50.33%	1.05%	1.33%
Securities, commodity contracts, and other financial investments	0.85%	99.15%	13.13%	41.95%	1.35%	1.44%
Insurance carriers and related activities	52.29%	47.71%	7.26%	2.21%	1.60%	1.35%

	Cost of Sales, %	Gross Profit, %	Net Income as % of Sales	Interest as % Sales	Taxes as % of Sales	Depr. and Amort. as % of Sales
Funds, trusts, and other financial vehicles	0.00%	100.00%	70.62%	5.19%	0.74%	1.61%
Depository credit intermediation	0.05%	99.95%	18.33%	43.10%	2.23%	2.24%
Bank holding companies	0.62%	99.38%	17.51%	33.32%	1.77%	3.61%
Real estate services	15.17%	84.83%	19.77%	2.87%	2.99%	2.09%
Rental and leasing services	19.72%	80.28%	11.51%	8.81%	2.48%	19.33%
Lessors of nonfinancial intangible assets	7.70%	92.30%	37.97%	0.75%	2.12%	4.58%

Information	Cost of Sales, %	Gross Profit, %	Net Income as % of Sales	Interest as % Sales	Taxes as % of Sales	Depr. and Amort. as % of Sales
Publishing industries	23.01%	76.99%	17.78%	3.34%	2.56%	3.90%
Motion picture and sound recording	24.80%	75.20%	11.12%	11.57%	1.55%	12.16%
Broadcasting (except internet)	19.25%	80.75%	8.58%	5.10%	1.84%	13.48%
Internet publishing and broadcasting	18.32%	81.68%	10.98%	6.00%	3.12%	7.15%
Telecommunications	13.52%	86.48%	11.29%	7.31%	2.70%	9.27%
Internet service providers, search portals, data processing	10.14%	89.86%	9.36%	3.02%	2.22%	7.72%
Other information services	18.17%	81.83%	10.87%	3.71%	2.28%	4.30%

Manufacturing	Cost of Sales, %	Gross Profit, %	Net Income as % of Sales	Interest as % Sales	Taxes as % of Sales	Depr. and Amort. as % of Sales
Food manufacturing	62.73%	37.27%	11.51%	2.43%	2.01%	2.03%
Beverages and tobacco products manufacturing	43.00%	57.00%	17.94%	3.50%	7.26%	3.08%
Textile mills and textile product mills	67.40%	32.60%	5.97%	1.31%	1.69%	1.93%
Apparel manufacturing	61.70%	38.30%	7.28%	1.26%	1.96%	1.25%
Leather and allied product manufacturing	59.91%	40.09%	8.85%	1.27%	1.63%	1.42%
Wood product manufacturing	71.06%	28.94%	6.97%	2.32%	1.57%	2.08%
Paper manufacturing	64.36%	35.64%	11.31%	3.45%	1.34%	2.89%

(continued)

T A B L E   A-1

Industry Profitability—Corporations (continued)

Manufacturing	Cost of Sales, %	Gross Profit, %	Net Income as % of Sales	Interest as % Sales	Taxes as % of Sales	Depr. and Amort. as % of Sales
Printing and related support activities	58.65%	41.35%	6.77%	1.72%	2.24%	3.60%
Petroleum and coal products manufacturing	83.14%	16.86%	8.58%	1.17%	1.62%	1.18%
Chemical manufacturing	45.21%	54.79%	23.11%	2.66%	1.06%	2.99%
Plastics and rubber products manufacturing	68.70%	31.30%	6.00%	2.03%	1.52%	2.56%
Non-metallic mineral products manufacturing	61.66%	38.34%	9.97%	2.77%	2.02%	4.05%
Primary metal manufacturing	75.24%	24.76%	7.65%	1.78%	1.22%	2.51%
Fabricated metal product manufacturing	63.76%	36.24%	9.26%	2.81%	1.88%	2.60%
Machinery manufacturing	63.71%	36.29%	8.63%	2.65%	1.35%	2.59%
Computer and electronic product manufacturing	54.99%	45.01%	16.59%	1.09%	1.22%	3.22%
Electrical equipment, appliance, and component manufacturing	49.58%	50.42%	6.37%	14.75%	1.00%	5.50%
Transportation equipment manufacturing	68.16%	31.84%	6.89%	3.33%	0.99%	4.16%
Furniture and related product manufacturing	64.15%	35.85%	6.66%	1.24%	2.01%	1.51%
Miscellaneous manufacturing	48.91%	51.09%	15.11%	2.35%	1.65%	2.68%

Transportation and Warehousing	Cost of Sales, %	Gross Profit, %	Net Income as % of Sales	Interest as % Sales	Taxes as % of Sales	Depr. and Amort. as % of Sales
Air-rail-water transportation	25.73%	74.27%	8.28%	3.98%	3.84%	7.10%
Truck transportation	32.00%	68.00%	4.88%	0.95%	3.68%	4.02%
Transit and ground passenger transportation	34.31%	65.69%	5.33%	1.52%	4.26%	4.79%

	Cost of Sales, %	Gross Profit, %	Net Income as % of Sales	Interest as % Sales	Taxes as % of Sales	Depr. and Amort. as % of Sales
Pipeline transportation	32.39%	67.61%	21.35%	4.86%	3.91%	7.34%
Other transportation and support activities	36.45%	63.55%	7.18%	0.68%	2.83%	2.69%
Warehousing and storage	29.55%	70.45%	8.44%	4.01%	3.53%	4.46%

Agriculture, forestry and fishing	Cost of Sales, %	Gross Profit, %	Net Income as % of Sales	Interest as % Sales	Taxes as % of Sales	Depr. and Amort. as % of Sales
Agricultural production	43.86%	56.14%	10.01%	1.97%	1.94%	4.42%
Forestry and logging	62.01%	37.99%	7.98%	2.26%	1.82%	3.91%
Fishing, hunting, and trapping	56.83%	43.17%	7.97%	1.01%	1.86%	2.72%

Mining	Cost of Sales, %	Gross Profit, %	Net Income as % of Sales	Interest as % Sales	Taxes as % of Sales	Depr. and Amort. as % of Sales
Oil and gas extraction	44.33%	55.67%	25.04%	3.00%	2.69%	5.41%
Coal mining	56.45%	43.55%	5.42%	2.37%	5.31%	7.14%
Metal ore mining	43.32%	56.68%	26.22%	2.03%	1.68%	13.35%
Non-metallic mineral mining and quarrying	60.19%	39.81%	7.91%	3.25%	2.68%	7.31%
Support activities for mining	35.46%	64.54%	16.31%	3.43%	2.20%	7.87%

Source: BizStats.com

U.S. Funds Focused on Minority Markets

The following table notes a number of U.S. funds that target minority markets.

T A B L E B – 1

Private Equity Firms Focused on Minority Markets

Firm	Location	Geographic Preference	Industry Preference	Investment Type
21st Century Capital	Dallas, TX	National	Manufacturing, value-added distribution, service and media	Buyouts, recapitalizations, growth equity
Altos Ventures	Menlo Park, CA	Western U.S.	Information technology	First institutional round
Ascend Venture Group	New York, NY	National; Mid Atlantic; California	Applied technology with a focus on enterprise software, outsourced business services, and appliance devices; education sector	Companies poised to experience dramatic revenue growth
Black Enterprise/Greenwich Street Fund	New York, NY	National	Telecom, consumer goods, media, financial services, retail, information tech.	Expansion and acquisition financing; buyouts and successions
CSW Capital	New York, NY	North America	General industrial and consumer	Does not generally participate in startups, technology companies, or real estate investments.
Fulcrum Capital Group	Culver City, CA	Businesses located in and employing from Southern California's under-served urban communities	Commercial and consumer services companies; light manufacturing; communications; no turnarounds; real estate project finance; talent-driven entertainment; re-lending or technology; select start-up financing	Companies that are important in minority and urban communities

Firm	Location	Geographic Focus	Industry	Description
GenNx360 Capital Partners	Prospect, KY	Generally focuses on US but consider global investment opportunities	Industrial water treatment, specialty chemicals, and engineered materials. Industrial machinery & equipment components, industrial security services	Industrial business-to-business companies
Hispania Capital Partners	Chicago, IL	US Hispanic Market	Diversified	Well-established business that provide goods and services to the Hispanic community or are Hispanic-owned
ICV Capital Partners	New York, NY	US	Healthcare, food processing consumer products and services, commercial service, media and telecommunications, industrial manufacturing	Companies that are based in, hire from, or serve America's inner cities; owned and/or managed by ethnic minorities
Milestone Growth Fund	Minneapolis, MN	Minnesota	Minority-owned companies	Provide equity-type financing and management assistance to minority entrepreneurs
MMG Ventures	Baltimore, MD	Mid-Atlantic Region Selected Investments outside of this core area	Telecommunications, information technology, healthcare, and the computer software and services industries	Minority-owned and operated businesses that are poised for growth
Nogales Investors	Los Angeles, CA	National, West Coast	Any industry	Later stage expansion acquisition
Opportunity Capital	Fremont, CA	N/A	Communications, applied technology, healthcare, African-American funeral homes and cemeteries	Later stage companies seeking acquisition and expansion capital, preferred equity, or equity-linked instruments

(Continued)

Firm	Location	Geographic Preference	Industry Preference	Investment Type
Oracle Capital Partners	Detroit, MI	Headquartered or significant presence in the state of Michigan	Healthcare services, industrials/manufacturing, consumer products, commercial services, technology	Preferred equity or equity-linked
Pacesetter Capital Group	Richardson, TX	Southwestern US: Mostly Texas, Oklahoma, California New Mexico, Colorado, Arizona, Arkansas, and Louisiana	Broadcasting (radio television and cable), telecommunications, manufacturing and services. Enterprise software, technology infrastructure involving later stage semiconductor	Diversified private equity funds
Palladium Equity Partners	New York, NY	Most investments in US base firms. Some investments in Latin American and international firms or management teams.	Business and financial services, food, healthcare, manufacturing, media, and retail, with a particular focus in Hispanic market opportunities	Buyouts, recapitalizations, corporate spin-outs, growth financings, and restructurings
Pharos Capital Group	Dallas, TX	Globally	Healthcare technology and business services	Growth and expansion capital
Reliant Equity	Chicago, IL	U.S.	Diversified	Buyouts of growth-oriented fundamentally-sound middle-market businesses
RLJ Equity Partners	Bethesda, MD	N/A	N/A	N/A

Rustic Canyon/Fontis Partners	Pasadena, CA	Southern California and the Southwest	Media consumer goods and service companies	Expansion and late stage companies
				N/A
Smith Whiley Company	Evanston, IL	N/A	N/A	Private equity, tax credit finance, and structured finance
Stonehenge Capital	Columbus, OH	National	Media and communications industry	Early to mid-stage investments in underserved segments of media and communications industry
SYNCOM Venture Partners	Silver Spring, MD	N/A	Media and communications industry	

Source: National Association of Investment Companies (NAIC) and company web sites.

INDEX